MW00658678

Patricia Pender is Senior Lecturer in English at the University of Newcastle, Australia. She is the author of *Early Modern Women's Writing and the Rhetoric of Modesty* (2012) and the editor, with Rosalind Smith, of *Material Cultures of Early Modern Women's Writing* (2014). A member of the editorial board of *Slayage*, she specialises in gender and popular culture, early modern literature and feminist theory.

INVESTIGATING CULT TV

Series Editor: Stacey Abbott

The **Investigating Cult TV** series is a fresh forum for discussion and debate about the changing nature of cult television. It sets out to reconsider cult television and its intricate networks of fandom by inviting authors to rethink how cult TV is conceived, produced, programmed and consumed. It will also challenge traditional distinctions between cult and quality television.

Offering an accessible path through the intricacies and pleasures of cult TV, the books in this series will interest scholars, students and fans alike. They will include close studies of individual contemporary television shows. They will also reconsider genres at the heart of cult programming, such as science fiction, horror and fantasy, as well as genres like teen TV, animation and reality TV when these have strong claims to cult status. Books will also examine themes or trends that are key to the past, present and future of cult television.

Published and forthcoming titles:

Battlestar Galactica: Investigating Flesh, Spirit and Steel, edited by Roz Kaveney and Jennifer Stoy

Being Bionic: The World of TV Cyborgs, by Bronwen Calvert

The Cult TV Book, edited by Stacey Abbott

Dancing with the Doctor: Dimensions of Gender in the New Doctor Who Universe, by Lorna Jowett

Dexter: Investigating Cutting Edge Television, edited by Douglas L. Howard

I'm Buffy and You're History: Buffy the Vampire Slayer and Contemporary Feminism, by Patricia Pender

Investigating Alias: Secrets and Spies, edited by Stacey Abbott and Simon Brown

Investigating Charmed: The Magic Power of TV, edited by Karin Beeler and Stan Beeler

Investigating Farscape: Uncharted Territories of Sex and Science Fiction, by Jes Battis

Investigating Firefly and Serenity: Science Fiction on the Frontier, edited by Rhonda V. Wilcox and Tanya R. Cochran

Love and Monsters: The Doctor Who Experience, 1979 to the Present, by Miles Booy

Sounds of Fear and Wonder: Music in Cult TV, by Janet K. Halfyard

Time on TV: Narrative Time, Time Travel and Time Travellers in Popular Television Culture, edited by Lorna Jowett, Kevin Lee Robinson and David Simmons

Torchwood Declassified: Investigating Mainstream Cult Television, edited by Rebecca Williams

True Blood: Investigating Vampires and Southern Gothic, by Brigid Cherry

TV Horror: Investigating the Dark Side of the Small Screen, by Lorna Jowett and Stacey Abbott

Ideas and submissions for Investigating Cult TV to
s.abbott@roehampton.ac.uk
pbrewster@ibtauris.com

I'M BUFFY AND YOU'RE HISTORY

BUFFY THE VAMPIRE SLAYER AND CONTEMPORARY FEMINISM

PATRICIA PENDER

I.B. TAURIS
LONDON · NEW YORK

Published in 2016 by
I.B.Tauris & Co. Ltd
London • New York
www.ibtauris.com

ISBN: 978 1 78076 745 1 (HB)
978 1 78076 746 8 (PB)

eISBN: 978 1 78672 010 8
ePDF: 978 1 78673 010 7

A full CIP record for this book is available from the British Library
A full CIP record is available from the Library of Congress

Library of Congress Catalog Card Number: available

Typeset by Out of House
Printed and bound in Great Britain by T.J. International, Padstow, Cornwall

MIX
Paper from responsible sources
FSC
www.fsc.org
FSC® C013056

In Memoriam
Kylie Quinane 1970–2010

‘We will never not be fighting.’
Joss Whedon

Contents

List of Illustrations

Acknowledgements

As the book that follows makes embarrassingly clear, I have been writing and thinking about *Buffy* for more than 20 years: first in undergraduate essays written at the University of Sydney in the mid 1990s (on the 1992 film), then as a graduate student at Stanford University in California and Assistant Professor at Pace University in New York, and back full circle to the University of Newcastle in Australia where this book finally took shape. The debts I have accrued during the long gestation of this project are consequently considerable.

To begin at the beginning, I would like to thank my Sydney friends in student politics, who helped me flesh out my fledgling ideas about *Buffy* and feminism and with whom I ran a 'Buffy and the Vampire Slayers' team for student government which was miraculously elected: Michelle Swift, Gina Laurie, Kirsten Tranter, Natasja Worsley, Catherine Burnheim, Lena Nahlous, Ben Ho, Eugene Ho, Simon Clarke, Anna Davis, Polly Porteous and Caitlin Vaughan. Flatmates in various shared houses at this time had to put up with an inordinate amount of *Buffy* watching. My thanks to Michelle Swift (again), Nicola O'Shea, Storm Stanford, Jane Shadbolt and the late lamented Kylie Quinane for their, if not infinite, then certainly very admirable, patience with my obsession.

Work towards this book began in embryo at Stanford University where I was fortunate to be able to design and teach my own undergraduate seminar, Girls on Film: Cultural Studies in Third Wave Feminism. I thank the Feminist Studies Department for this opportunity, particularly Penny Eckert, Nikhila Pai and Caitlin Delohery, and Stanford's Institute for Women's and Gender Studies, where a graduate dissertation fellowship gave me the boon of productive conversations about the diverse interdisciplinary meanings of feminism, particularly with Falu Bakrania, Celine Parreñas Shimizu and Miriam Ticktin. My work on *Buffy* was again supported institutionally in my move to Pace University. I thank the Women's and Gender Studies Department for opportunities to teach not only Girls on Film but also Men and Masculinities, and the colleagues who gave me fantastic support and critical feedback: Sid Ray, Tom Henthorne, Jonathan Silverman, Catherine Zimmer, Amy Foerster, Aseel Sawalha, Meghana Nayak, Nancy Reagin and Martha Driver. I particularly wish to thank the marvellous students in my Girls on Film classes at Stanford and Pace, and Jonathan Silverman, for publishing the work of five of these students in a 'Third Wave Feminism Suite' in his co-edited composition textbook, *The World is a Text*.

At the University of Newcastle I have been fortunate in finding wonderfully simpatico friends and colleagues. For assistance or simply support in wrestling with the issues in this book I thank Ros Smith, Dianne Osland, Keri Glastonbury, Brooke Collins-Gearing, Tiffany Tsao, Caroline Webb, Mark Gauntlett, Camilla Russell, Hamish Ford, Rebecca Bierne and Jane Shadbolt. Financial assistance in the form of internal grants from the University of Newcastle enabled me to employ a group of research assistants without whom this book would never have reached completion. For their invaluable help, research smarts and welcome enthusiasm, I thank Vanessa Bowden, Alexandra Day, Elizabeth Kinder, Ellen McGeoch, Claire Maddocks and Elizabeth McGrath.

My work on this book has also been enriched by conversations and friendships spanning several years and continents. For their support, sustenance, care and occasional chastening, I thank Kate Lilley and Melissa Hardie in Sydney, Sara Hackenberg, Russell Ward, Kirsten Tranter, Danny Fisher, Cat Luedtke and Jayson Hill (now all in the Bay Area), Skye Patrick and Didi di Almeida (who used to be in the Bay Area), Jo Littler in London, Kris Woofter and Trish Salah in Canada and Virginia Ross, Ed Wright and Kum Rathnayaka in Newcastle. Rhonda Wilcox and David Lavery deserve special thanks for their tireless work and generosity in building the *Buffy* studies community, for taking a risk in publishing my first *Buffy* essay and for the support they have shown me in the many years since then.

For gifts too innumerable to mention I thank my extended family, particularly my parents, Anne Pender and Gordon Pender, my aunts Emily and Maggie and my cousin Ness, who found me my very own Mr Pointy stake. To James, who lived with this book on a daily basis and who made me laugh when I didn't think I could, no thanks is enough, and I promise we can watch something else now. This book is for Kylie, and for all the girls who battle the big stuff on a daily basis. Love you long time Kyles. Wish you were here.

Introduction: How to Do Things with *Buffy*

The cult television series *Buffy the Vampire Slayer* is now indisputably one of the most widely analysed texts in contemporary popular culture. The end of the series in 2003 did not herald the passing of a fleeting academic fancy, as many must have expected, but has instead ushered in an unprecedented number of monographs, edited collections, conferences, book chapters, journal articles and even university courses that grapple with the *Buffy* phenomenon in one way or another. *I'm Buffy and You're History: Buffy the Vampire Slayer and Contemporary Feminism* attempts to engage the energy of the avid audience of *Buffy* fans and at the same time appeal to the interests of scholars in feminism, cultural studies, and film and television studies more broadly, with the aim of cementing *Buffy*'s position as an essential – even canonical – text in the feminist analysis of contemporary popular culture.

Gender analysis has been central to popular and academic critiques of *Buffy* from the series' inception, and debates about its feminist rhetoric, politics and potential continue to engage readers and viewers, scholars and fans. The status of the series' creator Joss Whedon as an 'out' male feminist has served both to promote and to complicate this enterprise. All too often, for instance, *Buffy*'s status as a feminist text operates as an *a priori* assumption rather than a claim susceptible to interrogation. The passion the series continues to elicit in both fans and scholars means that its gender analysis can tend to be simply celebratory rather than genuinely critical. As a scholar who has engaged with *Buffy*'s reception and its ambiguous status as a feminist text for the last 20 years, and who has published regularly about the series during its extended afterlife, my aim in writing this book has been to produce a more sustained, nuanced and critical gender analysis of the series than is yet available, one that interrogates *Buffy*'s diverse rhetorics of feminism at both narrative and metanarrative levels.

My central argument is that *Buffy* is manifestly a feminist text, one that engages with transnational and postfeminist rhetorics in certain story arcs and seasons, but which is more centrally and thoroughly engaged with reconfiguring, and sometimes challenging, the ideals of US second-wave feminism for a wide third-wave audience. In further positing *Buffy* as a queer feminist text, I refer less to its representation of 'positive images' (which are in any case contestable) than to the series' deliberate queering of classic Hollywood narratives and its self-conscious construction of queer viewing positions. Believing that a fresh gender reappraisal of *Buffy* will allow us to interrogate and scrutinise some of the guiding principles and methodological fault lines that inform feminist cultural studies more broadly, in the chapters that follow I attempt to test the limits and enduring appeal of familiar disciplinary dichotomies between pleasure and politics, transgression and containment, scholar and fan.

This book is structured as a series of analyses that might be grouped under the rubric 'How to do things with *Buffy*' or, more accurately, 'How to do (feminist) things with *Buffy*'. After two introductory chapters that situate the series within various feminist fields (studies of girls, film, television, and post-feminism), each subsequent chapter investigates *Buffy*'s engagement with and contribution to a different strand of contemporary feminist theory: third-wave feminism, transnational feminism, queer studies, studies of masculinity and fan studies. Each of these chapters contains a brief summary of the development of that particular field, and goes on to test that theory against specific textual (and in the case of fan studies, extra-textual) examples from *Buffy*. In some cases my choice of examples is obvious and straightforward; in others, I have tried to approach the theoretical object via more oblique examples. For instance, studies of masculinity in *Buffy* have focused almost exhaustively on Buffy's rival lovers – Angel and Spike. In order to circumvent binary structures that are themselves becoming pervasive within *Buffy* studies (good Angel/bad Spike – or, depending how you roll, bad Angel/good Spike), my study of masculinity focuses instead on Riley, an altogether less popular choice (both for Buffy and for scholarship). Likewise, my analysis of queerness focuses on the fascinating but overlooked minor character of Andrew, rather than the overt lesbian storylines of Willow and Tara.

My aim in each instance has been to produce a chapter that can function as a case study in feminist analysis, which includes discussion of the relevant theoretical debates and a demonstration of those theories in action – in textual criticism – thus facilitating the reader's own use of those theories in different textual contexts. To the greatest extent possible, therefore, I have written each chapter with an eye to stand-alone coherence (and I apologise in advance for any repetition this strategy inflicts on readers). These chapters could be excerpted for use in a course on feminist theory or feminist cultural studies or film and television, with each chapter initiating discussion of a different aspect of contemporary feminism, using *Buffy* as the base text, but expanding in directions that are most useful for its readers. Of course use of the whole book is my ultimate goal; it has been designed as a survey of five strands in feminist theory that I find most salient and significant today, to facilitate use of the book as a set text in the kinds of courses mentioned above. At the same time, I have eschewed (I 'ope!) an 'overly' academic approach to these subjects, with the aim of appealing to lay readers who still constitute the bulk of *Buffy's* audience, despite appearances to the contrary.

Chapter 1, '"I'm Buffy and You're … History": *Buffy* Baffles the Binaries', revises my first *Buffy* publication, an essay which rehearses tenets central to the methodology I bring to *Buffy* scholarship.[1] This chapter introduces what I call the Good Buffy/Bad Buffy dichotomy: is *Buffy the Vampire Slayer* a groundbreaking, empowering and transgressive text, or is its political potential compromised, commodity-driven and contained? Put simply, is *Buffy* good or bad? I interrogate the polarised positions in this debate by examining the ambivalent gender dynamics of the series. Paying particular attention to representations of seriousness and silliness, to the avowedly political and the shamelessly post-modern, I suggest that *Buffy* is a television text that delights in deliberately and self-consciously baffling the binaries; the juxtaposition of mundane reality and surreal fantasy in the lives of the Slayer and her friends evokes a world in which the sententious morality of black and white distinctions is itself demonised as an unnatural threat from an ancient past.

Chapter 2, '*Buffy* in History: Feminisms Pro and Faux, Post and Most', positions *Buffy* in four important critical contexts: the scholarship of girl studies, film and television criticism, second- and third-wave feminism, and the emerging literature on post-feminism. At the time of writing, the original *Buffy* television series is ten years old, and we make a mistake, I believe, if we confuse our ongoing academic interest in the series as an indication of its contemporary currency. Historicising *Buffy*'s appeal and its rhetoric (both then and now) is crucial if we are to avoid making essentialising claims about the series' politics. This chapter locates *Buffy*'s emergence in the unique political and cultural climates of the 1990s and early 2000s and draws important distinctions between the politicised animus of riot grrrl, the grassroots, explicitly feminist movement that started in Seattle, and the more commercial 'girl power' aesthetics of later 'faux' feminist reverberations such as the Spice Girls. It goes on to look at connections between second- and third-wave feminism in *Buffy the Vampire Slayer* from the perspective of the current cultural moment in which rhetorics of 'post-feminism' have gained considerable traction in mainstream media's representation of girls and women.

My third chapter, '"Kicking Ass is Comfort Food": Buffy as Third-Wave Feminist Icon', also revises an earlier publication.[2] In this chapter I examine *Buffy* through the problematic of third-wave feminism, situating the series as part of a larger cultural project that seeks to reconcile the political agenda of second-wave feminism with the critique of white racial privilege articulated by women of colour and the theoretical insights afforded by post-structural analysis. I suggest that if one of the primary goals of third-wave feminism is to question our inherited models of feminist agency and political efficacy – without acceding to the defeatism implicit in the notion of 'post-feminism' – then *Buffy* provides us with modes of oppositional praxis, of resistant femininity and, in its final season, of collective feminist activism that are unparalleled in mainstream television. At the same time, the series' emphasis on individual empowerment, its celebration of the exceptional woman and its problematic politics of racial representation remain important concerns for feminist analysis. Focusing primarily on the final season of the series, I argue that Season 7 of *Buffy* offers a more straightforward and decisive feminist message than the show had previously attempted, and that in doing so it paints a compelling picture of the promises and predicaments that attend third-wave feminism as it negotiates both its second-wave antecedents and its traditional patriarchal nemeses.

My fourth chapter, 'Whose Revolution has been Televised?: Race, Whiteness and "Transnational" Slayer Suffrage', continues the critical race analysis of the series' final season begun in the previous chapter. In extending the Slayer's powers to young girls across the globe, *Buffy*'s Season 7 begins to redress – albeit belatedly and incompletely – the national, cultural and racial privilege the show assumed over its seven-year cycle. Bringing ethnic diversity and racial difference to the Slayer story, a generous reading of *Buffy*'s finale might see it as an exemplary narrative of transnational feminist activism. A more critical reading might see it as yet another chapter in a long, repetitive story of US imperialism. I suggest that the idealised vision of universal sisterhood with which *Buffy* concludes needs to be read against the immediate political context in which its final season screened – a context that illuminates some of the same gestures of cultural imperialism that the series elsewhere successfully critiques. *Buffy*'s celebration of what is effectively an international military alliance under ostensibly altruistic American leadership demands special scrutiny. In the context of then-President George W. Bush's 'War on Terror' and the spurious universalism of his 'Coalition of the Willing', *Buffy*'s final gesture of international inclusivity is imbued with unwittingly inauspicious overtones.

Chapter 5, 'Becoming Worthy of Buffy: Performing Masculinity in a Patriarchal World', explores the gender dynamics surrounding the least popular of Buffy's romantic relationships, that with her much-maligned Season 4 paramour, Riley Finn. The series is justifiably famous for turning conventional teenage clichés ('High school is hell', 'My mother is an alien') into spectacularly literal, horrific incarnations. In *Buffy*, the rituals of girlhood are similarly and spectacularly fraught. Buffy's first date, her high school prom and various early sexual encounters are all presented with a hyperbolic hysteria that somehow serves to foreground, rather than minimise, the fundamental pathos of growing up: adolescence is *unheimlich*, and adults don't know the half of it. Buffy's love objects play a central role in her *Bildungsroman*, and have attracted a prodigious amount of scholarly and fan attention. This chapter traces her surprising relationship with Riley and the ways in which he attempts, within the gender politics of the series, to 'become worthy' of its protagonist. If Angel's abjection is the paranormal punishment for his demonic 'deflowering' of Buffy and Spike's insidious appeal gets inextricably more complex as he serves as the shadow to Buffy's increasingly conflicted desires, the respite offered by Riley's all-American normality is exposed, as all such spectres should be, as less than straight and sure.

Chapter 6, '"From Beneath You It Devours": Andrew and the Homoerotics of Evil', considers *Buffy*'s queer politics through the micro-lens of a recurring minor character. Andrew presents a rich test case for queer readings of *Buffy* because his representation evolves over time and invokes several of the more misogynist, homophobic stereotypes of homosexuality as well as more open-ended or potentially progressive readings of homoerotic desire. I argue that the series does so wittingly, that is, self-consciously and deliberately, so that homophobia and misogyny are actually *thematised* at the level of narrative and are not merely, or perhaps not *only*, residual subtextual echoes. In Season 6, for instance, Andrew is represented variously as the 'invisible' queer ('Who are you?'), as a clueless queer member of a tight homosocial unit ('I like Timothy Dalton!') and as the closeted gay man acting out homophobia through the sexual objectification of women ('Free cable porn!'). In Season 7 these resonances reach their highest pitch when Andrew is portrayed as a stereotypical version of the 'homosexual as killer'. At the same time, Andrew's characterisation is more complex than these examples would suggest. His development in Season 7 takes him on a bumpy, sometimes reluctant, journey of remorse and redemption, opening possibilities for queer readings of spectatorship and cultural production that retrospectively reverberate across the series.

Chapter 7, '"Why Can't You Just Masturbate Like the Rest of Us?": The Erotics and Politics of *Buffy* Fandom', continues my analysis of Andrew and considers him as a figure for the fan, author and teacher in the meta-critical seventh-season episode 'Storyteller'. In 'Storyteller', Andrew's romanticised recollections of his fandom as successful super-villainy clash jarringly with Buffy's depiction of these same fannish practices as basically vegetative: in Buffy's scathing synopsis, Andrew is less evil than fungal; he is not evil himself, but if he is around it long enough he picks it up 'like a mushroom'. What Whedon and Co. present here are two competing narratives of Andrew's fandom: the first – Andrew's – emphasises mastery; the second – Buffy's – is distinctly bathetic; instead of master, Andrew is mushroom, absorbing evil through a process of osmosis. However, in 'Storyteller' Andrew is also positioned as an author or auteur. The device of the text within a text makes Andrew the director of his documentary, *Buffy, Slayer of the Vampyrs*. By extension, then, Andrew operates as a figure for the series' creator, Joss Whedon. Finally, Andrew is also positioned as pedagogue. As the author/director of a documentary designed for training future slayers, Andrew is a teacher producing a teaching text. He thus operates as a figure for *Buffy* scholars. Without giving too much away, it is safe to say that 'Storyteller' trades in a richly scatological lexicon that simultaneously eulogises and theorises the complex relationships that exist between fans, authors and scholars.

In the second part of Chapter 7, I explore differences between the sexual politics of the *Buffy* series and the *Twilight* saga by considering the popular video mash-up, *Buffy vs Edward (Twilight Remixed)*. In the words of its creator Jonathan McIntosh, this 'remixed narrative' is an example of 'transformative storytelling serving as a pro-feminist visual critique of Edward's character and generally creepy behavior'.[3] *Buffy vs Edward* provides immediate gratification for the feminist *Buffy* fan by exposing the possessive, intrusive and generally 'stalkery' behaviour of the *Twilight* saga's male hero, a critique that is ably supplemented by McIntosh's exegesis and its online response. In this chapter I ask what kind of pleasure is entailed for *Buffy* fans in 2009 and indeed today by triumphing over Edward/*Twilight*. Is there a feminist agenda involved here, and if so, what kind of feminism?

My final chapter, '"Where Do We Go from Here?": Trajectories in *Buffy* Studies', attempts the delicate operation of assessing the field, its hazards and its potential for future growth. I suggest that the *Buffy* series will continue to play an increasingly important role in academic forums and university classrooms, and that an assessment of the current state of scholarship is therefore timely. In the musical episode 'Once More, with Feeling', Buffy's anthem, 'What Can't We Face?' celebrates the sense of community that is itself a celebrated feature of the show. But as several critics have noted, this song is a wishful affirmation of unity in the face of decided differences, and I suggest that the state of *Buffy* scholarship is no different. Similarly, when Buffy warns Giles, 'I'm just worried that this whole session's going to turn into some training montage from an '80s movie', she voices a fear that the discipline and rigour of their training is about to be cheapened by caricature, portrayed with a sentimentality that drains it of significance. Shared appreciation of a popular culture text should not blind us to the fact that the field of *Buffy* studies unwittingly courts trivialisation if it pursues critical consensus at the expense of a dynamic discussion of differences. In this chapter, I consider several developments in *Buffy* studies (the fan/scholar slippage, the rise of auteur theory) that I believe require careful consideration. Rather than indicating weak points in the field, however, I argue instead that rigorous debate about these contentious issues offers some of the most promising directions for future *Buffy* studies, and of its potential impact on cultural studies more broadly.

This book represents 20 years of my thinking, arguing and writing about a single television series. Despite sporadic attempts to leave *Buffy* behind, I have been called back again and again by its unrepentant humour, its unapologetically fierce politics and its sophisticated, nuanced use of rhetorical strategies. *Buffy* is a text that was both timely and prescient; its (literally) hell-raising heroine struck a chord with audiences both young and old, and (thanks to developments of TV on DVD) its current reach extends far beyond that initial market. The seven seasons that make up *Buffy the Vampire Slayer* constitute a text that will only increase in importance as we keep striving to understand how popular cultural productions portray our society's political and ethical problems and in doing so offer us critical and creative ways in which we might challenge them.

1

'I'm Buffy and You're ... History': *Buffy* Baffles the Binaries

In Buffy's world, any encounter with the unknown, be it person or demon, initially forces us to evaluate it according to simple criteria: is it friend or is it foe? The starkly polarised moral universe of vampire slaying provides an uncanny double for political debates that circulate in contemporary cultural studies. Feminist critiques of popular culture frequently mobilise a strategy similar to Buffy's slaying technique when they question whether any given text is part of the solution or part of the problem: is *Buffy the Vampire Slayer* a groundbreaking, empowering and transgressive text or is its political potential compromised, commodity-driven and contained? Put simply, is *Buffy* good or bad? In this chapter I interrogate the polarised positions in this debate by examining the ambivalent gender dynamics of the series. Paying particular attention to representations of seriousness and silliness, to the avowedly political and the shamelessly post-modern, I suggest that *Buffy* is a television show that delights in deliberately and self-consciously baffling the binaries; the juxtaposition of mundane reality and surreal fantasy in the lives of the Slayer and her friends evokes a world in which the sententious morality of black and white distinctions is itself demonised as an unnatural threat from an ancient past.

Just a girl

Pike: Buffy, you're not like other girls.
Buffy: Yes, I am.

Buffy the Vampire Slayer (1992)

The quote above is taken from the 1992 film version of *Buffy the Vampire Slayer*, which pre-dates the television series by five years yet highlights one of the central thematics of both texts: namely, the ambivalent position Buffy occupies between authentic adolescent and supernatural Slayer. Not surprisingly, assessment of the transgressive political potential of *Buffy the Vampire Slayer* frequently involves examining the heroine's relationship to contemporary cultural stereotypes. At issue in this debate is the extent of Buffy's resemblance to and difference from 'regular' teenage girls, and her subsequent efficacy as an empowering feminist role model. On the one hand, Buffy is celebrated, in the words of Alyssa Katz, as 'a supremely confident kicker of evil butt'.[1] On the other hand, she might justifiably be accused of subscribing to, and therefore reinscribing, commercial and patriarchal standards of feminine beauty: she is young, blonde, slim and vigilantly fashion conscious. In what follows I examine the rhetorics of transgression and containment that characterised the initial academic and popular media response to *Buffy the Vampire Slayer*. Focusing in particular on the first three seasons of the series, I hope to illuminate the ways in which the unspoken assumptions that underwrite much of this criticism work inadvertently to circumscribe – to contain, in effect – the political and transgressive potential of the series.

If one of the principle motivations of popular cultural studies is to decode the political subtext of any given work, then of central concern for students of the *Buffy* phenomenon is the question: is Buffy feminist? Assessing the late 1980s/early 1990s surge of 'women in action' represented by such figures as Sigourney Weaver's Ellen Ripley, Michelle Yeoh's Wing Chun, Sarah Michelle Gellar's Buffy the Vampire Slayer and Lucy Lawless's Xena: Warrior Princess, authors Anamika Samanta and Erin Franzman pose the question this way:

> No longer damsels in distress, women are kicking ass and saving the world from doom – in Hollywood technicolor. But is happiness really a warm gun? [...] Is this a sign? Are we on our way to mass physical empowerment? Or are we just headed for a whole new pack of stereotypes to live down?'[2]

Rachel Fudge poses the question slightly differently in the journal *Bitch: Feminist Response to Pop Culture*: 'Is Buffy really an exhilarating post-third-wave heroine, or is she merely a caricature of 90's pseudo-girl power, a cleverly crafted marketing scheme to hook the ever-important youth demographic?'[3] However the question is phrased, the concerns are remarkably similar: does Buffy represent an empowering feminist role model or a return to, and reinscription of, repressive patriarchal stereotypes? While the first critical responses to this central question vary markedly, they are alike in affirming the either/or structure of the 'good Buffy/bad Buffy' binary. Collectively, such criticism relies on a model of feminist agency that itself has important political implications.

In her 1999 article, 'Media criticism: The sad state of teen television', printed in *New Moon Network: For Adults Who Care About Girls*, Lynette Lamb canvases a range of television serials targeted at teenage girls, among them *Buffy the Vampire Slayer*, *Sabrina the Teenage Witch* and *Felicity*, and concludes: 'Women and girls are portrayed no more fully or honestly than they were when I was a teenager 25 years ago. Indeed, in some regards the situation is worse'. Lamb argues that '[l]ike so many teens on prime time TV, Sabrina's and Buffy's major preoccupations are their appearance and their boyfriends, in roughly that order'.[4] Lamb is relatively singular in her outright condemnation of *Buffy* as 'bad'. Other critics express unqualified approval of the series. For example, Jennifer L. Pozner writes in 'Thwack! Pow! Yikes! Not your mother's heroines' that 'profeminist options are springing up on almost every network'.[5] She identifies *Buffy the Vampire Slayer*, along with *Xena* and *The Simpsons*, as 'three of the most subversive and campy programs on TV' and writes that Buffy, 'cornered by three snarling freaks [...] does what most high school girls wish they could do – thanks them for dropping by, tells them she's not in the mood, and kicks them into another dimension, literally'. Pozner applauds, '[h]ow's that for a role model?'[6] Despite their opposing judgements of the series, the model of feminist agency mobilised by these critiques is quite similar. Lamb upholds one end of the 'good Buffy/bad Buffy' binary, while Pozner maintains the other. In the majority of critical responses to the series, however, the binary distinctions 'feminist/not feminist' and 'transgressive/contained' operate and circulate in a more fluid fashion.

A third style of critique suspends initial judgement of the series' politics in order to explore its conflicting representations of femininity and feminism. Thus Micol Ostow, in a 1998 article entitled 'Why I love Buffy', confesses that 'I've never known quite how to explain my penchant for the program, but the bottom line is that *Buffy* and *Buffy* alone is the reason that I bothered to learn to set the timer on my VCR'.[7] Ostow applauds the show's 'sheer camp appeal' but at the same time maintains that, 'one can hardly consider Buffy a feminist icon'.[8] She suggests that 'for every few positive messages that it sends girls [...] it creates some problematic scenarios'.[9] Rachel Fudge argues that 'while she may not be your typical feminist activist', Buffy's 'anti-authority stance, her refusal to be intimidated by more powerful figures (whether the school principal or an archdemon)', has 'deeply feminist potential'.[10] Fudge suggests that 'Buffy is an ongoing lesson in this sisters-doing-it-for-themselves ideology' and maintains, in an interesting aside, that

> the impulse that propels Buffy out on patrols, night after night, foregoing any semblance of 'normal' teenage life, is identical to the one that compels us third-wavers to spend endless hours discussing the feminist potentials and pitfalls of primetime television.[11]

The meta-critical gesture that compares the task of the vampire slayer and the task of the feminist critic is not elaborated by Fudge, despite its potential to illuminate the institutional and intergenerational dimensions of Buffy's appeal. Critiques like those proffered by Ostow and Fudge suspend black and white judgement of the series in the interests of examining the ambivalence of *Buffy*'s political content, yet they cannot defer that judgement indefinitely. Indeed, while celebrating Buffy's strength, her commitment, her sassiness, such analyses are haunted by the dark spectre of her patriarchal containment, embodied, ironically enough, in her popularity, her commercial success, in effect her *Sassy*-ness. Fudge writes: 'Buffy could be the poster girl for an entire decade of girl-oriented mass media/culture. For better and most certainly for worse, she's *Sassy* incarnate, an angsty alternateen with a penchant for Delia's-style slip dresses.'[12] Ostow's 'Why I love Buffy' tribute suggests that 'some might find her utter femininity problematic';[13] the authors of 'Women in action', who insist that critics have so far failed to appreciate 'Buffy's potential as a post-feminist icon', nevertheless characterise the series' star, Sarah Michelle Gellar, as a 'Barbie doll-doppelganger';[14] and the recurring animadversions cast upon Buffy's tank tops, high heels and, most repetitively and insidiously, her cleavage, suggest that, Slayer aside, Buffy herself is something of a stumbling block for feminist criticism.[15] As Fudge states: 'Yup, she's strong and sassy all right, but she's the ultimate femme, never disturbing the delicate definition of physical femininity […] The Buffster, for all her bravado and physical strength, is a girly girl through and through.'[16] In the final analysis, such critiques cleave to the either/or binary of 'good Buffy/bad Buffy' as much their second-wave feminist counterparts. They suggest that Buffy can either be a feminist or a femme; there is no middle ground.

Paradoxically, then, the spectre that haunts the early feminist critiques of *Buffy*'s political content is the spectre of the protagonist's gender, the representation of her girlishness. Rachel Fudge summarises this position succinctly when she states that 'Buffy's unreconstructed, over-the-top girliness in the end compromises her feminist potential. Though this excessive femininity veers toward the cartoonish, in the end it's too earnest – too necessary – to be self-parody.'[17] Buffy's femininity is repeatedly reconfigured as a species of *femme-inanity*, and it is this facet of her character that is presented, time and again, as contradicting, and thus undermining, her transgressive political potential. Such analyses leave off their discussion of the gender dynamics of *Buffy the Vampire Slayer* at precisely the point that they become most interesting to me. How, for instance, does the exaggerated or cartoonish representation of Buffy's femininity mediate its 'earnestness'? Does Buffy's femininity in fact *require* amelioration? And how does an understanding of her 'over-the-top girliness' as 'necessary' to her 'make-up' challenge the very political judgements that are frequently made about her character?

In what follows, I would like to rethink the terms of the debate staged around Buffy's femininity by questioning the logic of the transgression/containment model. The model of feminist agency usually employed to analyse *Buffy* dictates that Buffy is 'good' if she transgresses dominant stereotypes, but 'bad' if she is contained in cultural cliché. Yet this binary logic itself works to restrict a range of possible viewing positions and to contain *Buffy*'s political potential. As Jonathan Dollimore has argued:

> containment theory often presupposes an agency of change too subjective and a criterion of success too total. Thus subversion or transgression are implicitly judged by impossible criteria: complete transformation of the social (i.e. revolution), or total personal liberation within, or escape from it (i.e. redemption).[18]

By examining *Buffy*'s ambivalent constructions of authenticity and originality, I hope to illuminate the series' own self-consciously parodic references to gender role-playing: 'Sorry, I'm an old-fashioned girl. I was raised to believe that the men dig up the corpses and the women have the babies' ('Some Assembly Required', 2.2). I suggest that a more productive reading of the politics of *Buffy the Vampire Slayer* is one that examines the challenges it poses under a rubric of feminist camp – a reading strategy flexible enough to recognise not only the ambivalence of the show's political content but also the constitutive incoherence of the very models usually employed to describe it.

The lite ages

> 'I am the Chosen One and I choose to be shopping!'
>
> *Buffy the Vampire Slayer* (1992)

In her 1964 essay, 'Notes on Camp', Susan Sontag defines camp as 'a failed seriousness, a love of exaggeration and artifice, the privileging of style over content and a being alive to the double sense in which things can be taken'.[19] In *Guilty Pleasures: Feminist Camp from Mae West to Madonna*,[20] Pamela Robertson highlights the efficacy of camp for a feminist politics: 'For feminists, camp's appeal lies in its potential to serve as a form of gender parody. Gender parody becomes a critical tool, a way of initiating change in sex and gender roles.' Robertson suggests that 'camp's attention to the artifice of feminine images of excess helps undermine and challenge the presumed naturalness of gender roles and to displace essentialist versions of an authentic female identity'.[21] Feminist camp thus operates in two, potentially conflicting, directions: it revels in an aesthetics of surface play and eschews the depth model of moral seriousness, and at the same time it foregrounds the inevitably performative nature of gender role-playing.

Buffy provides ample illustration of the doubled operations of feminist camp. Xander Harris, Buffy's early admirer and sidekick, provides one focus for the show's camp comedy. An archetype of 1990s 'embattled masculinity', Xander struggles with the machismo stereotypes of classic narrative film as he negotiates his role as handmaiden to Buffy's Slayer: 'Cavalry's here; cavalry's a frightened guy with a rock, but it's here' ('Becoming Part II', 2.22). In the episode 'Bewitched, Bothered and Bewildered' (2.16) a disgruntled Xander conjures a spell that will make him the focus of attention and desire, with unexpectedly dire results. As he endeavours to escape the rampaging hordes of women out to seduce him, Xander decides: 'That's it. This has got to stop. It's time for me to act like a man. And hide.' The poignancy of such moments is underscored by Buffy's occasional assumption of the quintessentially macho stance of the action hero, as exemplified in the following challenge to her antagonist, Spike:

> I've lost friends tonight, and I may lose more. If you have information worth hearing then I'm grateful for it. If you want to make jokes then I will pull out your rib cage and wear it as a hat.
>
> ('Becoming Part I', 2.21)

Both the rejection of seriousness and the subtext of gender masquerade that are central characteristics of feminist camp are evident in these gender reversals.

A product of late 1990s popular culture, Buffy's protagonists participate in what Mark Dery, in a clever tribute to both Edvard Munch's 1893 painting and Wes Craven's film of the same name, calls 'The *Scream* meme':

> The *Scream* meme suggests that we're so ironic that we can't even take our own apocalypse – our lurking sense, on the eve of the future, of social disintegration and simmering discontent – seriously. This is the moment Walter Benjamin warned us of, when humankind's 'self-alienation' reaches 'such a degree that it can experience its own destruction as an aesthetic pleasure of the first order'.[22]

Consider Xander's gag in 'The Harvest' (1.02): 'The dead rose! We should have at least had an assembly'; Buffy's comment in 'Never Kill a Boy on the First Date' (1.05): 'If the apocalypse comes – beep me'; or the Scooby gang's response to Giles's belated diagnosis of an earthquake in Season 4's 'Doomed' (4.11):

Giles: It's the end of the world.
Willow/Xander: AGAIN??!!

The bathos of such exchanges is one of the series' signature textual strategies. Dery states that 'delight in the delivery from depth, from the dead weight of content, is quintessentially postmodern'. He associates 'The *Scream* Meme' with Frederic Jameson's notion of the 'camp sublime' which he describes in the following manner:

> camp in the sense that camp delights in depthlessness, celebrates surface; sublime in the sense that this 'peculiar euphoria' is the postmodern equivalent, for Jameson, of what Edmund Burke called 'the Sublime' – the vertiginous loss of self in the presence of nature's awful grandeur.[23]

In the late twentieth century it is mass media, rather than nature, that induces this 'vertiginous loss of self'. Dery writes:

> Increasingly, the media form the connective tissue of our lives. In the past, says J. G. Ballard, we assumed that the external world represented reality and that our mental worlds were the realm of fantasy. Now, he argues, these roles have been reversed: 'We live in a world ruled by fictions of every kind – mass merchandising, advertising [...] the increasing blurring and intermingling of identities within the realm of consumer goods, the preempting of any free or original response to experience by the television screen'.[24]

Unarguably a product of mass media, merchandising and advertising, *Buffy* also insistently comments on its own historical moment. Joyce Summers, Buffy's mother, voices a familiar concern in the following exchange with Buffy's mentor, Giles:

Joyce: I know she's having trouble with history. Is it too difficult for her, or is she not applying herself?

Giles: She lives very much in the now, and history of course, is very much about the *then* ... ('Angel', 1.07)

Targeted towards a generation whose sense of generation has been fostered by the multiplex cinema, video games and the internet, *Buffy* enjoys, to borrow the words of Mark Dery, 'playing slip 'n' slide on a slick of pure surface: self-conscious quotes, appropriated styles, glib asides'.[25] Buffy's response to an uncharacteristically sceptical Giles, 'I cannot believe that you of all people are trying to Scully me' ('The Pack', 1.06), might stand as symptomatic of the series' casual pop cultural frame of reference. Yet the operations of metaphor at work in the series as a whole attest to its canny acknowledgement and manipulation of the tropes of the world as text, of reality as fiction. As Alyssa Katz provocatively suggests in her review of the series: 'Only sociopaths experience their teenage lives just once. Everyone else relives them again and again, occasionally with professional assistance, and some of us actually find entertainment value in this process.'[26] Giles's comment to his troublesome charge in the episode 'Ted' (2.11) – 'Buffy, I believe the subtext here is rapidly becoming text' – might be read as the overarching textual strategy for the series as a whole.

Much of the comic effect of the *Buffy* series stems from its engagement with the twin poles of the camp sublime, and from its volatile shifts from the sublime to the ridiculous. Buffy, experimentally rebellious in the episode 'Reptile Boy', is stymied by the rapidity of the transition:

Buffy: I told one lie, I had one drink.

Giles: Yes. And you nearly got devoured by a giant demon-snake. I think the words 'let that be a lesson' are a tad redundant at this juncture.

('Reptile Boy', 2.05)

Xander's ironic lament in 'Teacher's Pet' (1.4), 'It's funny how the earth never opens up and swallows you when you want it to', points to the endless applicability of the high school/Hellmouth analogy. The analogy enacts an almost dizzying dance between the literal and the metaphorical. On a formal level, high school and hell are linked through the rhetorical figure of chiasmus, a trope which is depicted, appropriately enough, by the sign of the cross, and which relates each concept in a mutually reciprocal movement (thus high school equals hell and hell equals high school). This chiastic relation is exemplified by Buffy's response to Willow's apology that she can't help her friend study for finals: 'I'll wing it. Of course if we go to Hell by then, I won't have to take them. [sudden fear] Or maybe I'll have to take them forever' ('Becoming Part I', 2.09). Giles's warning about the slippage between text and subtext points to the well-recognised and almost interminable interpenetrability of the two motifs. It also points to a larger rhetorical pattern to the series that is less well recognised.

If the high school/Hellmouth analogy that structures the show has been widely celebrated in the popular response to the series, the similar chiastic relation which structures Buffy's character has been less generally acknowledged. While early critics paid lip service to the 'joke' of the ex-cheerleader turned demon hunter, they usually tried to separate these disparate elements of her character in their political analyses of the series. Hence the Slayer is celebrated at the expense of the girl, and the composite character is found inexplicably wanting. Yet the very title of the text enacts, on a microcosmic scale, the shift from ridiculous to sublime that is a celebrated feature of the series, and it insists on the chiastic relationship between its twin components, 'Buffy' and 'Vampire Slayer:' Buffy is the Vampire Slayer/the Vampire Slayer is Buffy. While such a reduction might seem to beg the unanswerable response 'Duh!', I believe the point is worth making precisely because so many critical responses to the show seem to miss it. The 'joke' of the cheerleading demon hunter is not a one-line throw-away gag, but the foundational myth and ongoing premise of the entire series.

In '*Buffy the Vampire Slayer:* Vampires, postmodernity, and postfeminism', A. Susan Owen produces a sophisticated distillation of the critiques this chapter has surveyed. She writes:

> Buffy's power is domesticated by her oft articulated longing to be 'normal' – to have a steady boyfriend (with all that entails) and to consume life uninterrupted by the demands of civic obligation. The narrative opposes the costs of leadership and political potency, with intimacy, stable relationships, and material comfort [...] Moreover, in spite of Buffy's narrative agency and physical potency, her body project remains consistent with the rescripted body signs of American commodity advertising. In other words, political potency is both imagined and reduced to matters of consumer style.[27]

In a provocative, but to my mind poorly substantiated, move, Owen characterises Buffy as 'postfeminist' and concludes: 'The series plays at transgression: as such it is quintessential television. But it remains to be seen whether transgressive play can challenge institutional relations of power.'[28]

While such critiques significantly extend the terms of political analysis relevant to *Buffy*, in doing so they can be seen to raise the familiar spectre of the transgression/containment debate, this time in a slightly different guise: does *Buffy* comment on twentieth-century popular culture or simply revel in it? And again, I would argue that this binary formulation is itself part of the bogey – a bogey that the series' own structure and rhetoric militate against. Buffy is strong, sexy and subversive, not despite her immersion in popular culture but because of it. Alternatively vacuous and vengeful, she is a composite character; her politics cannot be extruded from her post-modernity. Cultural critique which juxtaposes style and substance in a hierarchical and mutually exclusive relation will always end up stuck with an outmoded and impossible model of feminist agency. If Buffy's form and Buffy's content are upheld as distinct and incompatible categories, then the inexorable logic of the binary will dictate, with awful irony, that Buffy cannot be a feminist because she has cleavage.

That the alternative to the archaic *either/or* is an anarchic *neither and both* has become something of a critical truism in contemporary cultural studies. In Rachel Fudge's words, 'Buffy constantly treads the fine line between girl-power schlock and feminist wish-fulfillment, never giving satisfaction to either one.'[29] That *Buffy* nevertheless refuses the black and white moral distinctions of a more self-evident and sanctimonious style of politics is perhaps testament to the complexity of its cultural moment. It is certainly testament to the fact that the post-modern sublime, that 'vertiginous loss of self', is virtually indistinguishable from the 'peculiar euphoria' of the ridiculous. Instead of considering *Buffy* as a political blueprint for either feminist transgression or patriarchal containment – in the terms of Dollimore's 'impossible criteria', 'complete transformation of the social [...] or total personal liberation within, or escape from it' – we might more usefully identify *Buffy* as a site of intense cultural negotiation in which competing definitions of the central terms in the debate – revolution/apocalypse; feminist/misogynist; transgression and containment – can be tested and refined. A criticism that insists on the necessity of either/or distinctions will be doomed to conclude with the unsatisfactory suggestion that you can take the Slayer out of the girl, because you *can't* take the girl out of the Slayer. Buffy's response to the demon in 'Never Kill a Boy on the First Date' (1.5) might double for her response to the cultural critic that asks her to choose between her ostensibly split selves: 'I don't think we've been properly introduced. I'm Buffy and you're ... History'.

2

Buffy in History: Feminisms Pro and Faux, Post and Most

Combining elements of action, drama, comedy, romance, horror – and occasionally musical – *Buffy* sits uneasily within the taxonomies of television genre. Darker than *Dawson*, and infinitely funnier than *Felicity* (two primetime teen dramas that aired alongside *Buffy*'s first seasons), the series was explicitly conceived as a feminist reworking of horror films in which 'bubble-headed blondes wandered into dark alleys and got murdered by some creature'.[1] From its mid-season US premiere in 1997 to its primetime series finale in 2003, the chronicles of the Chosen One have generated, in the affectionate words of its creator and director Joss Whedon, a 'rabid, almost insane fan base'.[2] Subverting the conventional gender dynamics of horror, action and sci-fi serials, as well as the best expectations of its producers, the series has followed the fortunes of the Slayer as she has struggled through the 'hell' that is high school, a freshman year at UC Sunnydale, and the ongoing challenge of balancing the demands of family, friends, relationships and work with her inescapable duty to fight all manner of evil. As the voice-over to the show's opening credits relates: 'In every generation there is a Chosen One. She and she alone will fight the demons, the vampires and the forces of darkness. She is the Slayer.'

Film, television and feminist scholars have been quick to appreciate the implicit feminist message of the series as a whole. *Buffy* has been celebrated as a 'radical reimagining of what a girl (and a woman) can do and be',[3] as a 'prototypical girly feminist activist'[4] and as a '[h]ard Candy-coated feminist heroine for the girl-power era'.[5] Her ongoing battle with the forces of evil is seen as symbolic of several second-wave feminist struggles: the challenge to balance personal and professional life, the fight against sexual violence and the 'justified feminist anger' young women experience in the face of patriarchal prohibitions and constraints.[6] More theoretically, the series has been analysed in terms of its 'wayward' reconfiguration of the mind/body dualism and, as I argued in the previous chapter, its refusal of the 'inexorable logic' of binary oppositions.[7] In Chapter 1 I claimed *Buffy* as a feminist text, which seems as important a claim to make now, in the twenty-first-century's teens, as it did when I first wrote about the series at the end of its third season. In the decade that divides that publication from this, feminism itself has undergone significant shifts and transformations. This chapter attempts to place *Buffy* in feminist history of various kinds – in the development of girl studies as an academic discipline, in film and television history, in second-wave and third-wave feminist theory and in the recent scholarship devoted to post-feminism.

All about the girl

The original movie, *Buffy the Vampire Slayer*, for which series creator Joss Whedon wrote the script but was not ultimately responsible, was released in 1992 – near the start of an era that remains remarkable for its empowering depictions of girls in independent cinema.[8] The television series commenced in 1997 and could conceivably bank on its projected audience being familiar with at least some of the surprising female protagonists that had been displayed in the alternative films of that decade.[9] At the same time, girl studies was gaining traction within the academy as an important new multidisciplinary endeavour, combining insights from sociology, psychology, education and cultural studies, as well as many related fields. In sum, *Buffy* was first aired in an era where adolescent girls were achieving new social, political and cultural visibility.

In 1990s America, the 'teenage girl' was subject to intense scrutiny from the popular press, policy makers and feminist scholars alike. The decade is bookended by two important demographic studies, *Shortchanging Girls, Shortchanging America*, produced by the American Association of University Women in 1991, and *The Girls Report: What We Know and Need to Know About Growing Up Female*, commissioned by the US National Council for Research on Women and produced by Lynn Phillips in 1998.[10] Both provide valuable snapshots of the central concerns of girl-focused policy making in the period. Mary Pipher's *Reviving Ophelia: Saving the Selves of Adolescent Girls*[11] placed the psychological issues confronting teen girls on the national cultural agenda. Indicting a 'media-saturated culture' for 'poisoning' young girls, the book was a runaway success, selling over 1.6 million copies. Pipher asserted that American popular culture, music and advertising 'limits girls' development, truncates their wholeness and leaves many of them traumatized'.[12] Several years later, Lyn Mikel Brown's *Raising Their Voices: The Politics of Girls' Anger*[13] attempted to redress what she saw as Pipher's 'victim' perspective, by presenting a study of girls who 'actively *resist* dominant cultural notions of femininity'.[14] Brown pointed out how public discussion of girls' development 'passed over the clarity and strength of girls' voices', discussing 'the *losses* the girls in our study sustained over time' yet overlooking 'the fact that most of the girls resisted these losses in some capacity'. Focusing on 'girls' active resistance', Brown argued that, 'to girls' great credit, what we see is not complete confusion but pockets of expressed, sometimes quite organized, grassroots resistance'.[15] Across the decade, mass media also sensationalised and manipulated some of the new challenges facing American girls, focusing on date rape in elite universities, African American teenage pregnancy and the violence confronted by rural queer and transgender teens.

In popular culture, girls stole a variety of shows in unexpected ways. Teen girl audiences of cinema emerged as one of the most powerful demographics of the late 1990s, creating surprising hits out of movies ranging from the low-budget romantic comedy *Clueless* (1995) to the critically acclaimed award-winning *Boys Don't Cry* (1999). As Kathleen Rowe Karlyn reports, teen girls saved the romantic epic *Titanic* from financial disaster 'when groups of them flocked to theaters for repeat viewings of it'.[16] The success of *Clueless* earned it a TV spin-off, and the slasher parody *Scream* went on to be reprised in two sequels, the first of them starring

Buffy's Sarah Michelle Gellar. Television, too, saw a swift rise in teen girl protagonists, from the daily dramas of *Felicity* and *Dawson's Creek* to the supernatural adventures of *Sabrina the Teenage Witch* and the female trio of *Charmed*. In music, the underground riot grrrl movement, starting in Seattle, spawned a wider, emancipatory culture of 'Girl Power', a phrase later adopted, commercialised and ultimately undermined at the opposite end of the political spectrum by the short-lived though sensational popularity of the Spice Girls.

Within the academy, girls had been the subject of Angela McRobbie's groundbreaking research since the 1970s, reprinted and consolidated in the classic collection of essays, *Feminism and Youth Culture* in 1991.[17] In this study McRobbie considered such diverse topics as teenage sexuality, young mothers and girls' magazines, subjecting the key concerns of the Birmingham Centre for Contemporary Cultural Studies – social class, ideology, popular culture and political change – to challenging questions from second-wave feminism. In her most recent re-evaluation of this early work, McRobbie reflects upon her self-described 'misjudgements' of gender and culture. In particular, she is critical of declaring individual female consumerist pleasures 'subversive', as these pleasures are still constructed within a limiting capitalist power structure.[18] She claims to have been too hopeful about the role that women's magazines and media culture would play in feminist discussion, 'over-enthusiastic' about an industry that is ultimately at the mercy of fashion and advertising trends, and commercial interests, and which strives to uphold a generic vision of heterosexual, fashionable womanhood.[19] She suggests that she was 'complicit, without abandoning a feminist perspective, in accommodating to the genre itself, and reducing the level and intensity of critique, in favour of a kind of compromise position'.[20] By 2009 she had arrived at the position that women's magazine culture is more closely aligned with post-feminism, 'playing a vital role in the undoing of feminism' through 'aggressive individualism', 'a hedonistic female phallicism' and 'obsession with consumer culture'.[21] That said, *Feminism and Youth Culture* remains a crucial cornerstone in the evolving scholarship of girl studies. As one of the first feminist analyses of girls' popular cultures, McRobbie's work will always command respect, and her continued interrogation of her initial premises and concerns in subsequent work stands as a salutatory example to the field: she is a scholar deeply invested in the possibilities, failures and *futures* of feminism, one willing to revise inherited paradigms, even her own, in the search for a salient and satisfying feminist praxis.

New sociological studies of girls emerged in the 1990s and early 2000s, with Valerie Walkerdine's *Daddy's Girl: Young Girls and Popular Culture* (1997), Walkerdine, Helen Lucey and June Melody's *Growing Up Girl: Psychosocial Explorations of Gender and Class* (2001) and Bonnie J. Leadbeater and Niobe Way's edited collection, *Urban Girls: Resisting Stereotypes, Creating Identities* (1996), updated as *Urban Girls Revisited* in 2007.[22] Within cultural studies, Sherrie A. Inness's collection *Delinquents and Debutantes: Twentieth-Century American Girls' Cultures* (1998), Catherine Driscoll's theoretically savvy *Girls: Feminine Adolescence in Popular Culture and Cultural Theory* (2002), Anita Harris's *Future Girl: Young Women in the Twenty-First Century* (2004) and her edited collection *All About the Girl: Culture, Power, and Identity* (2004) all continued to identify female youth culture as an important site for feminist scholarship.[23] More commercial publications in the field included Susan Douglas's *Where the Girls Are: Growing Up Female with the Mass Media* (1994), Joan Smith's *Different for Girls: How Culture Creates Women* (1998) and Emily White's *Fast Girls: Teenage Tribes and the Myth of the Slut* (2002).[24] In film scholarship (and in addition to the works discussed below) *Sugar, Spice, and Everything Nice: Cinemas of Girlhood* (2002), edited by Frances Gateward and Murray Pomerance, preceded their companion volume, *Where the Boys Are: Cinemas of Masculinity and Youth* (2005), and Mary Celeste Kearney's *Girls Make Media* (2006) pushed the study of girls' popular culture from reception to production with her study of girl-made zines, videos and websites.[25]

Scholars of post-feminism, discussed further at the end of this chapter, have also focused on the girl as a crucial category of analysis. In their valuable collection, *Interrogating Postfeminism: Gender and the Politics of Popular Culture*, Yvonne Tasker and Diane Negra consider the figure of the 'girl' and the concept of 'girl power' in the context of post-feminism, arguing that the very prominence of the girl in popular culture raises new problems for feminist cultural studies. In their words,

> the 'girling' of femininity itself is evident in both the celebration of the young woman as a marker of postfeminist liberation and the continuing tendency to either explicitly term or simply treat women of a variety of ages as girls.'[26]

Tasker and Negra claim that '[t]o some extent, girlhood is imagined within postfeminist culture as being for everyone; that is, girlhood offers a fantasy of transcendence and evasion, a respite from other areas of experience'.[27]

As befits a popular phenomenon, a range of less academic, more commercial representations of post-feminism have also emerged. The slew of 'third-wave' anthologies produced in the 1990s (discussed in the following chapter) is a case in point. Two titles, Emilie Zaslow's *Feminism, Inc.: Coming of Age in Girl Power Media Culture* (2009) and Rebecca C. Hains's *Growing Up With Girl Power: Girlhood On Screen and in Everyday Life* (2012) straddle a middle ground between feminist theory and embodied practice by examining 'girl power' as a phenomenon of media and popular culture. These loosely anthropological studies explore how girls navigate the marketing of feminism and femininity in pop music and television, and consider how the 'girl power' movement is employed in various forms of media. Both studies rely on discussions with contemporary young girls; in Hains's work in particular these discussions are often left to stand for themselves as a testament to the real-world, ideological consequences of girl power on girls and women.[28] Zaslow defines girl power media culture as a phenomenon that is 'rooted in a neoliberal discourse in which urban teen girls come to understand female power as an individualistic stance rather than a collective achievement'.[29] For Zaslow, feminism is performed by these girls as a personal identity of strength and independence, rather than acted out through social and political activism.[30]

As even this cursory survey of the field suggests, feminist politics and feminist rhetorics are deployed in a variety of different, often conflicting, ways in the burgeoning scholarship on girls. The fact that the phrase 'girl power' can mean such different things in different contexts alerts us to the need for nuanced and contextualised feminist analysis. While they are seemingly self-evident, such phrases carry diametrically opposed meanings in, say, the context of the riot grrrl movement and the promotion of the Spice Girls. In the first scenario, the phrase emerged in an alternative, underground grassroots culture and was explicitly political and activist in nature. Girl power in this context is part of the development of third-wave feminism at the community level. In the second scenario, the phrase was co-opted from its original political context for commercial and arguably superficial purposes. Girl power in this context is individualistic rather than collective and the phrase itself is effectively de-fanged – robbed of feminist bite. Its widespread adoption in marketing everything from lip gloss to tennis shoes should more properly be considered post-feminist in flavour than feminist in intent.

Throughout this book I try to distinguish carefully between the types of feminism I discuss – from second-wave feminism, to third-wave feminism and post-feminism – because distinctions between these disparate political projects are crucial to maintain if we are to avoid the kind of flattening, misrepresentation and simplification that does profound disservice to our discipline and its politics. It seems to me that collapsing important difference between the variety of contemporary feminist messages in popular culture today can only benefit the 'forces of darkness', the conservative ideology that would persuade us that the moment of feminism has passed. In the discussion that follows, I examine developments in film and television criticism, second- and third-wave feminist theory, and recent articulations of 'post-feminism' in order to provide what I see as important social, cultural and political contexts for the chapters that follow.

Placing *Buffy* in feminist film and television history

Although it is only now being considered a distinct corpus, the canon of girl-focused independent cinema of the 1990s arguably started in 1988 with the box office flop and subsequent cult classic *Heathers*. *Heathers* starred the 16-year-old Winona Ryder, who had first attracted attention the previous year in Tim Burton's *Beetlejuice* (and who was urged by her agent not to accept the role because of the damage it would do to her career). It also featured Christian Slater and Shannen Doherty, before she emerged as Brenda Walsh in Aaron Spelling's successful television series *Beverley Hills 90210* in 1990.[31] Set in a fictional Ohio town, *Heathers* is a dark comedy involving clique pressure, peer exploitation, and popularity, as well as teen suicide and serial killing – certainly the darker side of Sears. While *Heathers* ultimately ranked no. 5 on *Entertainment Weekly*'s list of the 50 Best High School Movies in 2006 and, in 2008, ranked 412 on *Empire*'s list of the 500 Greatest Movies of All Time, at the beginning of the 1990s it was still essentially a sleeper, although it had introduced a new bitterness and snarkiness to the teen girl flick.[32]

Heathers is an early example of the controversial and subversive girl-focused independent cinema that flourished in the 1990s. Also included in what we might call the third wave of feminist films are Matthew Bright's explosive Red Riding Hood allegory *Freeway* (1996), staring a rampaging Reese Witherspoon as the barely literate Vanessa; African American director Leslie Harris's powerful low-budget first feature, *Just Another Girl on the IRT* (1993); Alison Anders's dramatic exposé of Latina girl gangs in *Mi Vida Loca* (1993); Karyn Kusama's kick-ass boxing flick *GirlFight* (2000); Alex Sichel's queer New York Story *All Over Me* (1992); Kimberly Peirce's transgender tragedy, *Boys Don't Cry* (1999); the still-sobering adaptation, *Girl, Interrupted* (1999); the Seattle based *Foxfire* (1996) featuring a young Angelina Jolie; and Jim McKay's *Girls Town* (1996), set in suburban New Jersey.[33] Translating the ethos of independent activists, publishers and musicians in riot grrrl bands, zines, and DIY websites, these films produced a cinema that is noted for its uncompromising confrontation with the realities of social and sexual inequality, its blistering anger and redemptive energy and its sometimes surprising search for alternatives to traditional gender stereotypes.

Despite differences in budget, audience and commercial success, these films all participate in what Kimberley Roberts calls 'the angry girl' genre of the 1990s – 'the body of film where teenage girl anger is articulated specifically as a weapon against gender crimes'.[34] As Roberts relates: 'many film heroines of the girl power era are pissed off and ready to do something about it – they are fighters who combat the forces against them, unapologetically and often violently'.[35] While Roberts includes such films in what she calls 'the popular feminist groundswell known as *girl power*', she explicitly associates them with the 'radical and overtly political' riot grrrl movement rather than the 'tamer and more palatable version' of girl power popularised by the Spice Girls.[36] According to the taxonomy of feminisms outlined in my discussion of girl studies above, I refer to such texts as third-wave feminist films, in contradistinction to the more commercial brand of 'girl power' films discussed below.

In this analysis, third-wave feminist films are explicitly interventionist, dealing with real life situations like sexual harassment (*Boy's Town*; *Foxfire*), domestic violence (*GirlFight*), homophobia and homophobic violence (*All Over Me*; *Boys Don't Cry*), rape (*Freeway*; *Girls Town*), incest (*Freeway*; *Girl, Interrupted*), unwanted pregnancy (*Just Another Girl on the IRT*) and mental illness or suicide (*Girls Town*; *Girl, Interrupted*). Set predominantly in the present – the single exception is *Girl, Interrupted*, which was based on the novel of the same name and set in the 1960s – these films are realist dramas, and while moments of humour are sometimes used to leaven the serious message, that message is on the whole very serious indeed. These are films that force viewers to confront gender inequality and the abuse of patriarchal power in direct and usually uncomfortable ways.

The 1990s also gave rise to a slew of lighter films that represent the more commercial face of girl power – what Roberts calls 'a structure of belief and a set of consumer practices that centre on the individual teenage girl's power to effect change in her universe'.[37] Such films include the perennially popular *Clueless* (1995), *Spice World* (1997), *Election* (1999) and *Legally Blonde* (2001); the lesbian and queer romances *The Incredibly True Adventure of Two Girls in Love* (1995) and *But I'm a Cheerleader* (1999); and teen Shakespeare adaptations featuring strong female heroines, *10 Things I Hate About You* (1999) and *She's the Man* (2006).[38] These films are all comedies or romantic comedies and their feminist impulses vary from unadulterated individual ambition (*Election*) through impulsive 'do-goodery' (*Clueless*) to protofeminist platforms (*10 Things I Hate About You*). Their protagonists often fight stereotypes (particularly in the biracial lesbian romance *The Incredibly True Adventures of Two Girls in Love*) but also sometimes pander to and play with them (the dumb blonde stereotypes of *Clueless* and *Legally Blonde* being obvious examples). Protagonists such as Kat in *10 Things I Hate About You* might be feisty and express contempt for 'misogynist consumer culture', but Kat arguably ultimately follows the text of Shakespeare's *Taming of the Shrew* in being 'domesticated' by the heterosexual romance narrative.[39]

Comedy, of course, does not by any means preclude politics, and it would be impossible and indeed misguided to attempt to homogenise the feminist and post-feminist ideologies behind such a disparate collection of films. Analysis clearly needs to be made on a case-by-case basis. Humour can be used in some cases to bolster a feminist message and in other cases to submerge any potential political message. As a scholar of *Buffy*, I am unwilling to deem any pop culture product vapid or regressive simply because of its genre or topic; at the same time, scholars of post-feminism have taught us to be wary of seemingly emancipatory narratives that hide a more conservative gender agenda. Regardless of their individual politics, however, both the third-wave feminist films of the 1990s and their more commercial 'girl power' counterparts are contexts relevant to both the 1992 film *Buffy* and its subsequent television incarnation.

Screening from 1997–2003, the television series *Buffy* was part of a groundswell of popular programming at the close of the twentieth century featuring strong female protagonists. Seasons 1 to 5 of *Buffy* screened in the US on The WB Television Network, famous for teen hits such as *Dawson's Creek* (1998), *Roswell* (1999), *Felicity* (1998), *Charmed* (1998) and *7th Heaven* (1996). From Season 6 in October 2001, *Buffy* moved to the United Paramount Network (UPN), where it screened alongside *Star Trek: Voyager*, *Star Trek: Enterprise*, a revival of *The Twilight Zone* and *Roswell*, which UPN also acquired from The WB.[40] As the previous chapter indicates, the initial popular and academic response to the series considered it alongside television shows such as *Xena: Warrior Princess* as well as films such as the *Alien* series (on which Joss Whedon had briefly worked). Television criticism of this period sometimes positions *Buffy* in the context of contemporaneous primetime series featuring arguably empowered female leads, such as Fox's *Ally McBeal* and HBO's *Sex in the City*. Scholars have also considered *Buffy* in the context of science fiction heroines, or what Elyce Rae Helford has called 'Fantasy Girls', and of the action genre and what Sherrie Inness calls 'Action Chicks'.[41] Collectively, such studies place strong female protagonists at the centre of discussions about gender relations in popular media in an unprecedented way. The initial enthusiasm elicited by these innovative shows in their infancy led inevitably to a renewed critical focus on their heroines as such series continued to flourish.

In the introduction to *Feminist Television Criticism: A Reader*, published in 1997, editors Charlotte Brunsdon, Julie D'Acci and Lynn Spigel portray a positive relationship between feminism and television, noting a move in feminist cultural studies away from simplistic dismissals of popular culture:

> Since the 1970s, feminists have become increasingly interested in television as something more than a bad object, something that offers a series of lures and pleasures, however limited its repertoire of female roles. For its part, over the last twenty-five years, television too has engaged with the themes and tropes of feminism [...] Indeed, much of the current entertainment output of television features strong women, single mothers, and female friends and lovers – that is, female types who are integral to feminist critique and culture.[42]

However, Bonnie J. Dow identifies some of the ongoing shortcomings of 'primetime feminism' as 'a white middle class, heterosexual bias, an assumption that a "seize the power" mindset and more vigorous individualism will solve all women's problems, and a conflation of feminist identity with feminist politics'.[43] Dow offers the following useful caution: 'we need to appreciate media for what it can do in giving us images of strong women; yet at the same time, we need to maintain a very keen sense of the limitations of media logic'.[44]

In their overview of feminist television criticism from its inception in the 1970s to the early years of the 2000s, Janet McCabe and Kim Akass identify several current themes. Representing a shift towards 'audience research and reception studies', feminist television analysis in this period considers television viewing practices and 'how actual women watched and made use of television'.[45] A contemporary preoccupation of feminist television studies is feminist versus feminine pleasure. Examples of this include text-based genre studies, such as Sujata Moorti and Karen Ross's discussion of the cultural meaning of reality television, its themes and subjects.[46] Analysis of television viewing pleasure also encompasses audience studies and the analysis of often problematic and post-feminist 'approved cultural scripts' found in popular television.[47] Jennifer Maher argues strongly that the apolitical, uncritical stance of post-feminism has had a detrimental effect on feminist media studies, stating: 'I am most disturbed by essays that, by embracing a "postmodern version of feminism", unduly praise every example of a hot girl who knows how to fight or can pay her own bills.'[48]

McCabe and Akass highlight the prevalence of pleasure, ambiguity and contradiction in feminist television study. They state that 'interrogating issues of desire and pleasure, identity and sexual politics, and ambivalence preoccupies the current feminist television scholarship with which we are involved'. These discussions, they assert, are 'rooted in an intellectual context indebted to third-wave feminism, and the product of various contradictory definitions and theoretical differences emerging in the early-1990s'.[49] As feminist television criticism examines the 'socio-cultural ideological context' of television production, the representation of female agency and victimhood, and of racial, cultural and economic minorities in popular media, are at the forefront of contemporary discussions.[50] McCabe and Akass describe feminist television analysis as 'theorising power, oppression and domination' in such a way that 'criticism here becomes a form of activism, allowing multiple voices and contesting opinions to co-exist in an unpredictable, and often uneasy, alliance'.[51] Feminist television scholars are increasingly examining the meaning of participating in a television culture that continues to subjugate and oppress, by asking 'why women invest – some by choice, others not – in misogyny and sexism'.[52]

In the introduction to her edited collection, *Third Wave Feminism and Television: Jane Puts it in a Box*,[53] Merri Lisa Johnson provides a useful snapshot of some of these contemporary debates. She notes that, like all popular cultural studies, the study of television must contend with the spectre of the culture industry mobilised by the Frankfurt school and its denunciation of participation and pleasure in mass culture as a form of co-option. She cites John Fiske, for whom the politics of popular culture is at best only 'progressive', it can never be 'radical':

> It is concerned with the day-to-day negotiations of unequal power relations in such structures as the family, the immediate work environment, and the classroom. Its progressiveness is concerned with redistributing power within these structures toward the disempowered; it attempts to enlarge the space

> within which bottom-up power has to operate. It does not, as does radicalism, try to change the system that distributes that power in the first place.'[54]

Johnson notes that Terry Eagleton takes this several steps further when he argues that 'pleasurable conduct is the true index of successful social hegemony; self-delight the very mark of social submission'.[55]

Assessing popular television in terms of feminist content also means facing up to the forthright critiques of cinematic viewing pleasure and false consciousness urged by second-wave feminists like Laura Mulvey in which, in Johnson's words, the desire 'to watch television appears, in this framework, to be merely another outlet for women's lust for annihilation'.[56] The position of the feminist viewer of television becomes impossibly invidious. Johnson questions:

> Just when the television show starts to feel really good, when it holds my attention and dramatizes the very feminist debates that compel me, am I to understand that this moment is the measure of my submission to the status quo? That I am sufficiently entertained, lulled into false consciousness? I am not only 'caught looking', I am *caught liking*.[57]

The position of the feminist television critic is equally invidious, caught between the desire for an elusive 'correct' pleasure and the manifold lures of 'masochistic' pleasure. While Johnson cannot offer a cure for this critical bind, she does offer a caveat:

> The pleasures of reading Eagleton and Mulvey are, it seems to me, at least as masochistic as the pleasures against which they warn us in aesthetic and cinematic products, in that both theorists require us to trash the delight that doubles as complicity.[58]

Like Johnson I have been moved by the bracing rigour and manifesto-like fervour of Marxist and second-wave feminist critiques of pleasure: the rousing rhetoric and militant call to arms articulated by Eagleton and Mulvey makes me want to be part of the solution not part of the problem.[59] But if the answer is media abstinence, as it so often seems it is, that is not a very satisfactory answer and it certainly doesn't seem to pose any solutions.

For feminist television scholarship to proceed in the current critical climate, Johnson ultimately advocates a 'balance between appreciation and skepticism, or pleasure and danger' and recommends a focus on 'the conversations made possible by various series without feeling the need to subordinate this positive approach to an obligatory deprecation of television culture'.[60] Building explicitly on the arguments put forward in my previous chapter, Johnson suggests that the most pertinent and useful questions that feminist media theory can ask at this point are not 'is this show feminist or not' or even 'is it feminist enough?' She proposes instead that studies take for granted the fact that 'all shows on television today contain a mixture of feminist, postfeminist, antifeminist, and pseudofeminist motifs'.[61] Johnson wants to 'counter the trend in feminist television studies of reading for the wry pleasures of catching patriarchy at its old tricks once again'. She claims that '[t]here is not enough work being done to articulate what we like about television, what it does for us, what we do with it – while always taking note of where it falls short – as well as where we do'.[62] This task, however, is not an easy one, because, as Johnson observes, 'in exceeding its status as bad object, television does not negate its bad-objectness'.[63]

Buffy at the brink of second-wave and third-wave feminism

So, where does *Buffy* sit in the spectrum of feminist rhetoric, politics and praxis that we encounter today? In one sense, that is the broad question that this book as a whole endeavours to grapple with. Since the chapters that follow are primarily interested in more recent formulations of feminism – third-wave feminism, transnational feminism, queer feminism and studies of masculinity – it makes sense to spend some time here considering how *Buffy* engages with second-wave feminism. Second-wave feminism is the version of feminism that series creator Joss Whedon and his fellow students at Wesleyan College would most likely have studied at university; it is the kind of feminism espoused by Whedon's mother and the work with Equality Now that he undertakes as her legacy. It is also arguably the species of feminism with which the name 'feminist' is still most closely associated in popular culture.

The immediate genre designation claimed by *Buffy the Vampire Slayer* is horror and the series' conscious revision of genre archetypes remains one of its enduring contributions to feminism and popular culture in general. The basic feminist strategy here is a reversal of gendered power dynamics: if second-wave feminism argued that power is not the natural property of men, that women can and should wield it as well, then *Buffy* shows us that in an appealing, if fantastic, way. The pleasure of viewing, however, is also the pleasure of vicarious empowerment. If institutionalised patriarchy is a systematic abuse of women, and psychology tells us that anger is the healthiest psychological response to abuse, then fighting back itself can be a form of empowerment. And fighting back, night after night, is exactly what Buffy does.

Second-wave feminism is fundamentally a campaign for rights. In its liberal version it is a fight for equal rights under existing power structures, and in its radical version it encompasses the desire to overthrow existing power structures through that very shift. In her interactions with institutionalised power, Buffy represents both forms of protest. She challenges the established power structure most obviously through her interaction with the Watchers' Council – the body of men who create, enlist and monitor Slayer activity. The story arc of Buffy's battle with the Watchers' Council takes place primarily in Seasons 1 to 3, although it resurfaces periodically, most prominently in Season 7, and is discussed more fully in the next two chapters.

Buffy also embraces some of the political priorities of second-wave feminism. Through her supernatural actions, Buffy is a champion of 'the oppressed' but she is also, in her more human guise, a figure *for* the oppressed. If the healthiest psychological response to abuse (via patriarchy) is anger, then it is also sadly true that without collective action only a few robust individuals are able to respond in this way. More common (human – indoctrinated) responses include the repression of anger, which leads to depression and disillusion, and the denial of the oppression, which leads, in second-wave terms, to false consciousness, to willed ignorance, stasis, blockage and potential collusion. *Buffy* shows us the hefty challenges of trying to maintain the fight while struggling with these pressures.

Irene Karras and Michele Byers are two scholars who have analysed *Buffy*'s position at the cusp of second- and third-wave feminisms. Karras suggests that the relationships between Buffy and her mother, and Buffy and the Watchers' Council, for example, 'act as metaphors for the tensions between second and third wave feminists'.[64] In Karras's reading, Buffy's mother represents the 'quintessential second wave feminist' and that 'more than just representing a teen's typical view that her mother is clueless about her life, Joyce can be said to have represented all the tenets of second wave feminism against which Buffy is defining herself'.[65]

Byers raises anew the contentious issue of bodies and beauty in the series. She acknowledges criticisms that assume that '*Buffy* cannot be feminist because of its star's body or looks', but also highlights the reductive nature of these arguments: 'Are breasts really what keeps a show from being feminist?' She asserts that the series must be viewed within its mass media, Hollywood context, and suggests that feminist critiques consider not just the bodies in *Buffy* but also 'the performance of these bodies'. Byers argues that 'these characters are more than pretty bodies on the television screen; they also raise interesting questions about gender and the potentialities of third wave feminism'.[66] With this in mind, Byers asserts that 'in the *Buffy* world, competence, strength, and independence are precisely what is being offered to women, not just breasts, abs, and lip gloss'.[67]

In an extension of this argument, Karras defends Buffy's femme beauty and fashion-consciousness, aligning her with 'girlie' third-wave feminism, the intersection of culture and feminism that she argues is unique to the third wave. Karras argues that Buffy claims her femininity as a source of strength; she is a 'prototypical girly feminist activist, intentionally slaying stereotypes about what women can and cannot do'.[68] Byers supports this reading of Buffy as a 'girlie' third-wave feminist, pointing out the 'paradox of feminine adolescence' as enacted by the female characters on *Buffy*: they are

> interested in appearances; they long to be found attractive and to find appreciation for their bodies in the eyes of their peers […] But each of the young women is also fiercely dedicated to her own unique powers and struggles, and all of the female characters on the show tend to reject dependency.[69]

Byers celebrates the series' 'refusal to make its female characters masculine'. Buffy and her female comrades are not made honorary males, nor are they denied their feminine gender performance or struggles; rather, in Buffy's world, 'the feminine enacts the heroic'.[70]

On the flipside, both Karras and Byers highlight the lack of visible diversity in the series' landscape. Karras describes this as 'one aspect of second wave feminism that Buffy does not necessarily update to the satisfaction of the third wave'.[71] Both argue that economic and racial intersectionality is a priority of third-wave feminism, and one that is not adequately reflected in the series. Byers writes that 'in discussions of feminism, there is, increasingly, a desire to recognise diversity in relation to race, class, sexual orientation, and ability, for example', but that despite this, 'Buffy's terrain remains firmly white, middle-class, heterosexual, and able'.[72] Although *Buffy* 'establishes a terrain where women are empowered, where they take action and evidence physical strength, intellectual temerity, and independence' – certainly a feminist standpoint – Byers suggests that the series 'articulates a world devoid of visible difference or where difference must be eliminated, raising the spectre of racism'.[73]

She warns, however, against dismissing the series as unfeminist for this reason, suggesting that '*Buffy* (and mainstream television shows like it) expresses a contradiction, a tension that exists between second- and third-wave feminism on a much larger scale', and that whilst

> *Buffy* is in some ways an excellent example of the third wave, displaying and attracting young, empowered women [...] the retention of a focus on the struggles of privileged girls and women (white, middle-class, and so on) ties *Buffy*, as a cultural text, to the second wave.[74]

Byers states:

> It is hard not to recognise *Buffy the Vampire Slayer* as articulating a vision of feminism, albeit one that is primarily white and middle-class. The radical images of femininity it offers its viewers are linked to this idealised version of womanhood and girlhood. *Buffy*'s popularity in critical and feminist circles must thus also be understood within this particular context.[75]

Karras and Byers go on to examine the series' connections to third-wave feminism, a topic I explore in more detail in the following chapter. Both identify the third-wave potential of the series' premise, Karras asserting that the show's subversion of the female victim role 'exemplifies the third wave's commitment to girl power', and Byers stating that 'although the traditional hero of mythology is inarguably male, with *Buffy* the heroic becomes not just reconciled with the feminine but ruled by it'.[76] Karras points out that rather than being disempowered by the expectations of adolescence and others' gazes, Buffy has the power to gaze back, and her 'revolutionary' strength 'exceeds that of any gender, including the demonic'.[77] According to Byers, the series dramatises 'the struggle that many young women face to be strong, independent, articulate, ambitious, and powerful. And this is done without erasing women's desire for connection.' Championing the second-wave celebration of sisterhood as well as individual strength and desire, 'this vision of girlhood and womanhood as articulated by *Buffy* is what makes the series a feminist text'.[78]

Karras identifies Buffy's unrelenting duty to slay demons and her passing that duty on to her friends as a third-wave characteristic. Buffy faces an 'inherited world of evil', and although she 'did not choose her fate, and does not always enjoy defending humanity [...] her reluctance never keeps her from doing her job as well as she can'. Her duties are more important than her other interests; 'she certainly does not let the guy – not even her one true love – get in the way of her work and self-fulfillment'. It is important, however, that she does not fight alone, instead passing her duties on to her friends of all genders. For Karras, 'the fact that in Buffy's world, men and women are equally capable of intense evil and goodness without sacrificing their sexuality reflects the third wave's internalisation of the second wave's feminist goals'.[79] Before moving on to explore the ways in which *Buffy* can be considered a third-wave text more closely in the following chapter, however, it is important to consider one final context for Buffy's feminism – in the recent emergence of post-feminist rhetoric and scholarship.

Problems with post-feminism

In Chapter 1, I noted that the critic A. Susan Owen suggested that *Buffy* should more properly be considered post-feminist than feminist, and critics since then sometimes blithely suggest that *Buffy* is post-feminist as if television itself (or blondeness or short skirts) was somehow synonymous with post-feminism. This book strenuously refutes this idea. If the medium itself somehow makes a popular text post-feminist we are caught in the bind Merri Lisa Johnson identifies, where certain Marxist or second-wave feminist critiques eviscerate any pleasure or political potential that can be found in popular cultural production. I like to think instead that some popular culture forms are capable of commenting on their moment and medium in a critical, if still commercial, way.

This is not to deny that some pop cultural products are post-feminist. They undoubtedly are. While it is an easy target, for me films such as *Spice World* fit the category of post-feminist perfectly because they seem to address feminist concerns but actually do something else entirely. Post-feminism is worth exploring in some detail at this stage because it can easily be misunderstood and misleadingly represented. I use the term cautiously and specifically. In a sense the term is a misnomer in the way that the term post-colonialism can be potentially misleading. The contemporary era can be described as post-colonial in the sense that some states that were previously colonies have now achieved independence. This does not mean, of course, that colonies do not exist in the current political climate. Similarly, it would be premature to say that we live in a completely post-feminist moment when feminists and feminism still clearly exist. Overestimating the success of the 'post' in post-feminism is as dangerous, I believe, as underestimating the reality of its effects. In this book I talk about post-feminist impulses in parts of the media, in politics, in popular culture, rather than positing that society as we know it, or culture as we experience it, is entirely post-feminist. It is important to understand that post-feminist impulses occupy a political spectrum from taking feminism for granted to outright denunciation. There are different trajectories of post-feminism (just as there are several spokes to second-wave or third-wave feminism) and some of these are more obvious and some more insidious than others.

In *The Aftermath of Feminism: Gender, Culture and Social Change*, Angela McRobbie provides a useful working definition of post-feminism when she describes it as the 'undoing' or 'dismantling' of feminism – 'a process which says feminism is no longer needed, it is now common sense, and as such it is something young women can do without.'[80] McRobbie sees post-feminism as evoking a situation in which 'feminism ha[s] achieved the status of commonsense, while it [is] also reviled, almost hated'.[81] She analyses this phenomenon, and the popular culture forms that respond to it and help construct it, by dissecting 'the forms of gender power which operate within an illusion of positivity and progress while locking young women into 'new-old' dependencies and anxieties'.[82] McRobbie argues that the tropes of freedom and choice 'which are now inextricably connected with the category of young women' present feminism as 'decisively aged' and 'redundant':

> feminism is cast into the shadows, where at best it can expect to have some afterlife, where it might be regarded ambivalently by those young women who must, in more public venues, stake a distance from it, for the sake of social and sexual recognition.[83]

In response, McRobbie undertakes what she calls 'a complexification of backlash',[84] an analysis that seeks to understand aspects of post-feminist culture such as

> the spotlight effect of power, or, in Deleuzian parlance the luminosities which bring young women forward, as individualised subjects, and which attribute to these young women, a range of capacities such that they can be understood as agents of change.[85]

McRobbie presents post-feminist thinking (and marketing) as a taking-for-granted of feminism, the uptake of a common sense understanding that then leaves feminism behind.

Yvonne Tasker and Diane Negra have similarly tackled the idea of post-feminism in their 2007 book, *Interrogating Postfeminism: Gender and the Politics of Popular Culture*. They argue that definitions of post-feminism are as ubiquitous as the definition is slippery.[86] They assert that:

> Postfeminist culture works in part to incorporate, assume, or naturalize aspects of feminism; crucially, it also works to commodify feminism via the figure of the woman as empowered consumer [...] [P]ostfeminism is white and middle class by default, anchored in consumption as a strategy (and leisure as a site) for the production of the self. It is thus also a strategy by which other kinds of social difference are

glossed over.[87]

Tasker and Negra point out that post-feminism does not always offer 'a logically coherent account of gender and power' but

> through structures of forceful articulation and synergistic reiteration across media forms it has emerged as a dominating discursive system. It generates and draws strength, for instance, from a rhetorical field that produces buzzwords and slogans to express visions of energetic personal empowerment (the borrowed African American idiom 'You go, girl!' the phrase 'girl power', etc).

At the same time, they argue,

> postfeminism draws on and sustains an invented social memory of feminist language as inevitably shrill, bellicose, and parsimonious. Thus, while feminism is constituted as an unwelcome, implicitly censorious presence, it is precisely feminist concerns that are silenced within postfeminist culture.

For these critics, 'reference to "the F word" underscores the status of feminism as unspeakable within contemporary popular culture'.[88]

Diane Negra consolidates this critique in her 2009 monograph *What a Girl Wants?: Fantasizing the Reclamation of Self in Postfeminism*. In her own terms, this book is about 'a popular culture that has just about forgotten feminism despite the constant, generally negative invocations of (often anonymous) feminists'. Exploring what are by now familiar post-feminist media tropes such as the princess, the return to home and the retreat to family, Negra writes:

> To the extent that she is visible at all, the contemporary feminist appears as a narcissistic minority group member whose interests and actions threaten the family and a social consensus that underwrites powerful romanticizations of American 'community'. By caricaturing, distorting, and (often willfully) misunderstanding the political and social goals of feminism, postfeminism trades on a notion of feminism as rigid, serious anti-sex and romance, difficult and extremist. In contrast, post-feminism offers the pleasure and comfort of (re)claiming an

> identity uncomplicated by gender politics, postmodernism, or institutional critique.[89]

Negra argues that post-feminism

> retracts the egalitarian principles of feminism (even if those principles were in some ways faulty or if their egalitarianism was never quite complete), taking hold as an ideological system in a period in which democratic equity may be seen to have curdled into entitlism.[90]

Buffy is never named as a feminist within the extended narrative of the series but nor does she, or the series to which she gives her name, adopt either belittling cheap shots about feminists or post-feminist smugness that that fight is over. Quite the opposite. The debates discussed in this chapter that oppose the popular to the political reflect and extend some of the binaries I explored in the previous chapter about Buffy's fitness as a feminist role model. As I have argued in Chapter 1, these binaries themselves sometimes short-circuit the discussion. The definition of terms is often too absolute to include hybrid genres – an irony given that these are the most common contemporary popular forms. Johnson cites feminist film scholar Linda Williams' reluctance to adopt 'the burden of orthodox position taking' in the field:[91] 'In her resistance to "a moralizing feminism" and simultaneous rejection of the "post-feminist" label, Williams paves the way for . . . "a more relaxed understanding of gendered fun."'[92] This book attempts to follow the call, raised by both Williams and Johnson, for a third methodology – not, I would emphasise, a compromise between two already flawed alternatives, but a new way to negotiate existing, often reductive, debates in the field in search of fresh answers to perennial problems.

Gayle Wald is one scholar whose work offers helpful models for bridging some of the methodological and theoretical impasses in contemporary feminist cultural studies. Wald has offered a wonderfully counter-intuitive and convincing revisionist analysis of the political import of 'even' such a commercial film as Amy Heckerling's *Clueless*.[93] In a different context – this time her analysis of girl audiences of boy bands – Wald argues against too simple a celebration of popular cultural forms, warning against the feminist scholar's desire to see what she wants in something merely because it is fun.[94] In these two seemingly opposed arguments, Wald establishes a delicate tightrope act for feminist scholarship to follow. We should not dismiss popular culture forms too readily because they often contain liberating or emancipatory messages that are not immediately apparent. At the same time, we should not be misled by pleasure, or by a surface veneer of emancipatory rhetoric, in assuming that these popular culture forms are in fact emancipatory. Despite the difficulty involved in following this advice, I believe Wald's model is eminently worth emulating. In the chapters that follow I attempt a kind of rigorous critical exercise that could help cultural studies resist some of the same problems that the popular culture texts themselves fall prey to. If one is to resist a condemnatory culture industry analysis – necessary if one is to consider popular culture forms as capable of anything other than dumbing-down and brainwashing – then space needs to be made for critical analysis that is neither kneejerk rejection nor simple celebration.

3

'Kicking Ass is Comfort Food': Buffy as Third-Wave Feminist Icon

Buffy: I love my friends. I'm very grateful for them. But that's the price of being a Slayer … I mean, I guess everyone's alone, but being a Slayer – that's a burden we can't share.
Faith: And no one else can feel it. Thank god we're hot chicks with superpowers!
Buffy: Takes the edge off.
Faith: Comforting!

('End of Days', 7.21)

> I definitely think a woman kicking ass is extraordinarily sexy, always […] If I wasn't compelled on a very base level by that archetype I wouldn't have created that character. I mean, yes, I have a feminist agenda, but it's not like I made a chart.[1]

In the context of the panoply of feminist positions explored in the previous chapter, what accounts for the extraordinary and enduring feminist appeal of *Buffy the Vampire Slayer*, and how has its ex-cheerleading, demon-hunting heroine become the new poster girl for third-wave feminist popular culture? The isolation and consolation Buffy identifies in her conversation with Faith (above) both address these questions, as does Whedon's acknowledgement of a 'feminist agenda' and his rejection of a programmatic 'chart'. In this chapter I examine *Buffy* through the problematic of third-wave feminism, situating the series as part of a larger cultural project that seeks to reconcile the political agenda of second-wave feminism with the critique of white racial privilege articulated by women of colour and the theoretical insights afforded by post-structural analysis. I suggest that if one of the primary goals of third-wave feminism is to question our inherited models of feminist agency and political efficacy, without acceding to the defeatism implicit in the notion of 'post-feminism', then *Buffy* provides us with modes of oppositional praxis, of resistant femininity and, in its final season, of collective feminist activism that are unparalleled in mainstream television. At the same time, the series' emphasis on individual empowerment, its celebration of the exceptional woman and its problematic politics of racial representation remain important concerns for feminist analysis. Focusing primarily on the final season of the series, I argue that Season 7 of *Buffy* offers a more straightforward and decisive feminist message than the show had previously attempted, and that in doing so it paints a compelling picture of the promises and predicaments that attend third-wave feminism as it negotiates both its second-wave antecedents and its traditional patriarchal nemeses.

The contours of third-wave feminism continue to be contested and refined today, despite the sense on the part of some post-feminist scholars that its particular political moment has passed. While aspects of third-wave feminism have since proliferated globally, the movement originated in local enclaves of independent activists, publishers and musicians in 1990s America – in riot grrrl bands, zines and DIY websites based in Seattle, New York and Philadelphia. Introducing a vibrant counter-culture for young women that spread from its initial locales to the continental US, riot grrrl has been celebrated for its uncompromising confrontation with the realities of social and sexual inequality, its blistering anger and redemptive energy and its sometimes surprising (and sometimes surprisingly comic) search for alternatives to traditional gender stereotypes. Rebecca Munford characterises riot grrrl as a 'girl culture' phenomenon, that creates 'speaking positions for girls and young women whose experiences and desires are marginalised by the ontological and epistemological assumptions of a feminism that speaks for them under the universalising category of "woman"'.[2] Ednie Kaeh Garrison points out that it was 'feminist critiques of feminism' that formed the origins of third-wave feminism.[3] Riot grrrl constituted part of a youth-led critique of the second wave's shortcomings, and explored the intersections of race, age, aesthetics, pop culture and consumerism. According to Garrison, riot grrrl 'makes use of a historically situated repertoire of cultural objects and images, codes, and signs in self-consciously political ways'.[4] It claims and employs 'punk aesthetics, politics and style', often considered male constructions, as a means of conveying 'feminist consciousness'.[5] In an increasingly technologised cultural context, riot grrrl's punk and grunge grassroots and DIY means of distributing ideas through music and zines were a challenge, Munford writes, to the conventionally 'gendered relationship between (male) production and (female) consumption' within cultural industries.[6] And while riot grrrl championed individual empowerment and intersectional definitions of feminism, it was a movement more closely aligned with collectivism and solidarity, on all-girl punk bands and sharing handmade zines. At the same time, however, another group of feminist writers was producing work that championed the individual experience over collective action.

The early 1990s saw the production of several popular essay collections, such as *To Be Real: Telling the Truth and Changing the Face of Feminism* and *Listen Up: Voices from the Next Feminist Generation*, declaring the need for a new movement for younger feminists. With essay titles such as 'Getting off on feminism', 'How does a supermodel do feminism?' and 'Chicks goin' at it', these collections aimed to create what they saw as a younger, updated feminism designed to address the priorities and contexts of a new generation.[7] These anthologies were loosely edited, consisting primarily of anecdotal ficto-critical works, spanning a spectrum from insightful to solipsistic and, occasionally, insufferably smug. Such collections represent the third wave's interest in plurality, contradiction and individual empowerment, celebrating a multiplicity of individual experiences rather than creating a unifying cause or voice. Individually, these works often championed personal or popular discourse and cultural critique over political feminist theory, and implied derision for earlier earnest and angry styles of feminism. As Claire Snyder remarks, 'this popular literature contains [...] major claims about how third-wave feminism differs from second-wave feminism – claims that contain some truth yet overstate the distinctiveness of the new movement from its predecessor'.[8]

Often credited with heralding the third wave, most notably by herself, Rebecca Walker's 1992 article 'Becoming the third wave' straddles both the activism of politically inflected third-wave feminism and the sometimes surprising historical short-sightedness of its more individualist incarnations. In this essay Walker reflects upon her own anger and feelings of disempowerment, and declares that a new generation of women must channel that anger into feminist action. Using a recent high-profile sexual harassment case as the catalyst for her call to arms, Walker argues that male privilege continues to disempower and silence women and 'restrict the boundaries of women's personal and political power'.[9] She attests that women are admonished for speaking out: 'the backlash against US women is real'.[10] Reflecting on her feelings of 'powerlessness' she describes her main reaction as rage: 'I am sick of the way women are negated, violated, devalued, ignored. I am livid, unrelenting in my anger at those who invade my space, who wish to take away my rights, who refuse to hear my voice.'[11] Walker calls for a 'Third Wave of feminism' that refuses to stay silent, and that takes the 'repressed anger' of a marginalised group and fights back, channelling those emotions into action: 'my anger and awareness must translate into tangible action'.[12] Walker's feminism is self-aware and educated, aiming to extend beyond rhetoric and 'reading feminist theory' into action; feminism must 'understand power structures with the intention of challenging them'.[13] She defines her vision of a third-wave feminism as one which permeates every aspect of one's personal and public life: 'to be a feminist is to integrate an ideology of equality and female empowerment into the very fiber of my life'.[14] Walker highlights both the importance of personal reflection, the 'search for personal clarity in the midst of systemic destruction', and of collective action, the reformation of a 'sisterhood with women when often we are divided'.[15] She emphasises the generational aspect of the wave model of feminism, addressing her calls to arms to all, but to 'women of my generation' in particular ('I owe it to myself, to my little sister on the train, to all of the daughters yet to be born'[16]). Finally, Walker's vision of a third wave of feminism denies the notion of post-feminism that was gaining popularity during the 1990s: 'the fight is far from over'. Her final sentence emphasises this as she proclaims: 'I am not a post-feminism feminist. I am the third-wave.'[17]

The 1990s also saw the emergence of several popular feminist books, journals and magazines that continued to champion and expand upon the notion of a new wave of feminism. These include Jennifer Baumgardner and Amy Richards's *Manifesta: Young Women, Feminism, and the Future*, which discusses the various, seemingly contradictory, offshoots of contemporary feminism not as evidence of any structural weakening, but as proof of feminism's continued relevance and increasing vibrancy and diversity.[18] It also includes indie magazines *BUST* and *Bitch*, which began in 1993 and 1996 respectively as alternatives to mainstream women's magazines and aimed to intertwine popular culture, media and daily life with feminist discourse.[19] These magazines represented a generation who grew up with feminism and viewed the world as unequivocally gendered in every aspect. In its initial goals *Bitch* aimed to 'point out the insidious, everyday sexism of popular culture, propose alternatives, and celebrate pro-woman, pro-feminism pop products'.[20] *BUST* in particular aimed to glorify 'Girl culture', celebrating feminine trappings such as makeup, shopping, adolescence and the body.[21] During this same period, collections of scholarly essays such as Leslie Heywood and Jennifer Drake's 1997 *Third Wave Agenda: Being Feminist, Doing Feminism*; Heywood's 2006 two-volume *The Women's Movement Today: An Encyclopedia of Third-wave Feminism*; and Stacy Gillis, Gillian Howie and Rebecca Munford's 2004 *Third Wave Feminism: A Critical Exploration* (and its 2007 expansion) aimed to give the third wave an academic framework and trajectory, attempting to outline key issues across its multidisciplinary, plural nature.[22]

Despite some cosmetic similarities to post-feminism, it is important to distinguish between third-wave feminism and both the depoliticised, individualistic brand of 'girl power' pedalled by the Spice Girls and the 'common sense' taken-for-grantedness that Angela McRobbie sees as symptomic of post-feminism's derisive popular representations of earlier feminist movements. Describing post-feminism as an 'active process by which feminist gains of the 1970s and 80s come to be undermined', McRobbie foregrounds the role of popular culture in this perception of feminism as outdated, unnecessary and unattractive.[23] In particular she identifies advertisements that appear to deliberately and self-consciously act out sexism, to show it as a redundant 'thing of the past', even expecting 'to provoke feminist condemnation as a means of generating publicity'.

This, McRobbie argues, generates 'generational differences', as the younger, 'visually literate' viewer is able to roll her eyes and laugh at the 'feminist puritanism' of the past.[24] Feminism is set up as a joke and is therefore disempowered; to object to sexist advertising (in light of Laura Mulvey's 1970s discussion of the male gaze and female objectification in popular media, for instance), 'nowadays would run the risk of ridicule'.[25] Munford points out that although 'girl culture' began as an 'eclectic and politically grounded phenomenon', its power was lost as it was assimilated into popular, male-controlled media for young women.[26] The Spice Girls, arguably the figureheads of this 'homogenised media representation' of 'girl power', knowingly distanced themselves from feminist histories, effectively declaring feminism outdated and unnecessary.[27] Although third-wave feminism finds some of the second wave's ideals outdated or limiting, it still aims to build upon this feminist history.[28] Conversely, post-feminism acts to diminish the importance and influence of feminist histories and continued feminist action.[29]

'Third-wave feminism' thus functions in the following analysis as a political ideology still under construction. Buffy makes a similar claim about her own self-development when (invoking one of the more bizarre forms of American comfort food) she refers to herself as unformed 'cookie dough' ('Chosen', 7.22). Garrison has suggested that the name 'third-wave feminism' may be 'more about desire than a reflection of an already existing thing', and Stephanie Gilmore proposes that, ironically, the defining feature of third-wave feminism 'may well be its inability to be categorized'.[30] Transforming such indeterminacy into a political principle, Rory Dicker and Alison Piepmeier state that one of the aims of their 2003 anthology, *Catching a Wave: Reclaiming Feminism for the 21st Century*, is to 'render problematic any easy understanding of what the third wave is'.[31] While there are arguably as many variants of third-wave feminism as there are feminists to claim or reject that label, making clear what one refers to when invoking the term is, I suggest, more important than ever, given the ways that third-wave feminism risks being collapsed into or colonised by a pervasive post-feminist media discourse. The characteristics I have chosen to focus on in this chapter are therefore those that provide the most striking parallels to *Buffy's* Season 7: its continuation of the second-wave fight against misogynist violence, its negotiation of the demands for individual and collective empowerment, its belated recognition and representation of cultural diversity (discussed in more detail in Chapter 4) and its embrace of contradiction and paradox.

Hot chicks, superpowers, and patriarchal nemesises (sic)

What propels *Buffy*'s feminist fandom? What inspires this excess of affect? Rachel Fudge addresses this question directly when she writes that the impulse that propels Buffy out on patrols 'night after night, forgoing any semblance of "normal" teenage life' is identical to the one 'that compels us third-wavers to spend endless hours discussing the feminist potentials and pitfalls of primetime television'. Fudge claims that Buffy 'has the sort of conscience that appeals to the daughters of feminism's second wave', women for whom 'a certain awareness of gender and power is ingrained and inextricably linked to our sense of identity and self-esteem'.[32] In her examination of Buffy as the third wave's 'final girl', Irene Karras argues that Buffy's appeal lies in her intentional 'slaying [of] stereotypes about what women can and cannot do'. Karras applauds the show's combination of sexuality and what she calls 'real efforts to make the world a better and safer place for both men and women'.[33] Michele Byers celebrates *Buffy the Vampire Slayer* as movement away from hegemonic gender roles in popular culture, dramatising young women's struggles with identity and societal codes.[34] Similarly, Sophie Levy argues that the series 'draws its power from adolescent femininity', creating a powerful mythology of the American teen girl and reconciling the heroic and the feminine.[35] Blending an exhilarating athleticism with a compulsion to activism, Buffy's spectacular agency – her literally 'fantastic' facility for kicking ass – has come to function as feminist comfort food.

When fellow Slayer Faith consoles Buffy with the thought '[t]hank god we're hot chicks with superpowers' (first epigraph), the gesture is offered as sympathy and support; it helps to 'take the edge off' the burden they 'can't share'. In this exchange, the Slayer's burden is assuaged in part by what Whedon refers to as her 'sexiness' (second epigraph); in part by the very exceptional qualities or superpowers that isolate her to begin with;

and perhaps ultimately by the sharing of confidences and, by extension, of responsibilities. The 'comfort' offered here is a complex conglomerate, and one that rewards further scrutiny. The title of this chapter, 'Kicking Ass is Comfort Food', comes from the episode 'The Prom' (3.20), which occurs immediately prior to Season 3's apocalyptic Ascension. Buffy has just been told by her lover, Angel, that – in the event that they survive the imminent end-of-the-world – he will be abandoning their relationship and leaving town. To complicate matters, a jilted senior denied a prom date has secretly been training hellhounds to attack partygoers wearing formal attire. Buffy's mentor Giles attempts to console his devastated charge with the conventional cure for a broken heart:

Giles: Buffy, I'm sorry. I understand that this sort of thing requires ice cream of some sort.
Buffy: Ice cream will come. First I want to take out psycho-boy.
Giles: Are you sure?
Buffy: Great thing about being a Slayer – kicking ass is comfort food.

('The Prom', 3.20)

Kicking ass becomes comfort food for Buffy when her supernatural abilities provide her with an extraordinary outlet for more conventional frustrations. Action – in this case a cathartically violent form of action – serves up a supernatural solace for a range of everyday, human afflictions. Kicking ass offers Buffy psychological and physical relief: it allows her to simultaneously redress straightforward social evils and to palliate more personal sorts of demon. For the feminist viewer, the spectacle of Buffy kicking ass is similarly comforting; equally exhilarating and empowering, Buffy provides the compound pleasures of both the hot chick and her superpowers. At the same time, as Elyce Rae Helford has argued, Buffy can stand metaphorically for young women everywhere who are angered by having 'their lives directed by circumstances or individuals beyond their control'.[36] In an era that can sometimes seem saturated with condemnations of feminism's increasing frivolity, Buffy's indomitable militancy – her unrelenting vigilance – can be consumed by the feminist spectator as primetime panacea. Buffy's predilection towards, and consummate abilities in, the art of kicking ass thus simultaneously soothe and sustain, inspire and incite the compulsion to feminist activism.

While over its seven-year cycle, the series addressed a staggering range of contemporary concerns – from the perils of low-paid, part-time employment to the erotic dynamics of addiction and recovery – it is significant that the final season of *Buffy* makes a decisive shift back to feminist basics. Season 7 eschews to a certain extent the metaphorical slipperiness and pop-cultural play that is typical of its evocation of post-modern demons and instead presents a monster that is, quite literally, an enemy of women. The principal story arc pits an amorphous antagonist, The First Evil, against the Slayer and her 'army', a group that has swelled to include in its ranks 'Potential' Slayers from around the globe. Introducing a hitherto unknown matriarchal legacy (and weapon) for the Slayer, staging the series' final showdown with a demon that is overtly misogynist and creating an original evil with a clearly patriarchal platform, Buffy's Season 7 raises the explicit feminist stakes of the series considerably.

Unable to take material form, The First Evil employs as its vessel and deputy a former preacher turned agent-of-evil called Caleb. Spouting hellfire and damnation with fundamentalist zeal, Caleb is, of all of the show's myriad manifestations of evil, the most recognisably misogynist: 'There once was a woman. And she was foul, like all women are foul' ('Dirty Girls', 7.18). Dubbed 'the Reverend-I-Hate-Women' by Xander ('Touched', 7.20), Caleb is a monstrous but familiar representative of patriarchal oppression, propounding a dangerous form of sexism under the cover of pastoral care. 'I wouldn't do that if I were you, sweet pea', Caleb at one point warns Buffy; 'Mind your manners. I do believe I warned you once' ('Empty Places', 7.19). At other times he calls her 'girly girl' ('End of Days', 7.21), a 'little lady' ('Empty Places', 7.19) and, once (but only once), 'whore' ('Touched', 7.20). Buffy's response (after kicking him across the room) is to redirect the condescension and hypocrisy couched in his discourse of paternal concern: 'You know, you really should watch your language. Someone didn't know you, they might take you for a woman-hating jerk' ('Touched', 7.20). In comparison with the supernatural demons of previous episodes, Caleb's evil might seem unusually old-fashioned or even ridiculous, but successive encounters with the Slayer underscore the fact that his power is all the more insidious and virulent for that. Mobilising outmoded archetypes of women's weakness and susceptibility – 'Curiosity: woman's first sin. I offer her an apple. What can she do but take it?' ('Dirty Girls', 7.18) – Caleb effectively sets a trap that threatens to wipe out the Slayer line. Within the context of the narrative, Caleb's sexist convictions – 'Following is what girls do best' ('Dirty Girls', 7.18) – and, more importantly, their unconscious internalisation by the Slayer and her circle, pose the principal threat to their sustained, organised, collective resistance.

Challenges for third-wave feminism: the exceptional white woman as exemplar

In its exploration of the dynamics of collective activism, *Buffy's* final season examines the charges of solipsism and individualism that have frequently been directed at contemporary popular feminism. 'Want to know what today's chic young feminist thinkers care about?' wrote Ginia Bellafante in a notorious 1998 article for *Time* magazine: 'Their bodies! Themselves!'[37] One of the greatest challenges Buffy faces in Season 7 is negotiating conflicting demands of individual and collective empowerment. Trapped by the mythology, propounded by the Watchers' Council that bestows the powers of the Slayer on 'one girl in all the world', Buffy is faced with the formidable task of training Potential Slayers-in-waiting who will only be called into their own power in the event of her death. In the episode 'Potential' (7.12), Buffy attempts to rally her troops for the battle ahead:

> The odds are against us. Time is against us. And some of us will die in this battle. Decide now that it's not going to be you … Most people in this world have no idea why they're here or what they want to do. But you do. You have a mission. A reason for being here. You're not here by chance. You're here because you are the Chosen Ones.

This sense of vocation resonates strongly with feminist viewers who feel bound to the struggle for social justice. However, such heroism can still be a solitary rather than collective endeavour. On the eve of their final battle, after decimating her advance attack, The First-as-Caleb makes fun of what he calls Buffy's 'One-Slayer-Brigade' and taunts her with the prospect of what we might think of as wasted Potential:

> None of those girlies will ever know real power unless you're dead. Now, you know the drill … 'Into every generation a Slayer is born. One girl in all the world. She alone has the strength and skill …' There's that word again. What you are, how you'll die: alone. ('Chosen', 7.22)

Such references make it clear that loneliness and isolation are part of the Slayer's legacy.

Balancing the pleasures and price of her singular status, Buffy bears the burden of the exceptional woman. But the exceptional woman, as Margaret Thatcher and Condaleezza Rice have amply demonstrated, is not necessarily a sister to the cause; a certain style of ambitious woman fashions herself precisely as the exception that proves the rule of women's general incompetence. As the mainstream media reflected upon Thatcher's influence in the wake of her death in 2013, opinions split dramatically on whether her legacy was a feminist one or not. Newspaper editorial headlines described her as a 'self-serving anti-feminist' and the 'ultimate feminist icon' in equal measure, and these polarised opinions represent two differing perspectives on what popular, contemporary feminism 'is'.

Journalists supportive of Thatcher's regime argued that her presence, as a woman who worked against parliamentary sexism to achieve a position of power, was enough to label her a feminist inspiration. From this perspective, she is celebrated for fighting her way from middle-class origins to the top 'against insurmountable odds', defying in this process 'others' notions of what women should be',[38] with some journalists identifying her famously ruthless character as the hallmark of an empowered, powerful woman: 'she would not capitulate to emotive, manipulative pressure tactics, even when the spectre of hollowed cheeks and sallow skin made her appear heartless'. Thatcher's visibility as a woman in the highest position of power, these journalists suggest, is the ultimate expression of gender equality, showing a generation of young people that women are capable of entering previously male-dominated fields.[39] She may have 'hated feminism' but her presence, 'the very fact that she managed to become Prime Minister […] meant a shift in mindset for both men and women that no amount of feminist rhetoric has ever achieved since in Britain'.[40] That she is still the only woman in British history to have achieved this level of influence, they argue, is a testament to her exceptional sense of self.[41]

This line of cultural commentary is overwhelmingly critical of contemporary feminism, dismissing it as valuing 'humorless blah-blah-blah' and rhetoric over action.[42] Conversely, journalists from the Left adopt a very different stance on what constitutes feminist action. From this perspective, Thatcher's gender and visibility are far less important than her beliefs and actions.[43] Simply being a visible, powerful woman in a male-dominated field is not enough: 'one woman's success does not mean a step forward for women', asserts Hadley Freeman; 'far from "smashing the glass ceiling", Thatcher made it through and pulled the ladder up after her'.[44] Thatcher dissociated herself from other women and from the women's movement and did little in terms of political action or rhetoric to help or empower other women, and for these reasons should not be remembered as a feminist icon.[45] Several writers point out that Thatcher 'promoted only one woman to her cabinet, preferring instead to elevate men', as well as her 'notable lack of female-friendly policies', arguing that not only did she do 'nothing to improve the lives of women' but that 'she espoused the very ideology and values that entrenched disadvantage for women and a host of other historically marginalised people'.[46]

Freeman argues that the notion of the exceptional woman is inherently anti-feminist; in her reading, Thatcher

> was a classic example of a certain kind of conservative woman who believed that all women should pull themselves up just as she had done, conveniently overlooking that not all women are blessed with the privileges that had been available to her.[47]

Jessica White describes Thatcher as 'profoundly anti-feminist':

> she was selfish: her tenure did not translate into increased opportunities for women. She does not seem to have had a clear positive effect on the ability of women to assume leadership roles in politics, and she definitely did not concern herself with equality.[48]

These journalists argue that a powerful political regime that does nothing to encourage equality or create opportunities for women cannot be considered feminist. They also counter the notion that Thatcher represents a positive feminist icon in her personal toughness and resilience, arguing that 'strength is not enough'.[49] In White's definition, 'feminism is not about strength [...] it is about making a better world for women'.[50] A powerful woman is not automatically a feminist, and a powerful woman who oppresses and ignores other women can never be considered feminist, 'no matter how tough she was'.[51] Thatcher's career may be one of 'remarkable individual achievement' but a successful, exceptional woman is not automatically a feminist woman.[52] It is salutary to explore the vastly different conclusions that these writers have concerning the exceptional woman, and their divergent interpretations of feminist action, in light of Buffy's transformation in Season 7.

In one of the more dramatic and disturbing character developments in the series as a whole, Season 7 presents Buffy's leadership becoming arrogant and autocratic, her attitude isolationist and increasingly alienated. Following in the individualist footsteps of prominent 'power feminists', Buffy forgoes her collaborative community and instead adopts what fans in the United States and elsewhere perceived as a sort of 'you're-either-with-me-or-against-me' moral absolutism ominously reminiscent of the George W. Bush administration – an incipient despotism exemplified by what Anya calls Buffy's 'everyone-sucks-but-me' speech ('Get It Done', 7.15).[53] The trial of Buffy's leadership is sustained up to the last possible moment, and its resolution repudiates recurring laments about the third wave's purported political apathy. 'According to the most widely publicized construction of the third wave', write Leslie Heywood and Jennifer Drake,

> 'we' hate our bodies, ourselves, our boring little lives, yet we incessantly focus on our bodies, and our boring little lives [...] 'We' believe that the glamorization of nihilism is hip and think that any hope for change is naïve and embarrassing.[54]

Jennifer Baumgardner and Amy Richards respond to such allegations directly when they write 'imagine how annoying it is to hear from anyone (including the media and especially Second Wave feminists) that young women aren't continuing the work of the Second Wave, that young women are apathetic, or "just don't get it"'.[55] Baumgardner and Richards state that they have reacted 'by scrambling to be better feminists and frantically letting these women know how much we look up to them'. Ultimately, however, they have 'refused to accept this myth'.[56]

Drawing attention to the Slayer's increasing isolation, The First highlights the political crisis afflicting her community, but in doing so he inadvertently alerts Buffy to the latent source of its strength, forcing her to claim a connection she admits 'never really occurred to me before' ('Chosen', 7.22). In a tactical reversal that Giles claims 'flies in the face of everything … that every generation has ever done in the fight against evil', Buffy plans to transfer the power of the Chosen One, the singular, exceptional woman, to the hands of the Potentials – to empower the collective not at the expense of, but by force of, the exception. In the series finale, Buffy addresses her assembled army in the following terms:

> Here's the part where you make a choice. What if you could have that power *now*? In every generation one Slayer is born, because a bunch of men who died thousands of years ago made up that rule. They were powerful men. This woman [pointing to Willow] is more powerful than all of them combined. So I say we change the rules. I say *my* power should be *our* power. Tomorrow, Willow will use the essence of the scythe to change our destiny. From now on, every girl in the world who might be a Slayer, *will* be a Slayer. Every girl who could have the power, *will* have the power. Can stand up? Will stand up. Slayers – every one of us. Make your choice: are you ready to be strong? ('Chosen', 7.22)

At that moment – as the archaic power of a recently recovered matriarchal scythe is wrested from the patriarchal dictates of the Watchers' Council – we see a series of vignettes from around the world, as young women of different ages, races, cultures and backgrounds sense their strength, take charge and rise up against their oppressors. This is a 'feel the force, Luke' moment for girls on a global scale. It is a revolution that has been televised.

In transferring power from a privileged, white Californian teenager to a heterogeneous group of women from different national, racial and socio-economic backgrounds Buffy's final season addresses, almost as an afterthought, the issue of cultural diversity that has been at the forefront of third-wave feminist theorising. Garrison has drawn attention to the connections between Chela Sandoval's articulation of 'US Third World Feminism' and US third-wave feminism, representing the latter as a movement fundamentally indebted to the feminist critique articulated by women of colour.[57] Garrison claims that, 'unlike many white feminists in the early years of the Second Wave who sought to create the resistant subject "women", in the Third Wave, the figure "women" is rarely a unitary subject'.[58] This understanding of third-wave feminism is borne out by Baumgardner and Richards, who argue that 'the third wave was born into the diversity realized by the latter part of the second wave', a diversity represented by the works of African American and Chicana feminists, Third World feminists of colour, and US Third World feminists.[59] Heywood and Drake make the third wave's debts to Third World feminism explicit when they state that the arguments that women of colour scholars introduced into the dominant feminist paradigms in the 1980s 'have become the most powerful forms of feminist discourse in the 1990s'.[60] They claim that while third-wave feminism owes

> an enormous debt to the critique of sexism and the struggles for gender equity that were white feminism's strongest provinces, it was US Third World feminism that modeled a language and a politics of hybridity that can account for our lives at the century's turn.[61]

From some of its earliest incarnations, then, academic third-wave feminism has presented itself as a movement that places questions of diversity and difference at the centre of its theoretical and political agenda. However, as Stacy Gillis and Rebecca Munford have pointed out, the 'extent to which third wave feminism has learned how to incorporate, rather than to exclude' remains an issue for ongoing concern.[62]

Rebecca L. Clark Mane problematises the third wave's claim of inclusiveness, asserting that uncritical tokenism and misinterpretation continue to influence the discussion of race in third-wave feminist texts. She argues that this has resulted in 'experiences of displacement by women of colour as well as the deflection of scholarship and theorisations that examine racial hierarchy as a constitutive factor in feminism'.[63] Similarly, Kimberley Springer suggests that the 'wave' model of the women's movement continues to exclude contemporary feminists of colour, relying on oversimplified terms and codes.[64] Discussing common misconceptions about third-wave Muslim feminists as well as their actual practices and goals, Sherin Saadallah argues that the fight for true inclusivity is not over and that limiting binaries of gender, culture and race are still 'predominant in many feminist writings'.[65] Examining what she sees as the serious limitations of predominantly Western third-wave feminism, Winifred Woodhull warns that the third wave risks repeating the exclusionary errors of earlier feminist practices. 'Given the global arena in which third wave feminism emerges', she writes, 'it is disappointing that new feminist debates arising in first-world contexts address issues that pertain only to women in those contexts'.[66] Woodhull claims that the significance and potential of third-wave feminism 'can be grasped only by adopting a global interpretive frame, that is, by relinquishing the old frameworks of the west and developing new ones that take seriously the struggles of women the world over'.[67] In its most rigorous and responsible guise, then, third-wave feminism's call for cultural diversity is the political response to the critique of white racial privilege articulated by second-wave feminists of colour, and the theoretical consequence of incorporating the discourse of difference elaborated by post-structural theory more broadly. In its less careful incarnations, as *Buffy* demonstrates admirably, it can perform the very strategies of occlusion and erasure that its more critical proponents are at pains to redress.

Buffy's racial politics are inarguably more conservative than its gender or sexual politics, a situation explored in more detail in the following chapter, and pithily summarised by one of the few recurring black characters of the show's first three seasons, Mr Trick: 'Sunnydale [...] admittedly not a haven for the brothers – strictly the Caucasian persuasion in the Dale' ('Faith, Hope, and Trick', 3.3). While the final season of the show sees an expansion of *Buffy*'s exclusively white, middle-class cast, with the introduction of character Principal Robin Wood and the international expansion of the Slayer line, such changes can easily be dismissed as mere tokenism. Season 7 makes repeated recourse to racial stereotypes – most notably in its primitivist portrayal of the 'First Slayer' and the 'Shadow Men' as ignoble savages, and its use of formulaic markers of cultural difference to distinguish the international Slayers. While these contradictions are explored further in the following chapter, it is important to note here that such contradictions have been identified as symptomatic of third-wave theorising, or indeed the lack thereof. In a similar vein, in her analysis of what she calls 'the globalization of Buffy's power', Rhonda Wilcox has argued that '*Buffy* can be seen as both a metaphor for and an enactment of globalization', one that contemplates both its negative and positive aspects. Wilcox claims that the series celebrates capitalist institutions such as the mall at the same time that it recognises and critiques the 'cultural presumption' inherent in the idea of 'all-American domination of the world [...] through the spread of technological goods and through governmental aggression'.[68] I would suggest that these readings are not as inimical as they might initially seem; Season 7's narrative implies that both of these readings are admissible, and perhaps, more radically, even mutually implicated.

Contradiction, paradox and third-wave politics

Terms like 'contradiction' and 'paradox' have been so overused in popular discussions of the 'post-modern' condition that they have arguably reached a saturation point where they mean everything and, ironically, nothing. I would like to draw a distinction between straightforward contradiction – where different parts of a philosophy are actually inconsistent and cancel each other out – and the rhetorical understanding of paradox, where apparently opposed positions can be considered mutually constitutive, allowing a deeper exploration of the grey area or 'third space' between them. Critical methodologies that help to excavate the third space between traditional binary oppositions such as man/woman, gay/straight, black/white, and margin/centre have been one of High Theory's most important contributions to the academic elaboration of identity-based politics, as their enthusiastic uptake by feminist, queer and post-colonial scholars attests. At the same time, it bears remembering that deconstructing such apparently self-evident edifices as the category 'human' – which has conventionally stood for white, straight, middle-class men – is by no means the exclusive province of academic theory; grassroots deconstruction gave impetus to the social justice movements of the 1960s and 1970s, and the battles of second-wave feminists must in this sense be counted a significant precursor to capital-D Deconstruction.

It is also important to recognise the difference between the informed assumption of fluidity based on the third wave's ideology of plurality and personal choice, and the post-feminist mantra 'Anything goes!', which waters down the previous political content of such slogans. If feminism is everything that a woman wants or does (or, in the case of Thatcher, simply her very existence), then feminism means everything and at the same time nothing: feminism and post-feminism are conflated. Despite the difficulties of defining third-wave feminism as a political and philosophical movement, I believe it is necessary to continue to distinguish and distance it from the populist post-feminist malaise that threatens to extinguish both second- and third-wave feminism's hard-won achievements.

Kathleen Rowe Karlyn identifies the post-structualist perspective that underpins one of the third wave's primary strategies as the denial of the 'positivist epistemology of the Second Wave', and the defining of categories such as 'male/female', 'black/white', 'heterosexual/homosexual' as 'pragmatic bases for identity politics more than transparent signifiers of the "real"'.[69] Under this ideology, third-wave feminism locates personal identities not as absolute, knowable states of being but as malleable and changeable creations, free to be borrowed, appropriated or 'pieced together ironically, playfully or with political intent'.[70] This vision of identity emerged as the third wave championed an intersectional, pluralistic feminism. Countering what was seen as the second wave's limiting ideal of a unified 'category of women', the third wave undertook to recognise differences in experience and individual perspectives.[71] The third wave does not aim to construct a unifying ideology or theoretical framework; as Leslie Heywood relates, 'contradiction, multiplicity, and ambiguity' are crucial elements to third-wave identity.[72] Snyder-Hall summarises this vision of identity succinctly, writing that 'third-wave feminism accepts the reality that multiple definitions of feminism exist simultaneously'.[73] She describes the third wave as a 'tactical response' to the changing interests of the academy, as post-modernism and post-structuralism began to destabilise second wave absolutes.[74] However, while scholars such as Heywood celebrate the third wave's 'non-essentialist approach to thinking about gender',[75] Snyder suggests that this pluralism has its limits in practice.[76] She argues that 'the conundrum that feminists need to make claims on behalf of women even as they reject a unified category of women' is not truly addressed in most current mainstream feminist writing.[77] Ironically, for Snyder, third-wave feminism's embrace of paradox and hybridity in identity, ideology and practice ultimately reflects the 'embryonic stage of feminist politics' – a judgement that reprimands and encourages in almost equal measure.[78]

It would be a mistake, I think, to underestimate or to collapse too quickly the contradictions embedded in *Buffy*'s cultural politics, contradictions that are in turn indicative of the crosscurrents that distinguish the third wave of feminism. The refusal of misogynist violence, the battle against institutionalised patriarchy and the potential of transnational feminist activism are issues that remain at the forefront of the third wave agenda, and are themes that *Buffy*'s final season explores with characteristically challenging and satisfying complexity. The fact that its success in critiquing its own cultural privilege is equivocal should be read less as a straightforward sign of failure than a reflection of the redoubtable contradictions that characterise third-wave feminism itself. Fudge has suggested that Buffy 'constantly treads the fine line between girl-power schlock and feminist wish-fulfilment, never giving satisfaction to either one'.[79] Adopting one of the signature rhetorical strategies of feminism's third wave, *Buffy* has consistently welcomed such apparent contradiction with open arms. I suggest that in its examination of individual and collective empowerment, its ambiguous politics of racial representation and its willing embrace of contradiction, *Buffy* is a quintessentially third-wave cultural production. Providing a fantastic resolution – in both senses of the word – to some of the many dilemmas confronting third-wave feminists today, *Buffy* is comfort food for girls who like to have their cake and eat it too.

4

Whose Revolution Has Been Televised?: Race, Whiteness and 'Transnational' Slayer Suffrage

> Here's the part where you make a choice. What if you could have that power *now*? In every generation one Slayer is born, because a bunch of men who died thousands of years ago made up that rule. They were powerful men. This woman [pointing to Willow] is more powerful than all of them combined. So I say we change the rules. I say *my* power should be *our* power. Tomorrow, Willow will use the essence of the scythe to change our destiny. From now on, every girl in the world who might be a Slayer, *will* be a Slayer. Every girl who could have the power, *will* have the power. Can stand up? Will stand up. Slayers – every one of us. Make your choice: are you ready to be strong?
>
> ('Chosen', 7.22)

In the previous chapter, I made a case for *Buffy* as a third-wave feminist text, noting that where the series lets this designation down most is in its tokenistic representations of racial otherness and its celebration, in the final season, of 'international' Slayer suffrage under the guise of what might also be seen as North American cultural and military imperialism. In this chapter I consider these concerns in more detail. While I do not think they disqualify the series' claims to third-wave feminist credibility – they are if anything *symptomatic* of North American third-wave theorising at the turn of the millennium – I believe they require critical examination because of the often submerged roles that race and whiteness continue to play in the popular discourse of feminist emancipation, particularly in popular culture. In this chapter I survey some of the critiques of race and post-colonialism that have been raised in *Buffy* studies and explore the problematics of whiteness that have been articulated by film and television critics of the series. I point to the surprising absence of anti-imperial critiques of Season 7's story arc in the scholarship to date, and offer readings of several episodes that foreground these concerns (and causes for concern) in this season. I end by looking at the representation of benevolent US world domination depicted in Season 7's finale in the context in which this episode screened, arguing that *Buffy*'s celebration of universal Slayer suffrage needs to be considered in the immediate historical context of President George W. Bush's rhetoric of the 'War on Terror' and First Lady Laura Bush's unprecedented invocation of women's rights in defence of the US invasion of Afghanistan.

A number of critics have engaged with the representation of race and post-colonialism in *Buffy the Vampire Slayer* and have examined how these dynamics intersect with the series' otherwise emancipatory gender politics. Kent A. Ono and Vivian Chin assert that both popular US media and late-twentieth-century feminism rely overwhelmingly on a white default, and they interrogate the ways this default is manifested across *Buffy the Vampire Slayer*. A recurring criticism is the show's positioning of middle-class whiteness as the norm, and the problematic use of demons to represent the marginal other.[1] Ono argues that the white female as hero in *Buffy* is contingent on the othering and literal demonising of people of colour as villains, with demons' social difference marking them as inherently and irredeemably bad. The demonised other is made killable – the ultimate marginal position.[2] Ono asserts that the series both directly and indirectly villainises people of colour by celebrating 'violence by primarily white vigilante youths against people of colour in the name of *civilisation*'.[3] Chin explores the complexities of Orientalism and identity in *Buffy*, and the ways in which vampires can 'masquerade' as both human and demon, familiar and foreign.[4] She argues that vampires in the text don 'quasi-Oriental' masks that allow them to 'play at being Oriental without actually being Oriental'; their otherness does not disrupt the dominant whiteness of *Buffy*.[5] Chin also discusses the intersection of race and the series' feminist model; Buffy, as the antidote to the 'helpless blonde' horror genre trope, must be blonde and therefore white for the subversion of gender stereotypes to be successful.[6]

In a related critical move, Ewan Kirkland has considered the ways in which the series' principal and supporting characters are coded as white, and highlights the erasure of any ethnic deviation from this norm, such as Willow's Jewishness.[7] Similarly, Naomi Alderman and Annette Seidel-Arpaci argue that despite the show's message of individual empowerment, acceptance in the Buffyverse is often only gained by homogeneity.[8] Elyce Rae Helford discusses racial homogeneity in terms of Kendra's appearance in Sunnydale, arguing that her experience serves to reinforce the privileging of white cultural values as heroic in the Buffyverse.[9] Lynne Edwards casts Kendra as the 'tragic mulatto' and views her aim to assimilate into the white community by adopting Buffy's cultural attitudes and behaviours as doomed to failure.[10] Reading Buffy's slaying practices and moral code through a post-colonial lens, Jessica Hautsch argues that *Buffy* can be seen to legitimise racist US colonial discourses of oppression and assimilation.[11] Ono concurs, concluding that the series enforces a 'neo-colonial' vision, which affirms established hierarchies and champions only that certain kind of white 'non-ordinariness' that the Scooby gang represents.[12] More emphatic is Neal King, who declares the series 'merrily racist', characterising Buffy's slaying as 'incremental genocide' with fascist leanings.[13]

Cynthia Fuchs provides an alternative perspective on the race politics of the series when she writes that *Buffy* depicts 'the whiteness of Buffy and her friends with a forthrightness that is rare on series TV, or in the broader culture'.[14] Citing Ruth Frankenberg's observation that 'whiteness makes itself invisible precisely by asserting its normalcy, its transparency, in contrast to the marketing of others on which its transparency depends', Fuchs asserts that 'Buffy's whiteness is anything but transparent. The series consistently investigates whiteness as a cultural construction and presumption, by parody, by metaphor, and occasionally, as with the First Slayer, by contrast.'[15] Conceding that Buffy herself 'is surely "white" in almost every sense of the term', Fuchs nevertheless argues that 'the very overstatement of that whiteness also highlights and draws attention to it (her name *is* Buffy and she does live in a place called Sunnydale, after all)'. Fuchs contends that part of the 'genius' of *Buffy the Vampire Slayer* 'lies in its ironic undermining of the very status quo it appears to epitomize'.[16]

In a salutary reversal of Ono's much-cited argument about the 'demonisation' of characters of colour in the series, Fuchs suggests that Buffy and her friends 'face frequent questions concerning their "race" metaphorized as their humanness'.[17] Fuchs argues that 'the series tends to displace raced identity and anxieties about race onto species-related anxieties, which are typically performed as various romances'.[18] While these relationships involve characters that 'look very white', they also, Fuchs contends,

> explore the compromises needed in order to cross cultural borders [...] Passing as normal (read: human), Buffy reveals the constraints and constructedness of the categories into which she is trying to pass, as well as those she is trying to elude ('monstrous', 'dead').

Ultimately, Fuchs sees value in the series' interrogations of race and whiteness, arguing that the ability of its central characters to 'transgress, to move in and out of such culturally constructed categories' in turn 'open[s] up those categories for viewers'.[19]

Fuchs' valuable contribution to race critiques of *Buffy the Vampire Slayer* does not address the final season of the series, in which questions of othering, race, whiteness and privilege take centre stage. A variety of critiques have been directed at the series' final season, aimed in the main at perceived flaws in its narrative action and at inconsistencies with the politics espoused in previous seasons. Arwen Spicer provides both narrative and metanarrative objections to Season 7 when she reflects severely on the credulity with which we, as viewers, are supposed to respond to Buffy's (admittedly) logically flawed battle plan to defeat the First Evil. Spicer argues that this represents a 'gutting' of the 'meta-narrative of feminist empowerment through dialogic communication' that the series has stood for until this point.[20] In addition to providing philosophical and theological readings of the final season's themes,[21] scholars have also criticised the 'obviousness' of Caleb's characterisation[22] and the *deus ex machina* appearance of both Willow's scythe and Spike's amulet.[23] Focusing on narratology and the tonal shift that starts in Season 6, scholars such as Paul Hawkins assess the series' changing focus from supernatural monsters to the horrors of real life, and the changing metanarrative meanings of the Slayer as mythological hero.[24] Gregory Erickson and Jennifer Lemberg argue that as the narrative grows darker and more traumatic, the series deliberately begins to disrupt its own narrative structure, consistency and character. In undermining coherence and undoing tropes, it begins to destabilise audience expectations.[25] Erickson and Lemberg discuss the use of the body as site for this rupture and subversion, while Rhonda Wilcox discusses the changing relationship between spirit and flesh. She argues that Seasons 6 and 7 stand apart from the rest as characters are forced to confront realities of mortality, injury, the limitations and pleasures of flesh and their own potential for monstrosity.[26] Michael Adams observes these changes in the language and style of the Slayer; as Buffy focuses on her mission, mortality and moral duty, puns and wordplay no longer meet her needs.[27] Finally, Lynne Y. Edwards and Carly Haines discuss the television networks that aired *Buffy* in the US, arguing that as the series moved to UPN for Season 6 and Buffy's grisly resurrection, the series became a symbol of industry change and a movement towards more diverse and darker, realistic storytelling.[28] With the significant exceptions discussed below, few critiques of Season 7 focus on the compelling issues of race or nation, although their deliberate foregrounding is one of that season's most startling innovations.

Whose revolution has been televised?

In her sophisticated analysis of racial dynamics in *Buffy the Vampire Slayer*, Trish Salah provides the following penetrating synopsis:

> Characters of colour on the show seemed to hover between being *token and taboo* symptoms of the show's anxiety around race. But while the show registered and resisted, in an occasional and recurring way, the racial homogeneity of its own tableau, and flagged outside its diegesis the possible operation of racism in keeping Sunnydale white, this did not translate into racially inclusive casting, let alone usher in an anti-racist rather than tokenizing and apologist politics.[29]

By extending the Slayer's powers to young girls across the globe, Buffy's Season 7 might be seen to begin to redress – albeit belatedly and incompletely – the national, cultural and racial privilege the show assumed through its seven-year cycle. Bringing ethnic diversity and racial difference to the Slayer story, a generous reading of Buffy's finale might see it as an exemplary narrative of transnational feminist sisterhood. A more critical reading might see it as another chapter in a long, repetitive story of US imperialism. As noted in the previous chapter, in Season 7 Buffy's radical innovation for defeating The First, her turning the tables on the traditions of the Watchers' Council, involves transferring power from one uberwhite, middlingly privileged, Californian teenager to a heterogeneous group of women from different national, racial and socio-economic backgrounds. But how diverse is the Potential pool? Exactly whose revolution has been televised?

Season 7's interest in the political category of global girlhood, and what I am calling the political trope of 'girls-around-the-globe', is registered as early as the first episode's opening montage. This episode aired, as Salah notes, 'one year into the war in Afghanistan and in the lead up to Iraq Invasion' and it 'opens upon an Orientalist vista'. Salah's description is worth quoting at length because of its detailed attention to the *mise-en-scene*:

> 'Oriental' themed music is playing, and the camera pans the skyline of a city at night; Istanbul, according to the title. The camera drops lingering on a man lazing at the top of a wall, and then follows a stone stairwell down to tiled and cobblestone streets. A dark haired girl is running through the streets, pursued by hooded men in long brown robes, wielding curved, ornately bejeweled daggers. The music changes, swelling, become recognizably Western and orchestral while retaining orientalist motifs. The running girl is observed by a man through a partially open doorway, who shuts the door, leaving her to her fate. Chased down a dead end alley, she climbs a drainage pipe to the roof, displaying a speed and agility that suggests athletic, if not superhuman, prowess. However this girl does not survive or slay the monster: as she scrambles to the roof, she discovers the robed men already there; one pushes her and she falls to the street below. More robed men jump upon her with raised daggers, and this girl is taken down, slaughtered by a crowd of brown robed men.[30]

In his commentary on this scene, composer Douglas Romayne states that:

> It was Joss's idea to keep the ethnic elements going as the chase ensued, utilising the energy of traditional Turkish percussion to

Figure 1: The Turkish Potential, 'Lessons,' 7.1

> underscore the intensity of the slayer running for her life. As the scene progressed orchestral elements were added to increase the fear factor, building to a frenzied climax as the slayer is held down and the knife is raised.[31]

The scene then cuts abruptly to a graveyard in Sunnydale, where Buffy is training her younger sister Dawn to defend herself against vampires. Her first words are: 'It's about power. Who's got it, who knows how to use it.'

In his DVD commentary on the opening montage, Whedon states:

> You know this is, like, not to be all deep and stuff but this is absolutely the primal scene for me because, because it's everything I made Buffy to get rid of [...] was the girl who couldn't get through it.[32]

Whedon thus starts Season 7 by offering us a series of binary oppositions: the 'girl who couldn't get through it' and the girl who can and will, coded respectively as brown and white; the Oriental difference of Istanbul and the familiar locale of Sunnydale, with danger lurking in both; and an 'old world' of patriarchy (the Turkish girl is the only woman in the extended all-male scene) versus a scene of pedagogical instruction in the 'emancipated' West, where Buffy inculcates her sister into the logics of power.

In this opening episode, appropriately titled 'Lessons' (7.1), Buffy's graveyard pedagogy and its critical reception by Dawn is crucial to the set up of the whole season. Employing a rather heavy-handed Socratic method, Buffy challenges Dawn:

Buffy: So who's got the power Dawn?
Dawn: Well, I've got the stake …
Buffy: The stake is not the power.
…
Buffy: Who's got the power?
Dawn: He does.

The 'lessons' here are all on the surface, but they deserve spelling out nonetheless. Despite her possession of the stake/phallus, Dawn does not have the power: 'He' does. Women can wield the stake/phallus, but the power ultimately belongs to men/vampires. The associations between men, vampires and patriarchy are made explicit and unusually didactic here. In contradistinction to Ono's theory that vampires are primarily figures for racial otherness, here, as occasionally elsewhere in the series, vampires represent a system of institutionalised patriarchy that literally imperils women. Buffy's ensuing instruction to Dawn makes this obvious:

Buffy: Never forget it. It doesn't matter how well prepared you are, how well armed you are. You're a little girl. Woman. You're a little woman.
Dawn: I'm taller than you.
Buffy: He's a vampire.

And lest we miss the real-world application of the metaphor, Buffy also drives this home: 'It's real. That's the lesson Dawn. It's always real.'

If these two parts of the opening scenes of 'Lessons' (7.1) are relatively innocuous individually, placed together as the split sides of a whole, they are considerably more freighted. In his DVD commentary to the graveyard scene, producer David Solomon states, '[t]his is the old subvert-the-moment-thing that we try to do at least one moment each first episode'.[33] The humour of Buffy stumbling through various politically incorrect labels for her sister and concluding, with understandable misgiving, with a version of Louisa May Alcott's nineteenth-century classic novel for girls is undeniable. At the same time, the visual and narrative logic of these scenes *in combination* presages something more insidious: the death of the brown girl is central to the 'lesson' for the white girl, in a way that uncannily mirrors the terms of Gayatri Spivak's classic post-colonial feminist critique in 'Three women's texts and the critique of imperialism'.[34] *Buffy*'s Season 7 shifts the ground of Spivak's nineteenth-century British colonial context to one of twenty-first-century US imperialism but the message is decidedly similar: the death of the brown girl is necessary to provide for the individual growth of the white girl into a (neoliberal feminist) woman. Instead of Charlotte Brontë's Bertha Mason destroying herself 'so that Jane Eyre can become the feminist individualist heroine of British fiction', Whedon and Co. present the Turkish Potential, in Spivak's terms, as the 'self immolating colonial subject for the glorification of the social mission of the colonizer'.[35] The Turkish Potential must be sacrificed in the service of white women's emancipation, so that Dawn may learn the danger that her sister believes is universal.

Spivak argued urgently in her game-changing 1985 essay that '[i]t should not be possible to read nineteenth-century British literature without remembering that imperialism, understood as England's social mission, was a crucial part of the cultural representation of England to the English', and she particularly cautioned that 'the role of literature in the production of cultural representation should not be ignored'.[36] Almost 30 years later, it seems equally important that contemporary popular cultural texts be understood as part of the broader representation of America to Americans, and that the role of US imperialism, in both its cultural and military permutations, be studied as part of this process. In 1985 Spivak felt the need (seemingly justified by defensive reactions to her critique) to assert that her reading of Charlotte Brontë's much-loved canonical novel did not 'seek to undermine the excellence of the individual artist' but rather to 'allow [...] some room to situate feminist individualism in its historical determination rather than simply to canonize it as such'.[37] As the most written about popular culture text to date, and one increasingly included in university curricula in a variety of disciplines, *Buffy the Vampire Slayer* has achieved canonical status in popular and academic contexts. It has accrued as well a corresponding resistance on the part of some *Buffy* champions to admit less than salutary readings of the series as part of its discourse, a point I will return to below.

If the representation of the Turkish Potential in 'Lessons' (7.1) carries an unexpected weight of imperialist baggage, what about the other Potentials? Surely there are enough of them to (to mangle the title of episode 15), 'Get It [the representational job] Done' (7.15)? The second episode of the season ('Beneath You', 7.2) opens with a German Potential running from robed men in a city designated as Frankfurt. Styled in homage to the striking appearance of Franka Potente's Lola in Tom Tykwer's 1998 film, *Run Lola Run*, she sports bright pink hair, black combat boots, orange lipstick and a nose ring.[38] If the Turkish Potential's demise visually references an Oriental 'old world' past, the German Potential is Western street smart and edgy with something of the futuristic flavour and fierce determination of the Replicant Zhora in Ridley Scott's 1982 classic, *Blade Runner*.[39] The scene of her ambush is a nightclub and her soundtrack is techno. As she dies, the scene cuts to Sunnydale, with Buffy awakening with a scream from a nightmare of the dying girl. Dawn is again present. Emerging from her dream, Buffy mutters: 'There was a girl.' Dawn quips chirpily: 'That would be me.' But Buffy continues sombrely: 'There were more like her Dawn, out there somewhere. And they're gonna die.' Dawn's eagerness to identify herself with the girl in Buffy's dream underscores the parallel being drawn between 'girls-around-the-globe' and 'the girl-next-door' or, in this case, the bedroom next door. And Buffy's role is, once again, to spell out the significance for her sister: if Dawn is not *that* girl this time, she will be unless the message of the Potentials (their sacrifice) is heeded.

After the first two episodes, introductions featuring the deaths of international Potentials are abandoned – the bookends of 'Old World' Turkey and 'Brave New World' Germany apparently sufficient to imply that the pattern is unrelenting and universal. And while a Benetton-like parade of multinational (and multicoloured) deaths would certainly be stretching the formula past efficacy, the way these two initial archetypes are made to stand for girls worldwide is noteworthy. After the second episode, diversity in the Slayer pool is signalled primarily by differences in class, race and

Figure 2: The German Potential, 'Beneath You,' 7.2

sexuality within the predominantly North American and British Potential pool assembling in Sunnydale. There is the Chicana lesbian Potential Kennedy, eventually the lover of Willow, the sceptical African American Potential Rhoda and the Southern belle Eve, killed in her hotel room before reaching the Summers' house ('Showtime,' 7.16). It is not until episode 14, 'First Date' (7.14), that we are introduced to another international Slayer, and when we do meet Chao Ahn, a Chinese Slayer characterised by excessive racial stereotyping, viewers can learn to be grateful for the temporary suspension of the international storyline.

The first (and presumably only) non-English-speaking Slayer to reach Sunnydale, Chao Ahn's presence highlights a major flaw in *Buffy*'s Season 7 leadership and tutelage, yet the linguistic barrier is primarily played for laughs, with Giles drawing bloodied stick figures to teach the new recruit about demons.[40] When Chao Ahn objects: 'I don't understand a word any of you are saying' ('First Date,' 7.14), her speech merely serves as a subtitled punch line to an American joke. The real issue of cultural and linguistic difference in the Slayer squad is deflected onto Giles, whose paternal, didactic Watcher's role, augmented here by his Britishness, positions him as the colonial father teaching Western customs. Giles fumbles

Figure 3: Chao Ahn and Giles, 'First Date,' 7.14

awkwardly around Chao Ahn, misinterpreting her responses and speaking on her behalf. He jokes that 'ice cream is a universal language', despite Chao Ahn's assertion that she, 'like many from Asia', is lactose intolerant. When Buffy asks him for a translation of Chao Ahn's response, Giles responds blithely, 'she's grateful to be in the land of plenty'. Even before she becomes an experienced Slayer, successfully helping defeat Caleb in the vineyard, Chao Ahn faces another threat, this one smiling and offering her dairy products. When Giles tactlessly offers her milk to help her sleep, she responds by shouting: 'You're trying to kill me!' As neither Giles nor Spike speaks Cantonese, Chao Ahn is effectively silenced, participating in physical training but unable to communicate with her American leader or educate herself about her enemy. She must literally assimilate into the ranks of the Potentials or perish. As Chao Ahn has arrived without her personal belongings, Giles takes her to the haven of the American everygirl, the mall. Xander, the 'heart' of the Scooby gang, notes with compassion, 'that's gotta be rough. Getting just, like, pulled out of your home, being told you're a Potential Slayer, not being able to bring anything.' But in general Chao Ahn is depicted purely for stereotypical comic relief. Her presence as a voiceless soldier in Buffy's army is uncomfortably at odds with the ideal of transnational Slayer sisterhood, suggesting that international Slayer suffrage, however well intentioned in theory, is more problematic in practice than any one American girl hero or wise British Watcher is prepared for.

The most significant representation of Slayer diversity, however, is surely the celebrated montage of young Potentials feeling their power that provides what we now think of as the political climax to the final episode of the series, 'Chosen' (7.22). The montage begins with a series of images of Potential Slayers Amanda, Vi and Rona preparing for battle, registering first the shock and then the affirmation and rush of their literal empowerment. It then cuts to a series of 'multicultural' representations of young women and women's oppression: a preteen white girl looking uncomfortable and self-conscious as she comes up to bat in a softball game (Figure 4), a black teenager looking momentarily faint, leaning on high-school lockers (Figure 5), a sari-wearing South Asian woman prostrate on the ground, perhaps in a posture of grief, a Japanese girl rising amazed from a family meal (Figure 6) and a battered white woman standing up to stop a blow from an abuser (Figure 7). We return to the young white girl playing softball, who begins to smile as she too begins to feel her own power. The montage concludes with this all-American symbol of innocence and goodness, smiling into the eyes of her opponent, about to whack them into the New Girl Order (Figure 8).

This celebration of transnational sisterhood warrants close reading. The montage extends international Slayer suffrage from the US to the African American US, and from there to South Asia and Japan, returning by way (perhaps) of the US Midwest. This possibly Midwestern Slayer's difference is coded mostly as class: a flannelette shirt hangs from a door knob; the woman is wearing a tank top, or what with exquisite taste Americans colloquially call a 'wife-beater'; she seems to be resisting some sort of wife beater; and she reads to me like white trash 'getting smart'. In fact, visually this woman signifies difference primarily by the fact that she is *larger* than all the others. As a gesture of benevolent inclusion, this is in rather poor taste: Buffy generously extends her powers to girls whose dress size has edged into double digits. The final image of emancipation is the preteen baseball batter – the all-American image of internationalism. Based on representation, this pool of Potentials is 'international' in

Figure 4: Potential Slayers Feel the Power, 'Chosen,' 7.22

Figure 5: Potential Slayers Feel the Power, 'Chosen,' 7.22

Figure 6: Potential Slayers Feel the Power, 'Chosen,' 7.22

Figure 7: Potential Slayers Feel the Power, 'Chosen,' 7.22

Figure 8: Potential Slayers Feel the Power, 'Chosen,' 7.22

the same way that a baseball competition called the 'World Series' consists almost exclusively of American teams, which is to say – only in name.[41]

Now, at this stage of a critique of *Buffy*'s racial politics, it is customary to make some sort of qualification. It's a qualification I've heard during excellent readings of race and post-colonialism in *Buffy* at conferences in Australia, the UK and North America and it goes something like this: 'Now don't get me wrong ...' (can you tell what comes next?) 'Now don't get me wrong – I REALLY LOVE *BUFFY*!' And it's at this point that my interest in our collective hermeneutic kicks in. Because it is a sad comment on *Buffy* studies if serious-minded racial critique is seen as an inappropriate response to the text. On one level we might all know this, or at least acknowledge it, but I think the point bears pressing. The implication of this qualification is that a critique of *Buffy*'s race politics somehow threatens our idea of the beloved object.[42] And *Buffy*'s status as a much loved but sometimes critically maligned *popular* culture text factors in here. After all, race and post-colonial critics of Shakespeare do not feel the need to 'nevertheless' testify to their passion for the Bard (ironically himself a popular culture producer).

I am as prone to this type of justification as anyone else. In fact, it is the way I think we are taught to read critically in popular cultural studies. *If Buffy* advocates successfully for a transnational feminist sisterhood, and *if* it simultaneously resists the temptation to idealise (and therefore instantiate) American aggression in the name of assistance, then Season 7 rocks, *Buffy* can retain the laurel for enlightened primetime broadcasting and I can rest easy in my sleep because I can reconcile my politics with the undeniable pleasure I take in the show. But I would like to advocate for a suspension of this kind of certitude, for some kind of check on our desire (or my desire) for a definitively 'progressive' or 'regressive' assessment of the show. I don't think Season 7 is *either* a fantastically emancipatory text displaying a new recognition of white racial privilege *or* a willing and witting endorsement of American military might. I *do* think Season 7 mobilises both of those discourses and that the real insights that might be gained from studying *Buffy* in this way concern our own complicities with and investments in those discourses.

In an important essay applying post-colonial critiques to Amy Heckerling's now cult film *Clueless* (1995), Gayle Wald warned that feminist scholarship must be wary of uncritically reproducing simplistically celebratory readings of popular culture that focus on gender performance 'as a privileged site and source of political oppositionality'. She makes the point that when we do this, 'critical questions of national, cultural, and racial appropriation can be made to disappear under the sign of transgressive gender performance'.[43] There has been a wealth of wonderful feminist criticism of *Buffy* but, with significant exceptions, there is a tendency to focus on the series' transgressive play with gender at the expense of considering other, less obviously liberatory aspects of the show. Instead, I want to suggest that a critical analysis of *Buffy*'s racial representations need not be considered a critique of the palpable pleasures provided by the show but rather, as Wald suggests, 'a critique of the production of pleasure through gendered and racialised narratives that signify [and which in *Buffy* studies have been celebrated] as new, transgressive, or otherwise exemplary'. My analysis of *Buffy*'s Season 7 is not designed as a critique of pleasure but, rather, a critique of the way our pleasure is produced by, dependent on and occasionally circumscribed by narratives of race and nation. My engagement with this material is also, ultimately, a critique of the need to justify that critique by the appeal to the fact that – despite everything – 'I REALLY DO LOVE *BUFFY*!'

Buffy and benevolent world domination

As part of this process, I argue that the idealised vision of universal sisterhood with which *Buffy* concludes needs to be read against the immediate political context in which its final season screened (and indeed against the long history of US 'intervention' in international affairs); a context that illuminates some of the same gestures of cultural imperialism that the series elsewhere successfully critiques. *Buffy*'s celebration of what is effectively an international military alliance under ostensibly altruistic American leadership demands special scrutiny in the political climate in which it aired. In the context of the indefensible arrogance of George W. Bush's 'War on Terror' and the spurious universalism of his 'Coalition of the Willing', Buffy's final gesture of international inclusivity is imbued with unwittingly inauspicious overtones. The opposition that I'm drawing here is another version of the 'good Buffy/bad Buffy' binary that haunts feminist responses to the show (and that I survey in the first chapter of this book): Does *Buffy*'s Season 7 present a utopian vision of global emancipation or a misguided celebration of, and justification for, US domination?

Scholars have been understandably divided by this question, whether it is explicitly articulated or not. Several critiques celebrate the moral code that informs Buffy's slaying throughout the series or focus on the metanarrative's championing of communal female empowerment. Shannon Craigo-Snell argues that in her nuanced moral stance, feminist ethics and refusal to act as a 'lone warrior', Buffy cannot be seen as a supporter of or participant in war. Samuel A. Chambers and Daniel Williford read *Buffy* as an 'anti-imperialist' text. They state that there is 'no room for righteousness in the Buffyverse', citing the frequent distractions or interruptions to Buffy's 'morally stuffy' or 'self-righteous' speeches as the creators' attempts to undermine her stance.[44] In a similar political vein, Jeffrey L. Pasley rejects what he sees as conservative readings of the series, praising the Slayer's altruism and identifying a 'liberal, incrementalist vision' of heroism in the text.[45]

However, others have expressed discomfort with the autocratic turn that Buffy's character takes in Season 7. Helen Graham describes Buffy's rhetoric as 'uncomfortably zealous'[46] and Dennis Showalter has questioned the increasingly military rhetoric with which she leads her campaign.[47] Neal King has compared Season 7's Buffy to a fascist leader,[48] while Jonah Goldberg, in his online essay 'Buffy the UN Slayer', recasts Buffy as a pro-war US neo-conservative.[49] The Slayer methodology has been used as a lens through which to examine American military planning,[50] and by the final season Buffy herself is seen to act out many of the imperatives of a successful military general.[51] Martin Buinicki and Anthony Enns argue that although she resists the excessive, 'outdated institutional' model of power that the Watchers' Council represents, Buffy ultimately affirms the importance of institutional power and punishment in maintaining order.[52] Pointing out that the Slayer 'cannot sustain solo hero status and is designed to perish', Kim Kirkpatrick suggests that Buffy only succeeds in the final season when she learns to resist patriarchal military rhetoric.[53]

But if Buffy learns throughout Season 7 to resist patriarchal military rhetoric, this does not mean she eschews military rhetoric altogether. In fact Season 7 is celebrated in some circles precisely as a vision of emancipated global girlhood militarised in the service of feminism. And this is certainly a powerful vision. But what sort of feminism is being championed here? The racial politics discussed above indicate that it is a version of feminism that relies on the colonial trope of the brown woman's death as sacrifice to white women's self-knowledge and subsequent empowerment. It is a version of feminism that trades in racist tropes of African American 'noble savagery' in its depiction of the First Slayer to highlight the more 'evolved' individualist politics of its blonde Californian protagonist. And it offers a beguiling rhetoric of 'girls-around-the-globe' that nevertheless relies on stereotypically Oriental markers of racial and cultural difference, most obviously in its representation of the Chinese Slayer Chao Ahn. In an unhappy confluence of discourses, whose echoes exceed coincidence, Season 7 also reprises the neoliberal rhetoric of women's human rights employed by Republican First Lady Laura Bush to justify the US 'War on Terror'.

On 17 November 2001, in an unprecedented move for an American First Lady, Laura Bush addressed the nation via radio in a speech entitled 'The Taliban's war against women'. She announced:

> I'm Laura Bush, and I'm delivering this week's radio address to kick off a world-wide effort to focus on the brutality against women and children by the al-Qaida terrorist network and the regime it supports in Afghanistan, the Taliban. That regime is now in retreat across much of the country, and the people of Afghanistan – especially women – are rejoicing. Afghan women know, through hard experience, what the rest of the world is discovering: The brutal oppression of women is a central goal of the terrorists.[54]

Bush appears to direct her critique specifically toward terrorists and the Taliban rather than Muslims worldwide, arguing that 'the severe repression and brutality against women in Afghanistan is not a matter of legitimate religious practice' and that 'Muslims around the world have condemned the brutal degradation of women and children by the Taliban regime'. 'Only the terrorists and the Taliban', she argues:

> forbid education to women. Only the terrorists and the Taliban threaten to pull out women's fingernails for wearing nail polish. The plight of women and children in Afghanistan is a matter of deliberate human cruelty, carried out by those who seek to intimidate and control. Civilized people throughout the world are speaking out in horror – not only because our hearts break for the women and children in Afghanistan, but also because in Afghanistan, we see the world the terrorists would like to impose on the rest of us.

With this threat in mind, Bush exhorts her compatriots to action:

> All of us have an obligation to speak out. We may come from different backgrounds and faiths – but parents the world over love our children. We respect our mothers, our sisters and daughters. Fighting brutality against women and children is not the expression of a specific culture; it is the acceptance of our common humanity – a commitment shared by people of good will on every continent. Because of our recent military gains

> in much of Afghanistan, women are no longer imprisoned in their homes. They can listen to music and teach their daughters without fear of punishment. Yet the terrorists who helped rule that country now plot and plan in many countries. And they must be stopped. The fight against terrorism is also a fight for the rights and dignity of women.

Invoking the upcoming American Thanksgiving holiday, Bush asks her listeners to be 'especially thankful for all the blessings of American life' and concludes: 'I hope Americans will join our family in working to ensure that dignity and opportunity will be secured for all the women and children of Afghanistan.'

There is much that is astonishing in Laura Bush's sudden public interest in women's rights and the methods she uses to drive her point home (not least her invocation of nail polish as a human right),[55] but there are also aspects of this media intervention and its public reception that are horribly familiar. 'Among many other legacies', writes Christina Ho, the 9/11 (2001) terrorist attacks and the Bush administration's response 'will be remembered by some for catapulting women's rights to the centre stage of global politics'.[56] As Ho relates, Laura Bush's rhetoric on women's rights gained the approval of some US feminists: 'For some feminists, any concern about women's rights is better than silence, even if it is based on Orientalist assumptions.'[57] 'Under other circumstances', as Sharon Smith noted, 'feminist leaders might have been expected to raise their voices against the transparent hypocrisy of the Bush administration'. Instead, mainstream feminists 'applauded Bush' and 'confused liberals joined the war chorus'.[58] Smith points out that 'mainstream journalists did not question the ferocity of [Laura Bush's] implied threat, however politely delivered, to spread the war to other countries. Nor did they dwell on the Bush administration's sudden about-face on women's rights.'[59]

Viewing the increased attention to women's rights in the aftermath of 9/11 as a 'cynical ploy',[60] Carol A. Stabile and Deepa Kumar argue that 'the central framework' employed to justify the US war 'was thoroughly Orientalist:'

> [I]t constructed the West as the beacon of civilization with an obligation to tame the Islamic world and liberate its women.

> This served to erase not only the political struggles of women in Afghanistan against both the Northern Alliance and the Taliban, but those of women in the West as well who, contrary to Orientalist claims about the eternal virtues of Western civilization, have had to organize and fight for what rights they enjoy today.[61]

Stabile and Kumar identify two narrative traditions that converge in popular political discourses about Afghan women, 'that of the protection scenario and that of Orientalism', noting that both traditions 'draw much of their rhetorical force from discourses of imperialism'.[62] According to the logic of the protection scenario, women, 'like the penetrable, feminized territory of the nation-state, must be protected from the predatory advances of some real or imaginary enemy'.[63] As the United States launched the 'War on Terror' in Afghanistan and then Iraq, Ho contends that 'the liberation of women from barbaric regimes became a powerful rationale for intervention'.[64] Stabile and Kumar remind us that 'This has never been an innocent or progressive discourse aimed at improving the lot of women and children':

> Militarism by the world's imperialist powers never improves the lives of women and children. Instead, by rendering women the passive grounds for an argument aimed at imperialist domination, the discourse of protection used by politicians and media alike – like the very fundamentalism it purported to attack – denied women any agency in the decision-making processes that affected their everyday lives and futures.

Smith concurs, stating that '[t]he Bush administration's alleged concern for Afghan women was nothing but a cynical public relations ploy. The only surprise is that it worked so well.'[65]

What, you might ask, does all this have to do with *Buffy*? I suggest that Laura Bush's address to the nation attempts to harness some of the same indignation at the treatment of women that *Buffy*'s Season 7 does, and while the resonances might be unwitting or unintentional (Joss Whedon certainly didn't support the 'War on Terror' and in an interview with *SFX Magazine* he refers to George W. Bush as 'that ass-wipe'),[66] both cultural texts advocate a form of 'modern' Western neoliberal feminism that presents its cultural and military mission as universal, benevolent and morally justified. Season 7 does this through the trope of imperilled and unenlightened 'girls-around-the-globe' whom Buffy will save and empower. Bush's speech does this by employing some of the same binary distinctions mobilised by Whedon and Co. that I have discussed above. Evoking the ostensibly transparent category of 'civilized people', Laura Bush contrasts 'all the blessings of American life' with the 'poverty, poor health, and illiteracy' imposed on Afghan women. Regardless of the Bush administration's appalling record on women's issues, in this speech the First Lady presents women's rights as universal human rights that her husband's administration is prepared to defend with its considerable military might: 'They must be stopped.' Transposing the US nation state into one enormous domestic unit – 'we respect our mothers, our sisters and daughters' – Bush invites her compatriots to the Bush family Thanksgiving table: 'I hope Americans will join our family in working to ensure that dignity and opportunity will be secured for all the women and children of Afghanistan.' An insidious familial discourse invites her listeners to celebrate and support the 'War on Terror' as the gracious and generous extension of American hospitality.

In the speech used as the epigraph for this chapter, 'Are you ready to be strong?', Buffy performs several similar rhetorical manoeuvres. But surely, you ask, her aims are pure? If we can't condone the bombing of Afghan women and children with the aim of their purported emancipation, we can surely support the empowerment of 'girls-around-the-globe' that doesn't involve their lives as sacrifice. It depends, of course, on your definition of empowerment, and Buffy's feminism, as we have seen, while radical and righteous in its local North American context, can seem surprisingly blind to the more suspect occlusions it performs in promoting the politics of that context as a global solution. There is also the question of choice. As Trish Salah notes, in 'inviting the other woman to "choose" to participate in her (white, western, girl) power as an alternative to being slaughtered by a primordial evil', Buffy propounds a discourse of choice that has been thoroughly critiqued in post-colonial feminist theory. Salah notes:

> This double negation of any choice against participating in a Western paradigmed global feminist sisterhood implicitly evokes the fantasy, articulated by Spivak, that the other woman

> chooses death [...] This recognition of a global sisterhood, it should be stressed, emerges out of a recognition of the deaths of the other women as others, which begs the question of what they will need to become to share in Buffy's power.

Salah notes that throughout Season 7's narrative arc, Whedon is 'determinedly politically correct – there is certainly no mention of Islam – the diversity of representation here produces submission to subordination as culturally specific and other, while dramatizing resistance through representations of white, American young women'.[67] In a canny, pre-emptive defence against those who might protest against her post-colonial critique of Charlotte Brontë's *Jane Eyre*, Spivak suggested that, rather than blaming the artist herself, '[i]f even minimally successful, [Spivak's own] readings will incite a degree of rage against the imperialist narrativisation of history, that it should produce so abject a script for her'.[68] Instead of blaming Joss Whedon and Co. for the shortcomings of their neoliberal feminist platform, I suggest a similar rage might be directed against omnipresent popular narratives of North American benevolence and supremacy because they have created so apposite an imperial script for the makers of *Buffy*.

5

Becoming Worthy of Buffy: Performing Masculinity in a Patriarchal World

One of the most fiercely contested battles in *Buffy* studies concerns the competing attractions of Buffy's rival suitors – Angel and Spike – and evaluations of their disparate performances of masculinity. This chapter sidesteps that contentious and by now well-covered terrain to focus on arguably the least popular of Buffy's romantic prospects, Riley Finn. What can Riley's reception tell us about the portrayal of masculinity more broadly? As we have seen, the series is justifiably famous for turning conventional teenage clichés ('High school is hell', 'My mother is an alien') into literal and horrific incarnations. In *Buffy* the rituals of girlhood are similarly and spectacularly fraught. Buffy's first date, her high school prom and various early sexual encounters are all presented with a hyperbolic hysteria that somehow serves to foreground rather than minimise the fundamental pathos of growing up: adolescence is *unheimlich*, and adults don't know the half of it. Buffy's love objects play a central role in her *Bildungsroman*, and have attracted a prodigious amount of scholarly and fan attention. Her very different relationships with Angel, Riley and Spike provide a range of models of masculinity from which Buffy might choose, while each of these characters in turn must work to 'become worthy' of Buffy, specifically within the gender politics that the series has established. Angel's abjection is the paranormal punishment for his 'deflowering' of Buffy,

Spike's insidious appeal gets inextricably more complex as he serves as the shadow to Buffy's increasingly conflicted desires and the respite offered by Riley's all-American normality is ultimately exposed, as all such spectres should be, as less than straight and sure.[1]

One of the central thematic through-lines of the series is Buffy's struggle to balance the demands of her supernatural duties as the Slayer and her desire to live what she sees as a normal teenage life. As several critics have pointed out, this struggle literalises the challenges many, if not all, adolescents experience when negotiating their entry into the adult world: the liminal position Buffy occupies between supernatural and human worlds mirrors and amplifies the liminal location of the teenager between child and adult roles. Throughout the first three seasons Buffy voices a recurring desire to be considered, and to consider herself, simply 'a girl'. Dancing at the Bronze on a first date with Owen in Season 1's 'Never Kill a Boy on the First Date' (1.5), for instance, Buffy responds to Owen's tentative question: 'Are you, uh, having fun?' with an equally wistful: 'Yeah. I almost feel like a girl.' Yet the literalisation of metaphor, discussed in my first chapter as one of the series' signature rhetorical strategies, here points to a more ambiguous and ambivalent representation of girlhood than Buffy's wishful (or wistful) thinking evokes. The very fact that Buffy repeatedly aspires to the normative performance of girlhood, and just as often fails in this attempt, suggests that the category of the girl is not as simple or self-evident as it might initially seem, either to her or to us as viewers.

Boyhood and, as Buffy ages, adult masculinity are categories similarly open to multiple and conflicting interpretations throughout the series. In fact, one of the consequences of *Buffy*'s sustained and sympathetic exploration of girlhood is that the series as a whole addresses ideas about the performance of masculinity with a degree of insistence and feminist sophistication that is unusual in mainstream television. Tangentially, this chapter asks what sort of boy or man might prove an appropriate partner for the protagonist of an avowedly feminist show. Which of the many models of masculinity paraded before Buffy as potential partners might satisfy viewer expectations about the Slayer's consort? And how do these various male figures – their bodies, their ethics, their politics – need to be disciplined or moulded into an appropriate feminist form? This chapter commences with a brief examination of Buffy's first foray into the world of dating and concludes by considering the single yet still-sought-after status Buffy occupies at the conclusion to the series. Its central focus on Riley Finn might surprise both Buffy fans and scholars, but I hope to show that in Riley, Whedon and Co. have provided a penetrating and explicit analysis of normative masculinity that has crucial repercussions for the feminist rhetoric of the series as a whole.

'Never Kill a Boy on the First Date': romancing normality

'Never Kill a Boy on the First Date', the fifth episode of Season 1, explicitly foregrounds tensions between Buffy's supernatural duties and what she sees as the normal, teenage imperatives of her life in Sunnydale. The episode centres on Buffy's bid for a break from a life continually 'on call': 'A cranky Slayer is a careless Slayer!' and Giles's warning, 'Buffy, maintaining a normal social life as a Slayer … is problematic at best'. As the events of the episode unfold, we become privy to the colossal understatement of Giles's warning; in retrospect his buttoned-up, British prevarication functions as a form of the rhetorical figure litotes – the use of understatement for deliberate effect. Maintaining a social life as a Slayer, we discover, is not only problematic but also potentially fatal.

Like many Season 1 episodes, 'Never Kill a Boy on the First Date' is set largely in the locale of the high school – the library, the school corridors, its cafeteria and its familiar Sunnydale environs – the underground labyrinth, the cemetery, the Bronze, Buffy's bedroom and the morgue. It focuses on the conventional coming-of-age motif of the first date, with its attendant fumbling invitation, misunderstandings, rival attractions and *pas de deux*. The supernatural component offers the additional complications of Buffy's secret identity, an ancient prophecy, a vampire showdown in the crematorium and the appearance of the Anointed One. The fact that the closing twist of the episode reveals this eagerly awaited evil exemplar as an innocent-looking young boy emphasises the fact that the central protagonists in this drama are all pre-adult. Older figures such as The Master and Giles are presented as either literally trapped and contained or otherwise ineffectual. Their subsequent reliance on the Anointed One and the Chosen One for the fulfilment of their respective missions underlines the gravity of such seemingly trivial rites of passage as the first date to the safety of this society as a whole.

Dating as an adolescent girl preoccupation is certainly portrayed with broad comedy for most of the episode. An early collision between the supernatural and human plotlines results in the following confused exchange:

Buffy: It's not that big a deal. It's just a bunch of people getting together.
Willow: It's a very big deal!
Buffy: It's not!
Willow: It is. (spots Giles) Tell her!
Giles: I'm afraid it's very big.
Willow: (smiles at Buffy) Thank you! (turns back to Giles, confused) Wait! What are you talking about?
Giles: What are *you* talking about?
Buffy and Willow: Boys!
Giles: Yes, well, I'm talking about trouble.

('Never Kill a Boy on the First Date', 1.5)

Unsurprisingly, Willow emerges as a staunch supporter of her friend's extracurricular priorities: 'Buffy has a really important date.' But Giles's response is similarly predictable, albeit somewhat heavy handed: 'Alright, I'll just jump in my time machine, go back to the twelfth century and ask the vampires to postpone their ancient prophecy for a few days while you take in dinner and a show'. Buffy's riposte, '[o]kay, at this point you're abusing sarcasm', offers a salient reprimand, in this rhetorically savvy milieu, of Giles's lack of linguistic finesse in this instance. However, her own defence: 'But … Cute guy! Teenager! Post-pubescent fantasies!' is equally unpersuasive and falls on deaf ears: 'Those will just have to be put on hold.' Dating here is presented as a trivial, and feminised, obsession, a sense later reinforced by Owen's well-meaning statement: 'I just find most girls pretty frivolous. I mean, there's a lot more important things in life than dating, y'know?' But despite the general dissing of Buffy's desire to date, several factors militate against too severe a censuring of this particular preoccupation.

Perhaps the least of these is Buffy's own portrayal of her predicament. Foiled in her first date with Owen, Buffy complains to Xander: 'I can't take this anymore. I feel like everyone is staring at me, the big, hideous, dateless monster.' The fact that this slight registers to her primarily as a social rather than a romantic failure is recorded in her unsolicited feedback to a passing student: 'What? Yeah, that's right, I have no life, c'mon, nothing to see here, pal, move it along!' The additional fact that it is Buffy who stumbles across the pertinent clues in this episode's case, despite her lack of book learning ('Ooo, two points for the Slayer, while the Watcher is yet to score!'), and that Giles's Watcherly restrictions on her social life are based on miscalculations that result in failure, provide further grist for Buffy's mill. But is her choice of romantic object – the capital-R Romantic, Owen – that offers the most compelling case for empathy with Buffy's dating project, and for viewer sympathy with its failure.

One of the first in a long series of inappropriate matches for Buffy, Owen Thurman is on first-name terms with his hero, the famously difficult American poet Emily Dickinson, and carries her poems as a 'kind of security blanket'. Buffy is initially drawn to him, it seems, because he wonders whether she can actually read. In Willow's estimation, Owen is 'sensitive, yet manly'. She relates: 'He's solitary, mysterious … He can brood for 40 minutes straight. I've clocked him.' In Xander's quite clearly defensive estimation, he's 'Mr Excitement'. Ironically, it is Xander's sarcastic sobriquet that proves closer to the mark. Owen's public predilection for the 'sequestered and uneventful' life of retirement masks a hidden desire for defying death. In Buffy's disillusioned conclusion: 'He wants to be Danger Man:'

> Buffy: Two days in my world and Owen really *would* get himself killed. Or I'd get him killed … Or someone else.

The interest Owen poses for a study of masculinity in *Buffy* is the way his sensitive new-age guy (or SNAG) persona is exposed as fraudulent, harbouring an underbelly of violent voyeurism, and the way that even before this exposure his attraction must be repudiated by Buffy in favour of the family romance of father (Giles) and siblings (Willow and Xander). The attraction of Owen's pre-emo, or neo-Victorian, sensibility is overwhelmingly upheld by his female peers in the episode (Cordelia in particular wants a piece of this action), and his inappropriateness as Buffy's consort is not so much the result of his persona's beguiling fraudulence so much as the inherent weakness of its initial premise: with what he might imagine to be disarming outmodedness, he wants to 'protect' her. Both Angel and Spike will later offer Buffy variations of Victorian chivalry (the 'neo' is obviously misplaced in their contexts) with suitably underwhelming results. Towards the end of their relationship, Riley will reprise the danger-seeking morbidity (and stupidity) of Owen in this episode. Through Owen, 'Never Kill a Boy on the First Date' foreshadows the different models of masculinity that will be offered to Buffy as potential partners throughout the series. More often recognised for its bravura verbal play, gestured to in this book's title, as well as scholarly and fan appreciation of its comic one-liners ('If the Apocalyse comes, beep me') and its creative linguistic play ('Sure, he's got a certain Owenocity'), the deeper import of this episode might lie in the way it rehearses the more significant challenges of Buffy's future relationships. Angel, Riley and Spike all have more than a little 'Owenocity' in them and it is often these aspects of their characters that make them problematic partners for this particular feminist protagonist.

'I am what they made me to be': Riley, hegemonic masculinity and relapse

Of all of Buffy's potential partners, none is more routinely ridiculed and rejected than Riley Finn, the 'corn-fed Iowa boy' ('Doomed', 4.11) that fans love to hate. Coming close on the heels of Buffy's highly charged failed relationship with Angel, Riley's romantic aspirations seem hopeless from the outset. This representative of 'normal' just doesn't feel normal to Buffy, as she relates in the Season 4 episode, 'Something Blue' (4.9):

> It's just, different, you know? A picnic. First of all, daylight – kind of a new venue, Buffywise. And the best part – he said he would bring all the food, so all I have to do was to show up and eat. Those are two things I'm really good at.

Figure 9: Riley Finn, 'The Initiative,' 4.7

The conversation continues:

Willow: He's nice?

Buffy: Very, very.

Willow: And there's sparkage?

Buffy: Yeah. He's – have you seen his arms? Those are good arms to have. I really like him. I do.

Willow: But …?

Buffy: I don't know. I really like being around him, you know? And I think he cares about me … but … I just … feel like something's missing.

Willow: He's not making you miserable?

Buffy: Exactly. Riley seems so solid. Like he wouldn't cause me heartache.

Willow: (Fake worry) Get out. Get out while there's still time.

Buffy: I know … I have to get away from that bad boy thing. There's no good there. Seeing Angel in LA … even for five minutes … hello to the pain.

Willow: The pain is not a friend.

Buffy: But I can't help thinking – isn't that where the fire comes from? Can a nice, safe relationship be that intense? I know it's nuts, but … part of me believes that real love and passion have to go hand in hand with pain and fighting … I wonder where I get that from?

Given this introduction, it is not hard to see why fans reacted to Riley's introduction negatively. What perhaps *is* surprising is the way the series pursued the relationship in the face of the fierce rejection of fans. In what follows I explore Riley's character in terms of its deployment of different models of masculinity. I argue that Riley's portrayal is designed to be deliberately and provocatively underwhelming, and speculate about what this might mean in terms of the series' overall negotiation of contemporary gender politics.

To begin with it seems important to state that the series' construction of Riley as lame and essentially unworthy should not be seen as unwitting or unaware. This is not a case of bad casting or inadequate character development, although both charges have been directed at actor Marc Blucas and at Whedon and Co. circa Season 4. Instead, Riley is carefully, almost painfully, introduced as a compromised romantic choice from the very beginning. In 'Fear Itself' (4.4), in response to Riley's earnest Teaching Assistant advice, Buffy responds: 'Well, thanks for the pep talk, coach', to which Riley returns: 'Don't make fun. I worked long and hard to get this pompous.' Instead of signalling a lack of acting chops, the fact that Blucas can rob this scene of self-deprecatory charm is actually cause for applause. It is hard to deny Whedon and Co.'s scripts their Scoobie-style gracelessness, and that fact that Riley remains stolidly and essentially humourless, despite his share of one-liners, is a more a remarkable feat of acting ingenuity than the result of inadequacy on Blucas's part.

If Buffy's initial response to Riley's 'courting' (his word) is equivocal, the terms in which she expresses her confusion are revealing. In the exchange with Willow quoted above, Buffy acknowledges, at least at an intellectual level, her need to move beyond her bad boy fixation – 'There's no good there' – but she also wonders, not without reason: 'isn't that where the fire comes from?' In response to Willow's question about whether there is any 'sparkage' in the budding relationship, Buffy's '[y]eah. He's – have you seen his arms? Those are good arms to have' seems to indicate more a desire to *have* Riley's arms that to be *in* Riley's arms.

The subsequent, sometimes seemingly gratuitous sex that Buffy and Riley resort to – which in 'Where the Wild Things Are' (4.18) goes to the extent of threatening the lives of all those close to them – is often presented as compensatory or as a shorthand form of communication that stands in

Figure 10: The Arms of Riley, 'The Initiative,' 4.7

for the more important conversations they are avoiding (as the silent episode 'Hush' demonstrates admirably).[2] There is also the unnerving detail, discussed in more detail below, that their sex life is being monitored via a hidden camera by Professor Maggie Walsh in commando central, forging a decidedly queer triangulation in which, both visually and metaphorically, Walsh as pimp penetrates Buffy as patron via Riley as prosthesis. The scopophilic economy of this season – its fascination with all things visual – is literalised in the device of the panopticon that subjects members of the Initiative and their friends to constant surveillance. But this is only the most extreme of the metaphors for voyeuristic viewing that infiltrate these episodes.[3] Seeming and sexuality are inextricably bound up in Buffy's romance with Riley, and these themes are mirrored in the subplots that involve supporting characters such as Willow, Oz and Spike.

The ways the various Scoobies respond to Riley provide important clues to his character. While Riley is able to enlist Willow's grudging assistance in his pursuit of Buffy, yielding such game-changing insights as the fact that 'Buffy likes cheese,' he pursues his interrogation in the face of Willow's obvious desolation at the loss of her boyfriend Oz. While he later succeeds in saving Willow's life, thereby earning her gratitude, Riley's initial tactlessness in hounding Willow in her grief remains an enduring impression. Xander first refers to Riley as Buffy's 'Teutonic boy toy' ('The Initiative', 4.7), to which she replies that, 'Riley's a doof. He's not Teutonic.' Later Xander will refer to Riley sarcastically as 'big guy' ('The Yoko Factor', 4.20) and 'Captain America' ('Shadow', 5.8). Spike, not technically a member of the Scooby gang but cohabiting with various members through most of Season 4, refers to Riley as 'the enormous hall monitor' ('Out of My Mind', 5.4) and 'Captain Cardboard' ('No Place Like Home', 5.5). Even Forrest, Riley's second in command in the Initiative, makes fun of his fellow soldier, calling him 'Mama's boy' ('Pangs', 4.8) and 'moron' ('The Initiative', 4.7).

Lest we fail to mention the elephant in the room, the fact that Riley is part of the military industrial complex raises obvious questions about his suitability as a potential partner. As a uniform wearing, serial number toting, chip-implanted member of a covert special operations unit, he represents the sort of hegemonic masculinity to which the Slayer and her circle have hitherto been diametrically opposed. In previous seasons, Buffy has successfully extricated herself from the patriarchal supervision of the Watchers' Council, and we watch her early enthusiasm for the Initiative's operations with undoubted misgiving.

Differences between Scooby-style investigation and the elaborate protocols and hierarchy of the Initiative are portrayed in broad binaries that nevertheless allow for a certain comedic bathos:

Walsh: So, the Slayer.
Buffy: Yeah. That's me.
Walsh: We thought you were a myth.
Buffy: Well, you were myth-taken. (smiles but sees that neither are going to laugh and stops)
Walsh: And to think all that time you were sitting in my class. Well, most of those times. I always knew you could do better than a B minus. Now I understand your energies were directed in the same places as ours, in fact. It's only our methods that differ. We use the latest in scientific technology and state-of-the-art weaponry and you, if I understand correctly, poke them with a sharp stick.
Buffy: Well, it's more effective than it sounds.

('A New Man', 4.12)

Walsh here prematurely supposes that '[i]t's only our methods that differ'. The previous episode, 'Doomed', has effectively juxtaposed the competing styles and ideological subtexts that motivate the Scoobies and their black-clad opposite numbers in researching what the latter call an HST, a 'Hostile Sub-Terrestial' and the former a Vahrall demon:

Willow: (looking over at Giles's book) Eew!

Xander: I second that revulsion.

Giles: Yes. 'Slick like gold and gird in moonlight, father of portents and brother to blight.'

Buffy: (reading over his shoulder) 'Limbs with talons, eyes like knives, bane to the blameless, thief of lives.'

(Cut to Riley debriefing his patrol team)

Riley: Three metres tall, approximately 100–120 kilograms, based on my visual analysis.

Graham: Special hazards?

Riley: Unknown. Probably nothing we haven't handled before. There is no pattern we can discern yet, so we got to assume that it is on a basic kill-crush-destroy.

(Cut to Buffy)

Buffy: This thing isn't digging up the bones of a child for fun.

('Doomed', 4.11)

The Initiative here demonstrates not only a distinct lack of poetry but, more importantly, a lack of imagination and critical questioning. The Scoobies measure in metaphors, Riley in kilos; the Scoobies rely on ancient books, the Initiative on scientific technology. The Scoobies query motivation, while Riley, in a move that will later be reinforced by Dr Engelman in 'The "I" in Team', discounts it. The arrogance of Riley's assumption that the Vahrall demon is 'nothing we haven't handled before' and is probably on 'a basic kill-crush-destroy' is countered by Buffy's insight that '[t]his thing isn't digging up the bones of a child for fun'. Lorna Jowett elaborates some of the fundamental distinctions between the Scoobies and the Initiative in terms of group dynamics and basic operating procedure when she writes that the Initiative 'is based on hierarchy rather than communal effort, encourages competition rather than cooperation, and, ironically, requires passivity (following orders) rather than initiative'.[4] Jowett sees Riley as

Figure 11: Riley's Cowboy, 'Restless,' 4.22

'primarily homosocial', living in the fraternity house of UC Sunnydale and functioning as part of the homosocial family of the Initiative. While Frances Early has presented Riley as 'a nurturing and caring new age man' in comparison with his Initiative counterparts,[5] Jowett sees Riley rather as a figure of 'paternalistic chivalry', citing series writer Doug Petrie's comment that Riley is 'a sexist doof'.[6]

What Jowett sees as Riley's paternalistic chivalry is well illustrated in a scene in 'The Initiative' where Buffy and Riley protect their secret identities from each other whilst trying to patrol the campus grounds:

Buffy: Whoa! Ok … It's a free campus. Who died and made you John Wayne?
Riley: I'm just trying to help.
Buffy: You think I need help? Believe me, I don't. You know, if you were a real gentleman, then you would just leave. You would go far, far away, now! Shoo!
Riley: Are you drunk?
Buffy: Yes! Go and report me.
Riley: I'm taking you home. Come on.
(He goes to grab her and lead her off.)

Buffy: Oh, did you ever think maybe I'm gonna take you home, huh? What? You think that boys can take care of themselves and girls need help?
Riley: Yeah.
Buffy: That is so Teutonic.

('The Initiative', 4.7)

The invocation of the Western's most iconic hero, John Wayne, foreshadows Riley's transformation, in the season finale 'Restless', into a cowboy bent on 'world domination'. Here, however, Buffy betrays an incipient impatience with Riley's outmoded paternal concern and she attempts to rout him at his own game: 'You know, if you were a *real* gentleman, then you would just leave' (emphasis added). Descending to the infantile 'Shoo!' in the effort to rid herself of Riley's unwanted protection, Buffy seems increasingly desperate in the face of his stolid immovability. And her frustration is shared by viewers. Ratchetting up this tension considerably in 'A New Man' (4.12) is Riley's ill-advised interference in Buffy's plans to rescue Giles, temporarily trapped in the body of a Fyarl demon:

Riley: Buffy, I can't take you with me.
Buffy: You're not taking me with you. I am going and I am letting you come along.
Riley: Buffy, it's not really your call. This is a military operation now.
Buffy (steely): Then call out the troops. Because nothing less than that is gonna stop me. This demon did something to Giles and I'm gonna kill it.

('A New Man', 4.12)

Riley's loyalty to his adopted Initiative family becomes increasingly strained as the season progresses (as do the familial metaphors themselves) but it is important to the establishment of his character that at the outset this loyalty is unthinking (in several senses) and that he (literally) swallows so easily the story he is drip-fed by his superiors. The idea that Riley even recognises the existence of 'superiors' is fundamentally anathema to the Scooby ethos and is subject to severe and sustained critique, as Buffy's gentle mockery of his James Bond accessories attests, when Riley returns briefly to Sunnydale in Season 6's 'As You Were' (6.15). Earlier, however, while Riley's confusion in the face of different value systems is rendered with pathos, it is not necessarily a form of pathos with which *Buffy* fans would be expected to feel any particular empathy. Stymied in his first attempt to engage Buffy's personal attention in 'The Initiative' (4.7), Willow and Riley survey the damage:

Riley: I can't believe it. I choked.
Willow: You really, really did.
Riley: You don't understand. I'm good at things. That's what I do. Work hard, apply myself, get it done.
Willow: Well, you failed extremely well.

('The Initiative', 4.7)

Riley's form of unthinking, high-achieving do-goodery is distinctly at odds with the Slayer and her friends, who have always been social outcasts, and his cheerful, robust support of the status quo, especially when this discriminates, as it invariably does, against difference, is greeted with understandable mistrust.[7] Riley's black and white mentality about demons is a case in point. The Initiative's efforts to eliminate Oz as a dangerous HST lead Buffy to pronounce: 'I never knew you were such a bigot', but this is a recognition that strikes viewers as decidedly belated, perhaps even long overdue.

What makes Riley so fascinating a case study for the performance of masculinity in *Buffy* is precisely because his earnest attempts to embody hegemonic gender expectations met with such resounding disdain, both from his fellow characters and from fans around the world. While the human institutions of Sunnydale, such as the government, workforce and university, are realistically represented as patriarchal, the supernatural world lurking beneath this is less rigidly structured, and the community the Scoobies create might be usefully considered an alternative counter-public, based on more progressive, usually liberal but occasionally radical ideals of equality, tolerance and respect for difference. While this counter-public is never explicitly named as feminist within the narrative, my second chapter contends that it is clearly represented as feminist in a way fans recognise and endorse, and this politic is ratified and occasionally elaborated by Whedon in his extra-textual public pronouncements on the show. For the Scoobies, then, Riley's commitment to normative models of masculinity is inevitably anathema, but instead (or perhaps as well) as dismissing him out of hand, I propose that through him Season 4 performs an extended, almost forensic dissection of the maintenance and policing of masculine models in contemporary patriarchal culture.

I have argued in my first chapter that too much is essentialised in gender discussions of *Buffy* and that this often ends up reifying gender binaries rather than challenging them. That the series' scenario entertains this simplification – that it provides a space for its consideration – is not enough reason to swallow it wholesale. However, as we have seen, certain developments in feminist theory have supported and encouraged essentialist analysis of gender difference at various points in time, and the study of masculinity, emerging alongside the academic institutionalisation of feminism in the 1980s, has also courted this risk of oversimplification in some of its different incarnations.

Scholarly interest in ideas about men and masculinity emerged from the feminist movements of the 1960s and 1970s. As second-wave feminism began to point out the vast inequalities between men and women, progressive men in the 1970s created a 'men's liberation movement' aimed at supporting their female counterparts.[8] Alongside this feminist men's liberation movement, a distinct movement known as the 'mythopoetic men's movement' formed in the 1980s, which encouraged men to explore what was seen as their innate masculinity through 'retreating into the wilderness' and 'exercises in spiritual interrogation'.[9] Under the encouragement of leaders such as Robert Bly, the mythopoetic men's movement was critical of women's emancipation and exhorted men to spend time with each other, rediscovering their masculinity and 'the warrior within'. The idea that there was an innate mode of masculinity inherent in each man suggests that, as with some strands of second-wave feminism, the mythopoetic men's movement employed a biologically determined gender analysis, producing rigid dichotomies of gendered behaviour as essential and immutable characteristics. From its beginnings, then, studies of men and masculinity approached the issues of women, feminism, privilege and equality from decidedly different directions, and similar schisms are apparent in the field today in terms of methodology, theoretical orientation and political persuasion.

Now an established area of research with a prolific primary and secondary literature, masculinity studies is a broad umbrella that covers such distinct undertakings as quantatitive sex-role research, enthnographic studies of particular cultures and subcultures, psychoanalytic analysis of interpersonal relations, such as fathering, and discursive analysis of cultural representations such as *Buffy the Vampire Slayer*. While the key terms of the broad field continue to be contested, Australian sociologist Robert Connell's groundbreaking research, particularly in his co-authored 1985 essay 'Towards a new sociology of masculinity'[10] and his 1995 book *Masculinities* (recently reissued with a reflection on the state of the field in 2005), played a significant role in 'creating an intellectual agenda and consolidating a field of study'.[11]

Most significant for my study of Riley is Connell's notion of hegemonic masculinity, and the elaboration by subsequent theorists of its conceptual corollaries: subordinated and marginalised masculinities, homosociality and homophobia. Hegemonic masculinity can be simply described as the dominant idea of how to perform manhood in a given culture and time. As David Buchbinder relates, hegemonic masculinity involves a 'constrained repertoire' of behaviour and traits that are sanctioned – and prioritised – by the patriarchal order.[12] Hegemonic masculinity refers implicitly to a hierarchical structure between men, with the extent to which an individual fits the ideal characteristics becoming an indicator of power. As Connell makes clear, hegemonic masculinity is thus 'not assumed to be normal in the statistical sense; only a minority of men might enact it. But it [is] certainly *normative*'.[13] Men compete with other men in order to achieve hegemony and assert their masculinity.

The Gramscian term 'hegemony' refers to the way in which dominant ideologies are formed through cultural leadership rather than being imposed by force. As John Hartley points out, this process of cultural reproduction means that ideology is constantly being remade and contested; hence 'hegemony can never be total'.[14] Michael Kimmel comments that ideas of hegemonic masculinity can be seen to change over time and between cultures,[15] and numerous scholars, including Connell, have pointed out that this contestation over hegemonic masculinity inevitably creates a hierarchy among men. In his recent book *Studying Men and Masculinities*, Buchbinder provides a pithy synopsis of these positions:

> Hegemonic masculinity, then, constitutes a conventional or ideal(ized) masculinity. It is that notion of the masculine to which men subscribe, whether or not they themselves embody

> it. [...] [I]t is important to realise that *masculinity itself is made up of a repertoire of possible ways of being a man (of performing manliness), out of which is constellated a set of particular traits, attitudes and behaviors that become understood as hegemonic masculinity*. It follows, therefore, that hegemonic masculinity is both historically and culturally contingent: it means something different to both different cultures, and to a single culture at different moments in its history.[16]

In a statement that bears closely on my analysis of *Buffy's* gender politics, Buchbinder asserts that

> to *hypostasize* that masculinity (that is, to assume its concrete reality, despite its being an abstract concept) and so to *reify* it (to make it into a tangible thing) is to attempt to fix it and render it stable *despite* its historical circumstance and cultural context.[17]

As noted above, it is Riley's role in the Initiative that marks most clearly his commitment to hegemonic masculinity. While the composite demon Adam, hideously reminiscent of Frankenstein's monster, might technically be Season 4's 'big bad', it is hard not to see in the Initiative, as Adam's creator, the primary 'evil' the Scoobies must confront. The 'creature' of Mary Shelley's gothic fiction *Frankenstein* is an apt analogy for Adam. Both have been assembled out of dead body parts: Dr Frankenstein's creature is assembled from the remains of human corpses while Adam is assembled from the remains of captured demons. Both Dr Frankenstein and the Initiative's Maggie Walsh transgress societal norms and laws in their ambition to create a new form of life, and in each case their hubris is seen as a form of overreaching justly punished by death. The classical figure Phaeton and Milton's Satan are literary precursors not of Adam himself, but of his creators in the Initiative, who presumed to bestow the gift of life or death, even to the undead.

As the belaboured rhetoric of that last paragraph attests, Buffy's intertextual allusions are not necessarily meant to be taken too far. As Willow comments to Buffy after an earthquake: 'Hey! I was in the library during the quake, almost got buried under some nineteenth-century literature. And I don't have to tell you how hard it is to dig through some of that stuff.

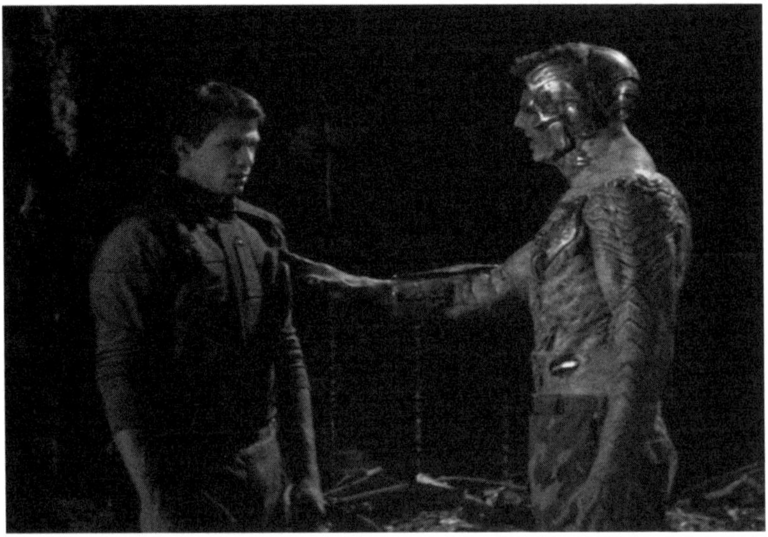

Figure 12: Riley and Adam, 'Primeval,' 4.21

You okay?' ('Doomed,' 4.11). At the same time, the joke would not be there if Whedon and Co. didn't mean people to laugh at it, and viewers with only a passing familiarity with nineteenth-century gothic fiction will be able to recognise, if only through contemporary cultural reference, Adam's analogy to Mary Shelley's *Frankenstein*. Modern audiences might not be able to distinguish between Dr Frankenstein and Frankenstein's creature, often mistaking and misnaming the creature for the creator, but Season 4 of *Buffy* teaches closer to the canonical literary text. The ambition and fear that drive the creators of Adam are more central to the narrative than the activities or clumsy cogitations of the creature himself. And Riley, despite his protestations, is linked to Adam by his status as the Initiative's 'creature.'

More specifically, Riley is Maggie Walsh's creature, and as a woman Professor Walsh might seem an unusual choice as leader for the homosocial unit of the Initiative. But as my discussion of Margaret Thatcher in Chapter 3 suggests, the 'exception woman' – defined by herself and others as the exception that proves the rule of women's general unsuitability for leadership – can in certain circumstances be the most effective figurehead for patriarchal rectitude and legitimacy. Maggie Walsh *is* masculinised in *Buffy the Vampire Slayer*, and by that I mean not that strength of purpose or leadership or tenacity or even violence are masculine traits per se, but that Walsh promotes them as such, with herself as their ultimate embodiment. In addition, she either creates or upholds (it is unclear which) a regime for the reproduction of normative masculinity in the men under her control that implicitly pits them against each other in their efforts to approximate, monitor and reinforce the behaviour that will earn her approval, and consequently the respect of their peers.

In a happy confluence of metaphor and methodology, Buchbinder describes the policing of masculinity under patriarchy through Foucault's figure of the panopticon – a figure already alluded to as central to Season 4's metaphorical structure and that is presented as Maggie Walsh's key to control. Buchbinder writes that 'no matter how "power-dressed" a woman might be, she is unable to confer masculinity upon men. Only other men can do that' and that 'this necessarily puts the individual male in a difficult and inevitably anxiety-producing position. His status as masculine depends on the judgment of those against whom the patriarchal order pits him as a competitor for phallic power.'[18] As Riley is drawn deeper into the feminist world of the Scoobies, it is ultimately Buffy to whom he will surrender the struggle for phallic power, but his patriarchal training is so effective that this surrender eventually erodes his self-respect to the extent that he can no longer function as a 'man' in the sense that he recognises. In the Scoobies' political world picture, neither Buffy's phallic power nor Riley's loss of it render either's gender performance problematic or illegitimate; it is Riley's patriarchal indoctrination that prevents him from imagining any successful masculine alternative, and which precludes him from fully participating in the new girl order. To assess the obstacles to Riley's becoming worthy of Buffy, however, we need to delve deeper into the discipline of the Initiative.

Foucault's *Discipline and Punish: The Birth of the Prison*[19] presents the idea of the panopticon, the design for a correctional facility developed by Jeremy Bentham in 1785, as an analogy for the functioning of power in contemporary society. Foucault states that the major effect of the panopticon is:

> to induce in the inmate a state of conscious and permanent visibility that ensures the automatic functioning of power.

Figure 13: Maggie Walsh's Surveillance, 'The "I" in Team,' 4.13

> So to arrange things that the surveillance is permanent in its effects, even if it is discontinuous in its action; that the perfection of power should tend to render its actual existence unnecessary; that this architectural apparatus should be a machine for creating and sustaining a power relation independent of the person who exercises it; in short, that the inmates should be caught up in a power situation of which they are themselves the bearers.[20]

The Initiative functions like the panopticon (that is, in analogy to the analogy of the operations of power in contemporary society) in several respects. It forces its members to police each other, promoting unthinking obedience as the epitome of correct procedure. It chastises recalcitrant members with the threat of ostracism for breaches of soldierly decorum; thus Riley's evolving sympathy for the Scoobies' alternative protocols are met with disbelief, disdain and eventually rigid disapproval. And it inculcates into its members/prisoners a belief in the omniscience *and* omnipotence of its leaders/jailers that serves to eliminate resistance and prohibit speculation about any possible alternative.

Buchbinder argues that although the analogy between the panopticon and patriarchy is 'not exact' it is still useful to think of the patriarchal order as a sort of panopticon, 'keeping all males under observation in order to control their behaviour to ensure that the criteria of masculinity are observed and maintained':

> In practical terms, this means that men are simultaneously panoptic subjects (the agents of the patriarchal panopticon) and panoptic objects (the focus of surveillance of the patriarchal panopticon). They both observe, and are observed by, one another, as a way of keeping male behaviours in line with the current norms of masculinity and acceptable gender standards.[21]

In Buchbinder's eerie summation: 'Such is the power of the kind of covert panoptic surveillance encouraged by the patriarchal order that, *even in private, men tend to behave according to the norms of masculinity as if they were under actual and continuous observation*'.[22]

Our understanding of Riley's behaviour in Season 4, and of Whedon and Co.'s possible intentions in subjecting a principal recurring character to such unabated fan derision, can be enhanced by this analysis of patriarchy. Rather than being simply an unsuitable love object, Riley is both a symbol and a symptom of all that feminist fans of the show instinctively reject and abhor. His struggle to repudiate that inheritance – his already over-ness and his primary training in patriarchy – provide for gripping if annoying viewing, partly because we don't want him to succeed. We actually want him to fail, to be over-*already*. Unlike Season 1's single-episode Owen, however, Riley is around for the long haul, and dutiful viewers are required to experience his encounter with alternative gender politics – through resistance, respect, revision, partial acceptance and relapse – in almost painful real time.

If it is unsurprising that fans of the show should feel impatience with Riley's narrative (we are, after all, designed to), it is more surprising that scholars of the series should replicate that response in their critical response to his character. With the exception of one essay promoting Riley as the only choice for a Buffy ready to settle down in a mature relationship (as if!),[23] the few critics to treat Riley as anything more than a passing reference seem to replicate without question the primary narrative's presentation of his basic irrelevance to the Slayer story. The insistence with which Buffy pursues this romance with 'normality' in the face of its obvious drawbacks – his deathly earnestness, his lack of imagination, his bigotry – suggests to me that we need to search beyond the immediate narrative rewards of Riley's failure to consider what role this might play in the series' metanarrative construction of an alternative gender politics.

One way to pursue this angle is to consider that, as much as Riley is a figure of hegemonic masculinity and believes firmly in this edifice, he is unable to perform it perfectly – as, of course, is everyone. Indeed, fissures within the edifice of hegemonic masculinity seem almost built into its structure. We learn unexpectedly, for instance, that Riley's Initiative code name is 'Lilac 1' and Buffy's immediate response – 'Very manly' – fractures his bravura performance of military professionalism and heteronormativity. Riley's failed or insufficient performance of hegemonic masculinity here introduces the spectre of marginalised masculinities, most obviously in its encoding of hypermasculinity as queer. Unsurprisingly, members of the Initiative employ practices of homophobic policing in their surveillance of each other – as with Forrest's aside that Riley is a 'Mama's boy' and his more direct rebuke: 'You used to be a contender, now you're the boyfriend of the contender.' More surprising, perhaps, is that Riley's masculinity is bifurcated from the outset, and that bifurcation is the ground of its instantiation: he is both the Number 1 of the hierarchical, homosocial Initiative and its lilac heart or wound.

Eve Sedgwick helpfully defines homosociality as 'the social bonds between persons of the same sex; it is a neologism', she argues, 'obviously formed by analogy with "homosexual", and just as obviously meant to be distinguished from "homosexual". In fact, it is applied to such activities as "male bonding" which may, in our society, be characterised by intense homophobia, fear and hatred of homosexuality'.[24] In a provocative Freudian analysis, Kimmel has read 'Masculinity *as* homophobia',[25] while Buchbinder suggests that homophobia, 'the [irrational] fear of homosexuality and of homosexuals', in effect constitutes 'the boundaries of masculinity itself, and so help[s] to construct the masculine'. 'Beyond this, *the patriarchal order itself can be seen to depend on the process of abjection*'.[26] Approaching

Figure 14: Riley and Maggie, 'The Initiative,' 4.7

this dynamic from a less psychoanalytic perspective, Benton J. Malin notes that practices of homosocial male bonding can be contradictory, as they involve a 'sense of brotherly contact, cooperation, and competition'. In particular, he argues that

> by placing men together in intimate contact, homosocial behaviour challenges conceptions of mainstream masculinity even as it supports others. As an arena where men might be encouraged to share their deepest feelings, or come into intimate physical contact, homosociality plays against a variety of stereotypically masculine traits.[27]

For example, bonding in a locker-room may induce hypermasculinity such as boasting about sexual exploits with women as a means of overcoming the physical closeness that might suggest homosexuality.[28]

The hypermasculinity performed by Initiative soldiers participates in such homophobic policing in maintaining, or attempting to shore up, the heteronomativity of the military unit. In his study of 'The organisational construction of hegemonic masculinity' in the US Navy, Frank J. Barrett presents the military as an exemplar of masculine role models and notes

Figure 15: The Initiative on Patrol, 'Pangs,' 4.8

the processes of reinforcing masculinity within the institution: 'Recruits learn the value of appearance, cleanliness, exacting detail, and respect for rank and tradition. They come to value conformity and obedience, and learn [to] display rules for exhibiting aggression and courage in the face of risk.'[29] As others such as Connell, Messner and Kimmel have done, Barrett emphasises that the construction of masculinity occurs through a process, involving the instilling of values such as those listed above, displays of which are then routinely tested for. Processes of surveillance and rewards, as we have seen with the example of the Initiative, are also used to reinforce the strict adherence to 'appropriate' characteristics. Barrett cites Arkin and Dobrofsky who, in 1978, argued that

> the military has socialized millions of men according to some traditional blueprint. As such the dominant male role model could largely be the product of the military, particularly in as much as those who are thus socialized have returned to society.[30]

Even outside his military connections, however, Riley physically represents the type of 'hard bodied' masculinity redolent of 1980s action films. His chiselled and torqued physique is the desired object of male and female gazes (Buffy: 'It would be good to have those arms'; Xander: 'Can I have sex with Riley too?'). In a fascinating essay on 'The White man's muscles', Richard Dyer analyses the presentation of the 'built body' in popular culture, arguing persuasively that this spectacle is tied with racial politics. He relates that the white body was rarely seen 'semi-naked' in popular films until the 1980s, partly because nakedness is vulnerable, but also because clothes signify wealth and status, yet when it was displayed in a particular fashion it could be used to explain white privilege, proffering a sort of biological explanation for inequalities.[31] According to Dyer, popular images of bodybuilding articulate the built body as white, drawing on traditions of ancient Greece and Rome; invoking a lifestyle of 'health, energy and naturalness' and sometimes adopting images of the barbarian. 'Many of the formal properties of the built body', Dyer contends, 'carry connotations of whiteness: it is ideal, hard, achieved, wealthy, hairless and tanned'.[32] Such images draw on the idea of *Übermensch* (beyond human) and in this way relate to fascism; but they also relate to traditional Christian images of the male body enduring suffering.[33]

Riley's relationship to his 'brother' Adam is pertinent here. Assembled from the most lethal parts of various demons, Adam is the ultimate *Übermensch*, underscoring by juxtaposition the fallibility, vulnerability and penetrability of Riley's human body. In terms of its racial inscriptions, Riley's body is Iowa white – a category existing primarily in the American cultural imaginary rather than in lived Midwestern reality. Like Dyer's bodybuilders, it is 'ideal, hard, achieved, wealthy, hairless and tanned'. The juxtaposition, however, is not only used to indicate difference. We learn that Riley is not all that he seems; he is both more and less than the love-struck suitor and upstanding military officer. He is in fact a weapon. Maggie Walsh's experiments have made of Riley a physical and psychological lab rat, with the aim, we presume, of producing the ideal human-soldier-machine. Riley is effectively a cyborg, albeit with a familiar, corn-fed face.

I would argue, then, that Riley is Season 4's primary marker of difference. It is not demons that pose the biggest threat to the Scoobies and their feminist counter culture; the greatest danger is the lure of the normal, with its insidious, attendant connections to patriarchal, and in this case state and military, hegemony. Riley, because and not despite his normality, is really the dark side for Buffy. Lilac notwithstanding, he is the place she could get lost in and not come out of. Troubled romances aside, Angel and Spike never present anything like this threat.

As the series progress, Season 5 sees Riley increasingly marginalised from the Scoobies and their concerns. Effectively cut off from his routine performance of hegemonic masculinity, Riley becomes incrementally estranged, despite his surface appearance as the normal, reliable, human boyfriend that Buffy claims to trust and know.[34] Buffy's encounter with Dracula in the opening episode of Season 5 prompts Riley to reassess his own, previously inviolable, sense of self against the 'monster' masculinity, represented by Angel and Spike, which he has previously rejected as aberrant. Dracula's brief appearance highlights how the masculinity that vampires perform does not threaten Buffy – they are after all explicitly linked to her role as Slayer – yet the brand that Riley performs (John Wayne, the Hall Monitor, the 'Action Hero' soldier) does in fact pose a danger because he has been constructed (by his cultural conditioning, by Maggie Walsh and ultimately by Whedon and Co.) as an archetype of normative masculinity that stands against everything that Buffy and the Scoobies have hitherto fought for.

Riley's reaction to his disintegrating gender identity leaves him with little option but to 'reset' to familiar modes of masculinity when he finally departs. In the third episode of Season 5, 'Out of My Mind' (5.4), Riley is tormented by losing the superhuman strength and power the Initiative's experiments have granted him and expresses a horror of becoming 'Joe Normal'. In consequence, he is willing to risk his life in a battle with Angel that Buffy disdainfully dismisses as 'some macho pissing contest'. Attempting to harness the lure of vampiric masculinity he believes appeals to Buffy, Riley later allows himself to be fed on by vampires – to feel, as he says, 'wanted'.

But whereas the 'dark' story arcs of characters such as Angel, Giles or Willow added development and depth to their portrayal, Riley's descent into darkness – like many aspects of his character – is deliberately underwhelming. Attempting to justify his juvenile behaviour, Riley relates that as Buffy grows stronger she becomes more distant and further 'out of his reach'; he does not feel himself her equal, just as he fails to measure up to the incarnations of monster masculinity to whom he is invariably compared (Angel, Spike and Dracula). Coupled with helpful observations from former deputy Graham, reminding him that instead of leading the mission he is now 'the mission's boyfriend' ('Out of My Mind', 5.4), Riley experiences a crisis of masculinity that is viewed by most of those around him with impatience and incomprehension.

The reasons behind this crisis and the way it is received are worth teasing out. Riley's desire to partner a strong, capable woman diminishes as he feels his own power ebbing. His claims to love Buffy's strength begin to ring hollow as we realise that, for him, her power is increasingly experienced as emasculating. When he and his commando buddies controlled the campus, Riley was happy to help hang the banner for the lesbian collective ('Something Blue', 4.9), but the loss of this privilege reveals his self-proclaimed respect for women to be more like benevolence (to be bestowed, albeit generously) than equality (with shared powers and responsibilities). In Riley's retreating patriarchal world, power is revealed to be a zero-sum game: there are only so many pieces of the phallic pie to go around and if Buffy has more of them then he doesn't want to play.

Despite attempts to shake the shackles of his previous military persona, Riley seeks solace in his inherited models of gender relations. In the eyes of Buffy, the Scoobies and the fan-base, this regression sets him apart as more 'other' than any other 'other'. In his Initiative career, Riley was designed to be a weapon – a cyborg – with a mission and purpose. The deeper message of Riley's negotiation with gender identity, however, is the parallel drawn between his military and civilian personas. It is not only medical intervention but also cultural indoctrination that has made Riley the kind of man he is. And he is a willing tool of both regimes. Riley is ultimately incapable of imagining, let alone implementing, a feminist ideology in either of the spheres he inhabits. He is left with a redundant model of masculinity that registers difference more starkly than any monster-of-the-week or Big Bad of the season. Riley eventually accepts Graham's offer to go 'deep undercover', to return to a familiar world of rules, routine and hierarchy, dominated by reliably black and white versions of right and wrong. With the possible exception of Xander, there is a sense of relief for the characters (and the audience) when he does so. This is where Riley belongs: in the familiar world of hegemonic masculinity, he is safe to relapse into his conditioned behaviour. As his self-confidence in his Season 6 cameo, 'As You Were' (6.15), suggests, he reverts (probably with palpable relief) to performing Captain America, the well-meaning but cartoonish soldier of duty, who was also, ironically, the result of a medical-military experiment.[35]

Not all done

Buffy's romance with normality takes a long time out for most of Seasons 6 and 7, with Spike claiming centre stage as the focus of her erotic attention. Ongoing and intricate debates in popular and scholarly venues about the rival merits of Spike and Angel as Buffy's consort make it unnecessary for me to rehearse them here. This terrain has been well traversed in *Buffy* studies, although the results are still gratifyingly undecided (one presumes – at least for Whedon and Co.). More pertinent for my project is the fact that in the tormented aftermath of another volatile, failed relationship with a vampire, this time Spike, Buffy's incipient romantic interest in Principal Robin Wood can only strike the viewer as her own relapse to doomed original principles.

Buffy's romance with normality is in this instance refreshingly short-lived: it only takes evidence of the fact that her potential new beau is attempting to kill her recently rejected old beau to bring Buffy to some sense of perspective. But in the interim we are treated to fleeting speculations about the 'mature' Buffy's 'normal' romantic predilections that strike this viewer at least as distinctly recidivist in nature. Wood, as principal, not unlike Riley as TA, is a figure of institutional authority whose advances IRL – in real life – might be summarily dismissed as sexual harassment. This does not trouble Buffy, or indeed the potentially more politically minded Willow. Instead, the narrative returns to fantasies of normality – of first dates and first kisses (with one's first boss) – that the increasingly dark Season 7 is at pains to accommodate. Luckily it does not seek to entertain this storyline at length, but its intrusion into the final plotline of the series' conclusion is worth noting: Buffy will resolve (or not) her relations with Angel and Spike in the episodes to come, but it is pertinent that her last-ditch attempt at a new relationship is with a figure who is supposedly 'normal' but who also embodies facets of normality that have proved dangerous to her in the past: an inability to accept her leadership as finally legitimate and a profound resistance to members of her chosen cohort.

Given the fierce rivalry between (and over) Angel and Spike, it is satisfying at the levels of both narrative and feminist politics that the creators of *Buffy* should leave her self-sufficient at the end: beloved by many, and manifestly befriended, but resolutely single. Rejecting as it does any grand reunion with either of her primary two suitors, and involving also an emphatic dismissal of alternate 'normal' contenders (such as Wood), the series concludes with its protagonist eschewing the conventional romance conclusion of union and instead sees her staking out the boundaries of her own becoming. As 'cookie dough', Buffy claims she is 'not all done yet', and defers the question of who will eventually get to 'eat' her to a later date. Cleverly, this scenario does not preclude further romance, but rather reserves those possibilities for the viewers' (let's face it, at this point quite graphic) imaginations. In terms of its treatment of men and masculinity, however, it is key that ultimately, the Chosen One retains the power to choose. We might ask, but Buffy (and Whedon and Co.) are not prepared to tell.

6

'From Beneath You It Devours': Andrew and the Homoerotics of Evil

While the compelling, histrionic heterosexual rhetorics of *Buffy the Vampire Slayer* have been energetically analysed, and the overtly lesbian narratives have begun to attract increasing attention, the flawed and often foiled homoerotic desires of the series' ostensibly straight male characters call out for further attention.[1] This chapter attempts to queer the character Andrew in *Buffy*'s Season 7 – a queering that may or may not be superfluous depending on your favoured viewing positions and pleasures. Indeed, it is questionable whether it is even possible, let alone worthwhile, to 'queer' Andrew because Andrew already seems so queer himself. If Andrew's queerness was written largely at the level of narrative (as Willow's and Tara's are, for instance) rather than suggested (no matter how broadly) at the level of subtext, this endeavour would be, as Buffy suggests Andrew's archival project is in 'Storyteller' (7.16), 'pretty pointless'. In a series that demonstrates such delight in the slippage between text and subtext, moreover, upholding distinctions between them might seem counterintuitive. But, equally, it seems to me that even if Andrew's queerness is highly legible and the source, for many viewers, of much of the humour in the season, the potential *meanings* of that queerness are not always so obvious and, in fact, could be conceived as considerable cause for contention. How do Andrew's desires change between Seasons 6 and 7? Does he offer a positive or negative image of homoerotic desire? And does the fact that Andrew's primary erotic attachment is to Warren – and, through him, to evil more generally – mean that the representation of this desire is *ipso facto* homophobic and misogynist or could it be interpreted in other less straightforward and formulaic ways? This chapter considers Andrew's desire for evil, and by extension Warren and Jonathan, in order to consider how a queer reading of these relationships might affect prevailing understandings of the operations of gender and sexuality in a series so invested in both.

First broadcast in 1997 following the film version of 1992, *Buffy the Vampire Slayer* went to air in the decade that gave birth to the New Queer Cinema and shares with it several key characteristics. In her 1992 essay, 'New queer cinema', B. Ruby Rich characterises the queer films of the 1990s, which included Jennie Livingston's *Paris is Burning* (1990), Todd Haynes's *Poison* (1991), and Tom Kalin's *Swoon* (1992) among many others, as 'homo pomo', and saw them as invested in 'appropriation', 'pastiche' and 'irony'.[2] New queer girl films (later additions to the new queer canon) that bear a closer relationship to *Buffy*'s content include *The Incredibly True Adventures of Two Girls in Love* (Maria Maggenti, 1995), *All Over Me* (Alex Sichel, 1997) and *But I'm a Cheerleader* (Jamie Babbit, 2000). In her 2004 re-evaluation of the movement, Michele Aaron argues that the films of the New Queer Cinema share a strategy of 'defiance': they tend to 'eschew positive imagery' and 'defy the sanctity of the past, especially the homophobic past'. They defy cinematic convention 'in terms of form, content and genre' and they also, tellingly, defy 'death'.[3] In its pastiche and irony, complex characterisation and defiance of the conventions of content and genre, *Buffy* shares many formal features with the New Queer Cinema. In its revision of historical narratives, fascination with death and play with positive and negative imagery, it shares significant ground in content as well.

Queer is an appropriate lens through which to look at both the world represented in *Buffy* and the text that is *Buffy*. Aaron speaks to the 'theoretically lucrative' valence of the term when she writes that queer represents

> the resistance to, primarily, the normative codes of gender and sexual expression – that masculine men sleep with feminine women – but also the restrictive potential of gay and lesbian sexuality – that only men sleep with men and, women sleep with women.[4]

In this way, queer, as a critical concept, 'encompasses the non-fixity of gender expression and the non-fixity of both straight and gay sexuality'. At its most expansive and utopian, Aaron argues, 'queer contests (hetero- *and* homo-) normality'.[5] In its theoretical applications, then, 'queer is not just about gender and sexuality, but the restrictiveness of the rules governing them and their intersection with other aspects of identity'.[6] Furthermore, Aaron makes clear that it is not just cultural production that demands queering but also the analysis of those productions: 'the queering of contemporary western culture is not just about the products alone, but about their theorization'.[7]

Buffy is a queer text at both the narrative and metanarrative levels; indeed there is reason to suggest that the series is most queer when it is not directly addressing explicitly homosexual content. Farah Mendelsohn has argued that representations of Willow's overtly 'gay' (the term preferred by the characters) relationships overshadow the homoerotic undercurrents of Willow's potentially queer relationship with Buffy.[8] Allison McCracken has argued convincingly for a queering of Angel's ostensibly straight male body, and she extends this queering to the viewing practices of *Buffy*'s legion of young female fans. She writes that the programme's serial structure 'permits girls' desires to shift and complicate over time, promoting the idea of sexual desire not as a fixed identity or goal-oriented pursuit (ending in a "solid" relationship), but as a queer continuum of erotic possibilities, opportunities and challenges'.[9] Significantly expanding the horizon of queer readings of *Buffy*, McCracken argues that the term queer

> acknowledges, as other descriptors cannot, the way in which *Buffy's* feminist focus works to queerly recode a relationship between a pretty blonde and a hunky male that could otherwise be read as 'straight'. Sexual norms are always set atremble when a female is on top and Buffy's feminism enables queer readings in a way that distinguishes the program from other instances of queerness on television.[10]

Andrew presents a rich test case for queer readings of *Buffy* because his representation evolves over time and invokes several of the more misogynist, homophobic stereotypes of homosexuality as well as more open-ended or potentially progressive readings of homoerotic desire. I would argue that the series does so wittingly – that is, self-consciously and deliberately – so that homophobia and misogyny are actually thematised at the level of narrative, and are not merely, or perhaps not *only*, residual subtextual echoes. In Season 6, for instance, Andrew is represented variously as the 'invisible' queer ('Who are you?'), as a clueless queer member of a tight homosocial unit ('I like Timothy Dalton!') and as the closeted gay man acting out homophobia through the sexual objectification of women ('Free cable porn!'). In Season 7 these resonances reach their highest pitch when Andrew is portrayed as a version of the 'homosexual as killer'. At the same time, Andrew's characterisation is more complex than these examples would suggest. His development in Season 7 takes him on a bumpy, sometimes reluctant, journey of remorse and redemption, and, as I suggest in my next chapter, 'Storyteller' in particular portrays Andrew simultaneously as a figure of the fan and of the author, opening possibilities for queer readings of spectatorship and cultural production that retrospectively reverberate across the series.[11]

It is useful to examine Andrew's early incarnations in order to assess how his character evolves. In 'Flooded' (6.4), we are introduced to Andrew and his buddies, Warren and Jonathan, who have banded together to form the 'Evil Trio'. In a flashback whose very inarticulateness bears eloquent testimony to the group's dynamics and to their compellingly redundant aspirations, Warren asks: 'You guys wanna team up and take over Sunnydale?' One month later, they have devised a bullet-pointed, white-boarded master plan: 'Shrink rays, trained gorillas, and Chicks! Chicks! Chicks!' Egregiously puerile and often unwittingly hilarious in their nerdly pursuits ('We can do anything! We can stay up all night if we want!'), in the early episodes of Season 6, the Trio sometimes function as an object of gentle satire and sometimes as an emblem of the darker sides of adolescent male posturing and competition. Perennial infighting and squabbling among the Trio make them the butt of obvious humour ('You're still sulking because I wouldn't make you a Christina Ricci robot'), but their initial portrayal also comes across as a rather tender homage to 'geek love' from a creator who has identified himself as the fanboy extraordinaire. Whedon is, after all, on record as saying that Buffy is 'a show made for losers, by losers'.[12] 'Flooded' provides a telling counterpoint between main plot and subplot, when Buffy's voice-over, 'I know, they're so cute you could die', seems to offer an analysis of the Trio but instead (or as well) refers to the childhood bed linen she offers Giles in the following scene. In one of those proleptic plantings that the Whedon team is famous for, this almost throw-away line will quickly acquire poignancy: there are many ways in which the Trio are not cute at all, and as their tests of Buffy over subsequent episodes indicate, she *could* very well die and ultimately, someone does.

Throughout Season 6, the Trio functions as a homosocial unit that has decidedly queer overtones. The 'horn' of their surveillance vehicle plays the *Star Wars* theme song and the language they use to describe their exploits is broadly metaphorical: Jonathan's jubilant announcement '[c]rime is our wormhole!' is followed by Andrew's extended meditation on the depth of this 'cavity' which is in turn foreclosed by Warren's, 'Dude, don't be a geek!' ('Flooded'). They regularly address each other with sexualised monikers, 'Penis' and 'Spanky', or evoke intertextual references to potentially queer popular texts: 'Shut up Frodo!' ('Gone', 6.11). A less obvious example of this strategy occurs when Andrew invokes queer modernist writer E. M. Forster by lamenting that they do not have 'a lair with a view' ('Dead Things', 6.13). Andrew summons demons through various phallic-shaped musical instruments – a small delicate flute in 'Life Serial' (6.5) escalating to a honking great didgeridoo in 'Normal Again' (6.17). The demons themselves are seen as phallic extensions: in 'Normal Again' Warren instructs Andrew to 'deploy your little friend'. There is not a lot of subtlety involved in these representations, but then I don't think subtlety is intended. In their early presentation of the Trio, Whedon and Co. relish the art of turning a double entendre into a single entendre: 'Give me my bone!'; 'Stop touching my magic bone!' If these guys are closeted, they are so only to themselves; the Trio inhabits a sort of Emperor's new closet, which frames and amplifies the homoerotic subtext they are at pains to repress.

Stevie Simkin sees the Trio as 'a group of anxious males who have retreated into, or never emerged from, a state of perpetual adolescence and fantasy' and he notes that a 'homoerotic subtext is clearly traceable in their relationships'.[13] As rabid fans of *Star Wars*, *Star Trek* and various competing versions of James Bond, the Trio's ostensibly grandiose schemes are regularly undercut by one of the series' signature rhetorical strategies – bathos: 'I think Timothy Dalton should get an Oscar and beat Sean Connery over the head with it!', Andrew rages in 'Life Serial' (6.5). Simkin points to 'the paltry nature of [the Trio's] ambitions, in comparison with the considerable powers they have developed magically and technologically' and draws attention to Andrew's lament in 'Gone' (6.11): 'But we had so many plans. Naked women, and all … well, all-all the naked women!'[14] Andrew's faltering regret registers a distinct lack of detail – he hasn't gone further than 'naked women' because this is probably not where his own fantasies lie – and despite what Simkin calls the queer 'trainspotting' pleasures that his ellipses provide, at this stage in the narrative he is certainly complicit with the group's overarching game plan of female objectification: 'We can make [Buffy] our willing sex bunny!' ('Flooded', 6.4).[15]

Lorna Jowett sees the Trio as the 'real-world' villains of Season 6, 'a homosocial group viewing women primarily as sexual objects'.[16] At various points in the series the group resembles, as Buffy's doctor tells her in 'Normal Again' (6.17), 'just three pathetic little men … who like playing with toys'. Warren evokes the spectre of homosexuality in a coercive fashion: 'When you girls have stopped playing with each other ….' And it is notable that it is Warren again, emerging as the leader of the group, who disciplines the others through the threat of exposure: 'Well you know what homophobia really means about you, don't you?' At a certain level, this construction of the Trio seems to be a clear case of what Ron Becker identifies as homosociality presented in a 'simple, typically homophobic opposition to homosexuality – through a shared exploitation of women or cooperative violence against fags'.[17] Warren's toxic misogyny sounds the dominant note of the Trio. His experiments on a former girlfriend, Katrina, take the form of rape, and it pays to remember that it is Warren who literally kills off the only out 'gay' relationship in the series when he shoots Tara whilst aiming for the Slayer. But while Warren's manipulations of the Trio's homoerotics are dastardly and ultimately deadly, Andrew's negotiation of this desire is portrayed with an overlay of pathos, and eventually empathy, that make his character less straightforward.

Andrew's queer credentials are flagged in 'Entropy' (6.18) when the Trio unexpectedly stumbles across live-action footage of Spike having sex with Anya in the Magic Box (pun probably intended). Initially unsure about what he is watching ('What are they …? Ooh!'), Andrew becomes transfixed by Spike and murmurs reverently: 'He is so cool'. Abashed by the raised eyebrows of his friends, he quickly compensates: 'And I mean, the girl is hot too.' The desire to be Spike and to have Spike is conflated in this scene. These tendencies are made explicit in 'Seeing Red' (6.19), where the Trio acquires the Orbs of Nezzla'khan. As Simkin notes, '[i]t is difficult not to interpret the orbs as phallic – or, more precisely, testicular: Warren even has a pouch, slung on his belt, designed to hold them.'[18] The testicular metaphor is played broadly for laughs. Watching an enhanced Warren overturn a security van, Andrew sighs: 'Man, I can't wait to get my hands on his orbs.' However, when abandoned by Warren later in the episode, Andrew is genuinely devastated. As Simkin notes, 'Andrew's despair has an overt romantic theme': '"How could he do that to me? He promised me we'd be together. He was just using me. He never really loved" – (catching himself) – "hanging out with us."'[19] Trapped in jail, Jonathan is somewhat salaciously but also phobically obsessed by the thought that a fellow prisoner wants to make him his 'butt monkey', but Andrew's grief raises his longing for Warren to another level.[20] Butt monkey jokes can no longer adequately assuage or express his desires.

By the time we get to Season 7's 'Storyteller' (7.16), Andrew is in the process of switching his fannish allegiance from evil to good, although this 'switch' is still performed through the male homosocial rhetoric favoured by classic film narratives in the buddy and outlaw genres. In their flight from the Slayer, Andrew and Jonathan attempt to bolster each other: 'We gotta make it right!', 'We're outlaws with hearts of gold!' In 'Storyteller', Andrew's romanticised recollections of successful super-villainy bump jarringly against his position as a hostage, or in his preferred terminology, 'guestage', of the Scooby household. Retreating from one of Buffy's pep talks to address the camera directly, Andrew offers us a glorified, revisionist narrative of his 'personal journey':

> Honestly, gentle viewers, these motivating speeches of hers tend to get a little long. I'll take you back in there in – in a little while, but in the in-between time, I thought you might want to know a little about me, your humble host. You see, I am a man with a burden. A man with a dark past. You see, I was once a *super villain.*

There follows a flashback to the 'Evil Workshop' in which an ultra-suave Andrew (in a black suit, shirt and tie) informs the geeky Jonathan and Warren (wearing jeans, t-shirts and protective eye goggles) of his latest invention: 'Thus the validity of the Bronsted-Debye-Huckel equation at low ionic strength has been amply tested, and the charges on the reactant ions are well known, if their reagents are properly characterized.' Stepping into the big shoes of Timothy Dalton, Andrew has, in his own imagination, acquired the masculine mastery to succeed his hero. Clearly attached to his experiment, he has anthropomorphised it in a distinctly virile, even kinky fashion. The 'kinda sweaty' smell of Andrew's prized concoction leaves the audience curious about its mixture of ingredients. The scene continues to show Jonathan and Warren's abject adoration of Andrew: 'Wow, you're the best Andrew.' 'Yep, and good-looking and smart too.' The innocent pleasure Andrew takes in the (fabricated) adulation of his friends is fairly endearing. It is not the least of Tom Lenk's admirable acting skills that he manages to make Andrew so accessible at the same time that he is so despicable. Andrew's declaration: 'In my plan, we are beltless!' is a delectably dorkish, if late-breaking, detail (admirably analysed by Linda Rust) and it is interesting to note that even in his own fantasy depiction, Andrew retains an essential gormlessness and immaturity that might seem to make him seem less culpable than he actually is. Andrew, as 'Storyteller' demonstrates explicitly, is far from innocent, and he must learn to take responsibility for the effects of his actions.

In the final season of *Buffy*, the Scooby gang battles an unseen 'Big Bad' whose signature calling card is the motto: 'From beneath you it devours'. Hiding in Mexico after the eviscerating effects of their last attack on the Scoobies, the remaining members of the Trio, Andrew and Jonathan, are plagued in dreams by a voice that intones '*Desde abajo te devora*'. Translating this warning as 'it eats you starting with your bottom', Andrew enacts a queering of evil that, if not unexpected, is at least surprisingly and explicitly sexual: to Andrew, the dead Warren has become the embodiment of The First and he offers, quite literally, a consummation devoutly to be wished. In Andrew's breathless, titillated translation, the big kahuna has become a master rimmer.

We are introduced to Andrew's recollections of his 'Mehico' sojourn because Buffy and the Scoobies are trying to shut the Seal of Danzalthar, an opening in the earth that Andrew activates when he kills Jonathan on Warren's orders. The trip to Mexico is presented as a sort of whitewashed *Y tu mamá también* fantasy for nerdlings (although rather than being triangulated by an attractive older woman, as in Alfonso Cuarón's 2001 film, the relationship between Andrew and Warren is triangulated by a younger, rounder man – Jonathan, aka 'the shortcake'). The 'Seal' is itself another instance of the series' indulgence in anal humour; a giant orifice complete with interlocking tooth-like panels, it resembles nothing so much as a sphincter dentata. Andrew is enlisted by the Scoobies to 'speak to it in its own language. 'Give it commands and stuff' – an exercise that positions him as an expert 'analinguist'.

Andrew's role as translator positions him between the real-time solidarity of the Scoobies' community and the severed remains of the Trio's homoerotic triangle. Flashbacks to 'Somewhere in Mexico, 2002' in 'Storyteller' (7.16) juxtapose the 'bromance' of Andrew's relationship with Jonathan with the more insidious and sexually charged depiction of his yearning for Warren. Thrashing and heaving in their shared double bed, Andrew and Jonathan erupt simultaneously from their joint nightmare: 'We're fugitives, haunted by our past, tormented by a message we don't understand.' 'We're hunted men, driven mad by forces beyond our understanding.' Jonathan's lament: 'I don't deserve this. I wasn't even that evil' has Andrew rushing to reassure his friend: 'I thought you were evil … I respected your ideas for evil projects, and I thought you had good follow-through.' Though the Scoobies are less than impressed with his blow-by-blow recollection of this tête-à-tête, it is significant that, at this stage, Andrew is still wedded to his infatuation with evil. Reassuring Jonathan about his evil performance anxiety, Andrew invokes the automated language of management consulting, adding a laughable corporate gloss to their joint enterprise.

When, in the present-time of the episode, Willow interrupts with: 'Whoa, I think we're getting a little off topic here', Andrew responds with: 'Shh, it's gonna get interesting. Jonathan's going to go to the bathroom.' And sure enough, Warren enters to interrogate Andrew about the knife he wants him to kill Jonathan with. Andrew is pathetically grateful for Warren's presence ('Oh, gosh. Gosh, I'm glad to see you') and Warren is able to manipulate his willing tool by flattering his fantasies ('Me too. You're looking good'). In a flirtatious scene (from Andrew's perspective) of reassurance, Warren allays Andrew's fears of 'pillow creases' by insisting on his legible masculinity, again registered through the homosocial codes of classic narrative cinema: 'No, no, it's good. You're a man on the run. You've got kind of a wild, desperate thing going on.' When it comes to the point of Warren's visit, however, Andrew stalls. Effectively talking to Jonathan's penis, with whose 'shy' functions he is clearly familiar, Andrew exploits his physical intimacy with Jonathan to buy more time with Warren.

It would be reductive to say that Andrew's desire for Warren is portrayed negatively *simply* because Warren is evil incarnate. The fact that Warren = evil does not necessarily mean that this representation = homophobia. But *Buffy* certainly treads a fine line in this respect. There are ways in which the series' depictions of Andrew produce an ostensibly queer version of the homosexual as murderer that bears disturbing similarities to the more overtly homophobic portrayals of mainstream cinema.[21] As Ron Becker notes:

> For what might be called post-closet TV, gay men who are *not* out – who fail to identify with the label waiting for them, who refuse to accept the straight world's tolerance, who expose the gaping hole in the post-civil-rights logic – are a real problem.[22]

One reading of Andrew's capitulation to Warren's insistence: 'Stab him! You have to! If you fail, you'll die a lost soul, and I'll hate you forever!' would be to see Andrew's closeted state as the cause for his moral failure: 'Got it. If I kill him with this knife, we live as gods.'

Andrew's own musical 'break away hit', 'We live as gods', represents a comic apex in his portrayal, one of the scenes in which he is most clearly 'gay', and a potentially disturbing comment on the self-deception to which his desires lead him – a comment that may or may not relate to his closeted state. Andrew's fantasy of a life joined to Warren and Jonathan takes the form of an idealised pastoral with overtones of *The Sound of Music* (a text that has been successfully queered by gay culture, as its frequent dress-up singalong reprisals attest). Set in what the script refers to as the 'Fantastic Fields', Andrew, Warren and Jonathan are dressed in togas, playing harps and frolicking in fields of daisies. Butterflies flit around and bars of gold lie about in piles. A unicorn (suggestively phallic but also mythically innocent) runs by them as they dance and sing 'We are as Gods'.

In his analysis of straight reception of queer mainstream film, Harry M. Benshoff outlines a typology of constructions of queer male identity in which, in addition to being 'psychologically and socially out of the closet' or 'both unconsciously queer and socially closeted',[23] that is, firmly in or out, *other intermediary positions are available.* Benshoff identifies one of these as being 'psychologically in the closet but socially out, a seemingly rare situation in which friends and family recognise queerness in an individual before he does'.[24] Andrew occupies this 'seemingly rare' position in Season 7. While he may be still psychologically closeted, he is at least socially out to Warren, who manipulates Andrew's patent desire for him to his own nefarious ends. As Ellis Hanson has argued, 'to be in the closet is not necessarily to be sexually out of sight, since discretion and secrecy are curiously readable modes of self-articulation'.[25] In 'Storyteller' (7.16), Andrew is arguably out to the Scoobies as well, who are the reluctant audience to his fantasy's repetition, and whose disapproval stems not so much from his object choice ('gay' is OK) as from his choice of object: Warren. Indeed it could be argued that Andrew's redemptive arc in Season 7 does not so much require him to renounce his queer desires as to find more a worthy object for them: Xander and, ongoingly, Spike.

How, then, do we critically assess Season 7's queer representation of Andrew? Discussing the proliferation of queer images in contemporary popular culture and expressing concern about the possible dilution of queer's oppositional stance that such proliferation entails, Thomas Peele argues that in popular primetime shows such as *Friends*:

> [S]ame-sex desire between men is regularly invoked to propel the action of the series, but it is never allowed to achieve sexual expression. Queer desire is tolerated and made use of, but it is never presented as a desirable state, at least among the men of the series.[26]

The fact that Andrew's sexual desires never receive overt expression (in fulfilment) in the series might seem to support this critique. The fact that Andrew's queerness is largely played for laughs also jeopardises the progressive potential of his portrayal. As Jes Battis has argued in his careful analysis of Xander, while male characters' negotiations with dominant forms of masculinity 'are meant to be funny and gentle':

> [I]t remains the case that, for queer audiences, every ironic jab at hypothetical queerness is a violent intrusion on someone's living queer reality. Jokes about turning gay, about the prospect

> of 'gaying' or being 'gayed up', are funny to straight audiences because *being gay* is funny to them; and they are funny to queer audiences because most queers experience this sort of humor as a kind of laughable irony, a playful self-criticism that is part of their tactics of survival in a predominantly heterosexual world. But for those whose living space is threatened by legislated homophobic violence, for those who are looking for representations of themselves in popular television and finding nothing, and for those who look up to *Buffy* as a show that rhetoricizes tolerance and inclusion, these ironic asides can appear patronizing at best, and insulting at worst.[27]

The 'funny' here is part of the problem.

Joss Whedon and Co. have developed an unusually intimate relationship with their loyal fan base, and as several critics have noted, the series occasionally makes opportunities to respond to fan feedback.[28] Whedon relates that some fans were disappointed with the 'vanilla' nature of Willow and Tara's lesbian relationship: 'Well, they're obviously gay. Why aren't they gay enough? They're not gay enough. You need to make them more gay.'[29] However, Whedon also reserves the right to subvert expectation, insisting that he has learnt that one of his main responsibilities as a storyteller is 'to be irresponsible': 'If I made *Buffy the Lesbian Separatist*, a series of lectures on PBS on why there should be feminism, no one [would] be coming to the party and it would be boring.'[30] The 'positive images' debate, whether focused on queer representation or feminist messages, can certainly be overly simplistic. Hanson notes that queer theory is valuable as 'a mode of deconstruction and analysis of sexual rhetoric' but that

> dogma inevitably produces insight at the expense of a certain level of blindness [...] Our critical vocabulary seems to render palpable only those pleasures it is destined to describe, such that our dogmas result in an impoverishment of language that masquerades as sophistication.[31]

In the case of Andrew, any account that assesses his portrayal simply as a character risks overlooking the important point that in his fannish proclivities he also functions as a figure for the audience; his desires therefore queer serial spectatorship in important ways. Andrew's purported 'effeminacy' is not even the issue here. One would hope that in a series so committed to the positive portrayal of female power and so critical of hegemonic masculinities, Andrew's femininity need not register as pejorative. As McCracken has argued, in the Buffyverse, 'the wounded, masochistic man is the ideal man, the man for all seasons'.[32] As the world-turned-upside-down carnival of 'Storyteller' demonstrates, and regardless of the viewer's sexual identity and identifications, the queer, feminised fan Andrew = us. To some extent, this is a generic predisposition. Alexander Doty notes that the central conventions of horror and melodrama 'actually encourage queer positioning as they exploit the spectacle of heterosexual romance, straight domesticity, and traditional gender roles gone awry'. In this sense, he argues, '*everyone's* pleasure in these genres is "perverse", is queer, as much of it takes place within the space of the contra-heterosexual and the contra-straight'.[33] Andrew's homoerotic viewing position, however, makes this position queerer. Doty contends that queer positions, readings, and pleasures

> suggest that what happens in cultural reception goes beyond the traditional opposition between homo and hetero, as queer reception is often a place beyond the audience's conscious 'real-life' definitions of their sexual identities and cultural positions – often, but not always, beyond such sexual identities and identity politics, that is.[34]

Cross-identifying with Andrew as fan, audiences from a range of sexual identities, both hetero and homo, can partake of his queer viewing pleasure.

Andrew's representation as a character in Season 7 is curious, complex and multivalent, employing a mix of homophobic stereotypes, more progressive depictions and overblown camp musical. At the narrative level, he is a decidedly queer character whose trajectory remains open-ended:

> Here's the thing. I killed my best friend. There's a big fight coming, and I don't know what's going to happen. I don't even think I'm going to live through it. That's, uh, probably the way it should be. I guess I'm …

Instead of finishing his sentence, Andrew looks at the camera, sighs, points the remote control and turns it off. At the end of 'Storyteller' (7.16), Andrew is unable or unwilling to identify exactly what he is. However, the episode does not ultimately code this inability as failure. The closing credits reprise Andrew's fantasy 'We are as Gods' in place of the regular Mutant Enemy animation, 'Grrr ... Argh'. Andrew retains the last word and his queer desires set the seal on this episode. Moreover, Andrew's role at the metanarrative level, as a figure of the fan and thus the audience, queers the text of *Buffy* in a more comprehensive fashion, offering an endearingly queer celebration of the 'perverse' pleasures of serial spectatorship that cuts across sexual identity politics. Andrew, after all, returns, in *Angel* Season 5 ('Damage', 5.11 and 'The Girl in Question', 5.20), as a junior 'Watcher', a role that formalises, and grants unexpected authority and distinction to, his position as queer spectator.

7

'Why Can't You Just Masturbate Like the Rest of Us?': The Erotics and Politics of *Buffy* Fandom

In June 2012, *Slate* magazine ran an article naming *Buffy the Vampire Slayer* the most written about popular culture text of all time. In an online search for scholarly articles on popular media texts, *Slate* noted that *Buffy* criticism far outweighed any other potential contenders: 'more than twice as many papers, essays, and books have been devoted to the vampire drama than any of our other choices – so many that we stopped counting when we hit 200'.[1] Since that time, popular culture texts such as *Lost*, *Mad Men* and *The Wire*[2] have attracted dedicated popular and scholarly scrutiny, but *Buffy* remains a firm contender for the 'most studied' award, always supposing anyone should have the resources today to calculate the extraordinary scope and reach of specific contemporary popular culture texts. *Buffy*'s centrality to the field of popular culture studies is partly a matter of serendipitous timing. As we have seen in previous chapters, the series was deliberately designed to be a cult television classic; it was also one of the first to engage directly with fans through the medium of the internet via message boards and websites; and it benefitted enormously from the exponential growth of series TV on DVD, making *Buffy* today – as much as in the last two decades – a movable feast, to be consumed on demand, available for multiple repeat performances, rather than an ephemeral text that, enjoyed once, disappears after first viewing.

In fact, *Buffy*'s phenomenal success is tied to its specific contexts of production and consumption in ways that, if further explored, promise to shed new light on contemporary popular culture, but that also lie outside the parameters of the present study. Its unique location in media history – in the infancy of internet fandom and benefitting from the growth of commercial marketing of series TV – makes of *Buffy* an exciting site for studies of contemporary convergence culture in all of its many manifestations.[3] Leaving this venture to others far better equipped to undertake it, in this chapter I look to the rhetorics – feminist and otherwise – that inform *Buffy*'s fan trajectory, not in its entirety but in specific textual instances. No book-length study of *Buffy* today would be complete without providing some account of its unusually rich and replete fan history, and I provide that here through an analysis of two idiosyncratic texts – one textual and one extratextual – by returning to the Season 7 episode 'Storyteller' (7.16), this time through a different critical lens, and by examining the popularly and critically acclaimed fan vid, *Buffy vs Edward*.

Studies of fandom have flourished over the past 40 years, evolving with what the editors of the compilation *Fandom: Identities and Communities in a Mediated World* call the 'the changing cultural status of fans'.[4] In their introductory chapter on the history of fan studies, Jonathan Gray, Cornel Sandvoss and C. Lee Harrington point out that fans now play a crucial role in media production and discussion, arguing that 'rather than [being] ridiculed, fan audiences are now wooed and championed by cultural industries'.[5] The contemporary field of fan studies is broad and varied, responding in part to Mark Duffett's point that 'almost everyone self-identifies as a fan in some sense', whether it be in sports, film or television, comics or novels, music or celebrities.[6] The 'fan' label can accordingly 'mean very different things in different contexts'.[7] Roberta Pearson, for instance, compares the behaviour and self-identification of fans of historical or 'high' literature texts versus fans of current, pop culture texts,[8] and Nancy Reagin and Anne Rubenstein have studied the development of fan cultures as early as the nineteenth century.[9]

What Gray, Sandvoss, and Harrington call the 'changing cultural status of fans' has affected the evolution of fan studies, with scholars recognising the diversity of fan objects, identities and practices, as well as the changing popular perceptions of fans. They argue that 'as cultural judgment has become increasingly detached from the state of being a fan, our attention shifts to the choice of fan object and its surrounding practices, and what they tell us about the fan him- or herself'.[10] Lynn Zubernis and Katherine Larsen point out that 'fans differ widely in the types of participation they seek out and the fan spaces to which they are drawn'.[11] For example, Nick Couldry, Will Brooker and Zubernis and Larsen examine some fans' desire to visit spaces or sites that are meaningful within their fandom, from the convention hall to the film set,[12] whilst a significant portion of fan studies is devoted to examining the growing range of online fan practices. This includes the study of online communities and conversations, the virtual distribution and discussion of fan-made work, the nature of online database information-sharing and the ubiquitous risk of 'spoilers'.[13] Many studies also examine the cultural shift that participatory technologies and media convergence have enabled in recent decades.[14]

Zubernis and Larsen suggest that despite the progress made in popular and academic circles to validate or defend fan practices, 'a pervasive sense of shame permeates both fan spaces and academic approaches to the subject'.[15] They examine the overlap between fannish pleasure and shame, and the therapeutic and transformative potential of fandom on an individual level coupled with the shame of perception and difference that continues to pervade fandom.[16] Zubernis and Larsen also assert that fan communities are not only self-aware but protective of their spaces, possessing a 'fear of being "studied" and misrepresented by outsiders'.[17] Perhaps in response to this situation, scholars are increasingly 'declaring' and integrating their fandom into their academic work; for instance, Zubernis and Larsen work from the position of immersed fans as well as academics, and examine this 'split' perspective as well as fans' often contradictory motivations and experiences.[18] They describe their own anxieties and experiences with attempting to 'simultaneously uphold fannish ethics and academic rigor'.[19]

Since their inception, then, academic studies of fandom have struggled against a variety of stigmas. Studies of television fandom first gained institutional traction with the pioneering scholarship of Henry Jenkins. His seminal study, *Textual Poachers*,[20] took as its object the culture created by popular media fans and the complex relationships between texts and readers. In this study, Jenkins presents fandom as an active and meaningful 'interpretive community', with unique methods of communication and production, modes of reception, frustrations, and aims.[21] Defending fandom against popular stereotypes, he introduces a model of fans as 'poachers' – active and selective readers – who, collectively operating from the margins of cultural industries, mine and transform often-flawed commercial texts to satisfy different interests. Jenkins asserts that these poaching fans 'transform the experience of watching television into a rich and complex participatory culture'.[22] For Jenkins, fandom is envisioned not as the hobby of the passive social misfit but as an active, intellectual and meaningful practice of 'popular resistance', denying both the authority traditionally afforded the writers of texts and the dominant narrative tropes they create.[23]

Jenkins's notion of the fan as poacher has been challenged, extended and modified in a range of subsequent studies, particularly in Matt Hills's widely read *Fan Cultures*.[24] Hills asserts that Jenkins's reading of fandom lacks psychological analysis and constructs a 'moral dualism' of fan/non-fan in order to create a celebratory, 'utopian' academic definition of fandom.[25] Hills suggests that Jenkins champions the fan as 'producer' in order to remove 'the taint of consumption and consumerism' from academic fan studies.[26] Coining the term 'fan-scholar' to denote fans who employ academic theories and methodologies to create work for fandom communities, Hills discusses the threat that this active denial of an academic/fan duality poses to academia's perceived power and authority over its subjects.[27] The scholar-fans – academics who identify as fans of the texts or genres they study – bring fandom into their study with their own 'specific academic agendas' and subsequent limitations of perspective.[28] Arguing for the breaking down of binary distinctions, Hills critiques contrasting perspectives of fandom, both popular and academic, and the restrictions of perception and privilege that have shaped them. Ultimately, Hills argues for perspectives on fan culture to be considered on a continuum, and for the destruction of moral dualism.

The study of fandom today encompasses a broad range of subjects, including convention attendance, online communities, fanzine production, fan fiction, slash fiction and vidding. The methods employed by this expanding field are of necessity diverse, ranging from detailed ethnographies of particular fan communities to studies of the convergence culture in contemporary media – involving analysis of marketing, programming, advertising and merchandising.[29] Various ethnographic fan studies have been conducted with different degrees of formality and perceived distance from or proximity to the subject. Camille Bacon-Smith's early contribution to the field, *Enterprising Women: Television Fandom and the Creation of Popular Myth* observes and analyses female *Star Trek* fan communities from a self-conscious academic distance.[30] Bacon-Smith's approach has been critiqued by Hills, who argues that although Bacon-Smith 'veritably scrapes away at the layers and layers of misdirection which the fan community presents to her as an initial "outsider"', her work relies on a self-consciously mythologised vision of outsider-ethnographer/detective observing insider-fan, and plays its own 'narrative games of expectation, disruption and delay with the reader'.[31]

David Bleich's early reader-response analysis considered data collected from surveys of students and mapped gendered trends of approaching and reading literature.[32] More recently, this data-collecting approach to ethnography has been employed by researchers of *Buffy* fandom.[33] Another mode of analysis is the 'fan-enthnographies' of scholars such as Jenkins. Although Hills denies the effectiveness of positivist, distanced ethnographic fan study, he also points out that 'the significantly affective nature of the fan's attachment renders ethnographic methodology problematic', and that '"asking the audience" cannot act as a guarantee of knowledge'.[34] He asserts that 'previous fan-ethnography has largely erred on the side of accepting fan discourse as interpretive "knowledge"', and that the ethnographic interview 'assumes that cultural activities can be adequately accounted for in terms of language and "discourse"', forgetting to consider how interview questions cause the fan 'to cut into the flow of their experience and produce some kind of discursive "justification"'.[35]

Some of these studies are deliberately subjective and specialised in their research of fan communities. Alexis Lothian, Kristina Busse and Robin Anne Reid, active participants in online fandom, ran a discussion with fellow community participants about their online practices and identities, considering themes that emerged in their conversations.[36] Many fans of queer fan fiction self-reflexively identified a feeling of 'connection between fandom and identity', their fannish practices serving as an extension, or virtual 'safe space' for exploration of sexual identity.[37] Informed by their discussion, Lothian, Busse and Reid characterised the sharing and discussion of fan fiction and fandom as a potentially queer practice, 'infinitely diverse in style and scope'.[38]

From its first entry to the academic stage, *Buffy* has been a prime site for fan studies. One of the earliest collections of *Buffy* scholarship, *Fighting the Forces: What's at Stake in Buffy the Vampire Slayer*,[39] included four essays on fan cultures: Justine Larbalestier's study of ways the series consciously acknowledges and interacts with fan practices; Kristina Busse's study of fannish readings of family, desire and vampirism in the series; S. Renee Dechert on music as a bridge between character and fan; and Amanda Zweerink and Sarah N. Gatson's observations of community and hierarchy in online *Buffy* fandom.[40] Subsequent studies have explored fandom's various constructions of characters and relationships, both popular and peripheral.[41] Many scholars analyse *Buffy*'s extensive online fandom, from Wendy A.F.G. Stengel's early discussion of online communication and fan fiction and Katrina Blasingame's study of the evolution of 'Buffy slang' and fandom vernacular to the studies of fan behaviour and identity in specific *Buffy* fan communities found in 2009's *Buffy and Angel Conquer the Internet: Essays on Online Fandom*.[42] The large amount of paper proposals on fan studies listed in the online journal *Slayage: The Journal of the Whedon Studies Association* is testament to the strength of scholarly interest in Buffy fandom.[43]

In what follows I consider *Buffy*'s textual treatment of the fan in the character of Andrew in Season 7's 'Storyteller' (7.16) before moving to the extratextual treatment of *Buffy* by fans – in this instance through the immensely popular and critically acclaimed fan vid, *Buffy vs Edward*. In 'Storyteller', the creative team behind *Buffy the Vampire Slayer* have offered us one of the series' most sustained and thoughtful examinations of the pleasures and problematics of fandom. With *Buffy vs Edward*, Jonathan McIntosh, the vid's creator, offers a beguiling but trenchant critique of the sexual politics informing Buffy's 'rival' in contemporary genre fiction and film, Edward Cullen from the bestselling blockbuster franchise *Twilight*.

Master vs mushroom: Andrew and the erotics of fandom in 'Storyteller'

In 'Storyteller' (7.16), Andrew functions as both adoring audience and as author of his own text. He is the ostensibly submissive groupie of the Scooby gang at the same time that he is the author/director of his own documentary, 'Buffy, Slayer of the Vampyrs'. The first half of this chapter is subtitled 'The Erotics of Fandom in "Storyteller"' but it could just as easily have been called 'The Erotics and Pedagogics of Fandom' (except that 'pedagogics' is such an inadmissibly ugly word). I am interested in both aspects of Andrew's character: the pleasure and the pedagogy bound up in the role of the fan. Now you know the drill: 'In every generation there is a Chosen One. She and she alone will fight the demons, the vampires, and the forces of darkness. She is the Slayer.' So … what happens if you're not the Slayer? This, in a nutshell, is Andrew's story, and the story of many a *Buffy* fan. Previous to 'Storyteller' ('Previously on *Buffy the Vampire Slayer*'), Andrew was not what you would call a fan of 'good'. In fact, as I've explored in the previous chapter, Andrew was first and foremost a fan of evil. We know that Andrew's back-story of fandom is relevant to the overall message of 'Storyteller' because we are provided with pertinent flashbacks. Andrew was once, or aspired to be, a Super Villain. The fact that he incorporates this history as part of his homage to Buffy emphasises his attachment to his earliest attachments:

> Honestly, gentle viewers, these motivating speeches of hers tend to get a little long. I'll take you back in there in – in a little while, but in the in-between time, I thought you might want to know a little about me, your humble host. You see, I am a man with a burden. A man with a dark past. You see, I was once a *super villain.*

In 'Storyteller' Andrew's romanticised recollections of his fandom as successful super-villainy clash jarringly with Buffy's 'previous' depiction of these same 'fannish practices' as, basically, vegetative: in Buffy's scathing synopsis, Andrew is less evil than fungal, he's not evil himself, but if he's around it long enough, she says, he picks it up 'like a mushroom'. What we have here are two competing narratives of Andrew's fandom: the first, Andrew's, emphasises mastery and is epitomised in the fake flashback in which he vanquishes the Evil Willow in 'Storyteller':

> You, Dark Willow, wield a force of mighty evil, it's true.
> But you are new to the game, little one.

The second, Buffy's, is distinctly bathetic; instead of master Andrew is mushroom, absorbing evil through a process of osmosis.

When we meet Andrew in 'Storyteller', he has become a groupie (or in his preferred terminology, a 'guestage') of the Scoobies, but that does not mean that he has broken his attachment to the glamour of Evil or to his partners in 'crime', the rest of the 'Trio', Warren and Jonathan. In fact, the First finds Andrew a fit tool because it can play on Andrew's frustrated romantic yearning for Warren, a desire that is portrayed in overblown camp (lest we miss the subtext) in Andrew's own 'break-away pop hit', 'We are as Gods'. Andrew is seduced by the First's promise that if he kills Jonathan he will be reunited with Warren. One of the darkest aspects of the carnivalesque delight of this episode is, psychologically speaking, Andrew's fantasy of redress and reunion in the face of the horror he feels at killing his best friend. Joss Whedon's love letter to his audience, his homage to the homage that his fans pay his text, is thus framed by a story in which the endearing, perhaps unwitting, fan/author (Andrew) nevertheless kills off his darling.

As the first scene of the episode opens, and as the shooting script states, '[c]lassical violin music plays as the camera pans across the room'. It shows a wall full of shelves stuffed with leather-bound books, a desk full of trinkets of interest such as skulls, quills, chemical bottles, an hourglass and a comic book laid open on a pedestal. A *Star Wars* poster hangs on the wall, with action figures displayed on a shelf in front of it. There's a fire in the fireplace beneath an elaborate mantelpiece, over which hangs an anime poster and tribal masks. The camera pans over to Andrew, who is sitting in a leather wing chair wearing a silk smoking jacket, holding a pipe in his right hand and an open book in his left. Andrew, while clearly waiting for the audience's attention, assumes absorption in the hefty tome in front of him and fakes surprise at the camera's intrusion: 'Oh, hello, there, gentle viewers.' The episode thus begins classically, even epically, *in media res* – in the middle of things.

We have stumbled across our author in a moment of private reverie, a moment given over to what Roland Barthes calls 'the pleasure of the text'.[44] Andrew proceeds to elaborate the particular pleasures of reading:

> You caught me catching up on an old favourite. It's wonderful to get lost in a story, isn't it? Adventure and heroics and discovery – don't they just take you away?

Figure 16: Masterpiece Theatre Andrew, 'Storyteller', 7.16

Andrew is clearly having a Masterpiece Theatre moment all to himself. And as we discover afterwards, he's having it on the toilet.

When he is rudely interrupted from his reverie by Anya's question '[f]or God's sakes, Andrew. You've been in here for 30 minutes. What are you doing?', Andrew's response is both portentous and unintentionally hilarious: 'Entertaining and educating.' Here, in glorious microcosm, are both the pleasures and the pedagogy of fandom. Andrew is offering to delight his gentle viewers. He is also offering to teach them. The fact that he's doing it from his invidious position on the loo (that's Australian for toilet) compounds the humour of the situation (and it's always a little redundant to explain humour, especially Andrew's, but bear with me for the moment). When Anya asks in frustration, and perhaps justifiable bewilderment, '[w]hy can't you just masturbate like the rest of us?', she sets up a parallel between fannish adoration and autoerotic activity that is impossible to ignore. Why must Andrew, and by extension, the audience, persist in his fannish practices? Why can't he, asks Anya, just masturbate like the rest of us? If the parallel Anya sets up equates the entertaining aspect of fandom with a form of masturbation, it also portrays the educative function of fandom as a kind of intellectual onanistics. The fact that Andrew is sitting on the toilet while he delivers his lecture also suggests that his lesson may be kind of crap – and I mean that literally. 'Storyteller' offers us an image of the fan as pedagogue pedalling a species of excrement or excess waste. As Anya says later, Andrew's story is not only 'kinky business' but also, potentially, 'pretty pointless.'

But this is just one side of the portrayal of fandom in 'Storyteller', and if it is mockery, it is certainly a gentle, even loving mockery. If Andrew's fannish practices are 'kinky' and 'pretty pointless', they are also deeply seductive. Buffy is the sole member of the Scoobies to hold out on Andrew's appeal. Dawn, Xander, Anya and even Spike are easily enticed into his project. The range of responses to Andrew in 'Storyteller' provides important information about the episode's treatment of fandom. Buffy, alone of the Scoobies, is surprisingly resistant. She rejects Andrew's desire to memorialise her mission in his documentary 'Buffy, Slayer of the Vampyrs.' When Andrew argues for the value of his fan text, '[b]ut it's a valuable record. An important document for the ages. "A Slayer in action"', Buffy responds with the threat: '"A nerd in pain." Would they like that? 'Cause we could do that.' What Buffy offers us here is actually an alternative reading of the episode as a whole. What Andrew sets out to film in 'Storyteller' is a testament to the Slayer in action, but what he ends up filming is precisely the story of a nerd in pain – his own story of remorse and redemption.

Other characters are more easily enticed into Andrew's project. Anya falls for Andrew's stellar director's pitch hook, line and sinker.

Andrew: Oh, I was gonna interview you later today, 'cause, you know, your unique perspective on the whole thing. Give it editorial balance and, uh, glamour ...

Anya: Balance is important. People don't always take that into account. I could bring that to you. Absolutely.

Xander is seduced by the lure of his own 'special intro': Xander, 'The man who is the heart of the slayer machine.' Dawn responds blushingly to Andrew's reading of her character: 'Dawn is a typical American teenager. Bubbly and sweet with a hunger for fun and a smile that lights up the room.' Even Willow endorses the pedagogical potential of Andrew's project; 'it does help the girls with training – you know, viewing the tapes.' But Buffy remains sceptical:

Buffy: Come on. No one else thinks this is idiotic?
Xander: Or is it important? I mean, Buff, I don't get why this is bothering you so much.
Buffy: Because it's a waste of time. Come on, someone has to agree with me. Spike?

Spike concedes, albeit disingenuously, as we later discover: 'Long as you're not pointing that thing at me, seems like a fine way to keep the boy busy' (a comment that seems to resonate with Anya's parallel with masturbation). Perhaps the real question here is voiced by Xander, appropriately enough given Andrew's slavish adoration of him in this episode: 'is it important?' Why does Andrew's project bother Buffy? We get some sense of this later in the episode, but the answers, at least to me, are not entirely conclusive.

When they are trying to close the seal, Buffy finally gets frustrated by Andrew's storytelling: 'Stop! Stop telling stories. Life isn't a story.' When Andrew sobs that he's sorry, Buffy responds: 'Shut up. You always do this. You make everything into a story so no one's responsible for anything because they're just following a script.' Buffy here is clearly in the director's seat, and Andrew is now following her script. While Andrew is an author figure in 'Storyteller', Buffy is clearly one too. When Andrew pleads: 'You don't need to kill me. You said we could all get through this.' Buffy responds: 'I made it up. I'm making it all up. What kind of hero does that make me?' A question that solicits Andrew's fannish response in a merely manipulative and lacklustre manner: 'No, you're doing great. Really. Kudos.' Andrew's response here is intentionally underwhelming, a moment of horror at the burdens of storytelling that Buffy, and perhaps the creators of *Buffy*, are involved with on a daily basis.

This is rather an odd place to end an episode. Buffy as character is sick of being filmed. Buffy as author is sick of making up stories. Andrew as storyteller is told to stop telling stories. Andrew as fan is told to '[s]top watching!' a directive that is given an ironic twist when he becomes a fledgling Watcher (capital W) in *Angel*'s Season 5. There is no single authoritative author here, and there are several types of audience. The juxtaposition of these roles, the slippage between them and the effort that the characters, and the episode, make to enforce distinctions between them enable an exploration of the various responsibilities and burdens of readers and authors. I suggest that they also mirror, in a suitably sly fashion, the peculiar mix of adoration and authority, of diffidence and ostentation that is symptomatic of *Buffy* scholarship itself. Andrew's documentary, 'Buffy, Slayer of the Vampyrs' is, self-consciously, a teaching text. It attempts to memorialise the Slayer and her circle, a task we engage in as scholars and fans as well. In 'Storyteller', Anya's question '[w]hy can't you just masturbate like the rest of us?' thus challenges the value of this/our enterprise, initiating a complex meditation on the responsibilities of readers, the pleasures of pedagogy and the burden of storytelling. The fact that Buffy fandom and Buffy pedagogy are construed as both masturbatory and waste (or crap) is not, however, the final word. Storyteller's final credits end, not with the 'grrr … argh' voice-over of other episodes but with the reprisal of Andrew's fantasy of inclusion: 'We are as Gods.' Whether this refers to the show's authors or audience is left open to interpretation but if either is admissible then I think we can extend it to *Buffy* scholars as well.

Metalepsis in the mash-up: Parsing the sexual politics of *Buffy vs Edward*

Under the name Rebellious Pixels, self-described 'pop culture hacker and transformative storyteller' Jonathan McIntosh uploaded the video *Buffy vs Edward: Twilight Remixed* to YouTube on 19 June 2009. According to a Rebellious Pixels blog post on 9 January 2013, the video had by then been viewed over 3 million times (at the time of writing, the view count on the video's YouTube page was over 3.5 million),[45] and fans have translated it into 30 different languages.[46] The video was not only hugely popular but also critically acclaimed, being featured in the *LA Times*, *Boston Globe*, *Salon*, *Slate*, *Wired*, *Vanity Fair* and *Entertainment Weekly*, and discussed on NPR radio. It was also nominated for a 2010 Webby Award in the Best Remix/Mashup category. The video is used in law school programmes, media studies courses and gender studies curricula across the United States and has ignited countless online debates over the troubling ways stalking-type behaviour is often framed as deeply romantic in movie and television narratives. Jonathan McIntosh's accompanying essay to the video, 'What would Buffy do?: Notes on dusting Edward Cullen', won the Short

Mr Pointy Award at the 2010 Slayage Conference on the Whedonverses.[47] While Rebellious Pixels describe the text as 'fair use transformative storytelling',[48] in a possible sign of the potential power of alternate fan readings and content, the video was the subject of a copyright claim by Lionsgate Entertainment in 2012 after they acquired ownership of the *Twilight* film franchise. Despite a fair use claim by Rebellious Pixels, Lionsgate successfully fought to earn advertising revenue on the previously non-commercial video, and later it was removed entirely. However, by 10 January 2013 the video had been reinstated without comment from either YouTube or Lionsgate, with the ads and the copyright warning dropped.[49]

Jonathan McIntosh describes *Buffy vs Edward* as a 'visual critique of gender roles and representations in modern pop culture vampire media'.[50] The video combines clips from *Buffy the Vampire Slayer* and the hugely popular 2008 film *Twilight* (the first of a series of five films based on the novels by Stephenie Meyer), splicing the two narratives together to form a new one. Famously, *Twilight* follows the relationship between the teenage vampire Edward Cullen and quiet, unassuming mortal Bella Swan. However, in this 'remixed narrative', the brooding Edward attends Sunnydale High and pursues Buffy, slayer of vampires, demons and creepy teen boys (or any combination thereof). The pop culture literate viewer clearly recognises the differences in gender roles and expectations within the two texts, foregrounded by McIntosh's splicing of footage. Posed in his original franchise as a powerful, dashing romantic lead, Edward here is given an alternate, far less favourable reading and, unlike Bella, Buffy is having none of his behaviour. Edward's dialogue, framed in the *Twilight* film as mysterious and captivating, becomes pathetic and puerile, his stalking and possessiveness over Buffy more bizarre overreaction than romantic gesture ('You know, being stalked isn't really a big turn on for girls'). Whilst in *Twilight* Edward is heralded as the ultimate heroic, old-fashioned heartthrob (he is, of course, over 100 years old), Buffy's swift, eye-rolling rejection of his advances in the remix represents an arguably more realistic reaction to his behaviour. After refusing Edward several times, she wakes up to find him in her bedroom ('I like watching you sleep, it's um, kind of—', 'Get out or I will drop you out head first!'), and takes the opportunity to unceremoniously dust him in the cemetery.

When I present this material at conferences, I start by screening the video mash-up in its entire six minutes, not because I think people haven't seen it: on the contrary; I believe the vast majority of an audience at, for instance, a Slayage conference will be familiar with this fan vid. But I think that it is also worth watching together, partly because what its creator Jonathan McIntosh calls its 'audio-visual language' offers a different kind of eloquence than any exegesis I can provide, and partly because a collective viewing experience is precisely what this mash-up offers, even to those viewing it privately on their personal laptops. To the lone *Buffy* fan, watching *Buffy vs Edward* offers immediate inclusion in an irreverent, highly partisan virtual community and I try to recreate that experience IRL – or 'In Real Life' – in my conference presentation.

The material artefact of the printed book does not, alas, yet provide that communal experience for readers of this present study; indeed, the different reading and viewing practices pertaining to print and the internet are germane to my discussion here. In the face of McIntosh's visual artistry, his dramatic juxtaposition of gender norms in *Buffy* and *Twilight*, 'Parsing the sexual politics of *Buffy vs Edward*' (the subtitle of this half of the chapter) seems, in fact, like bringing coals to Newcastle. The visual rhetoric of the mash-up is so compelling, entertaining and above all *familiar* that we 'know', more or less, what the remix is 'saying', and if we want clarification we can read McIntosh's lucid explication of his process and politics online. In his article 'What would Buffy do?' McIntosh explains:

> My re-imagined story was specifically constructed as a response to Edward, and what his behavior represents in our larger social context for both men and women. More than just a showdown between The Slayer and the Sparkly Vampire, it's also a humorous visualization of the metaphorical battle between two opposing visions of gender roles in the 21st century.[51]

McIntosh explains how he and his partner Anita, both media literacy advocates, were troubled by how the main characters in *Twilight* 'seemed to embody antiquated, sexist gender stereotypes':

> Teenage protagonist Bella Swan is written as passive, co-dependent and perpetually the damsel in distress. Edward

> Cullen, her love interest, is written as over-protective, domineering and possessive [...] Over the course of the film Edward is in turns patronizing, condescending and just downright creepy. He spies on Bella, he stalks her (for 'her own good'), he sneaks into her room to watch her sleep (without her consent) and even confesses to a deep, overpowering desire to kill her.[52]

As McIntosh points out, 'throughout *Buffy's* seven seasons, males that display the type of behavior Edward does are ridiculed or portrayed as dangerous (or both)'.

The approach this self-confessed 'Pop Culture Hacker' took to gender critique, however, was both careful and considered. He states:

> As an aspiring feminist guy, I wanted to speak out about issues of sexism and gender oppression in media but I wanted to do so carefully and intentionally. That's why I chose to focus my critique on Edward's patriarchal behavior in *Twilight* rather than on Bella's actions. I didn't feel it was my place to lecture her on desire (even in remix form), especially since her character is already disempowered by the original screenplay to the point of absurdity.[53]

On the whole, McIntosh has been surprised and pleased by the reception of his remix, glad that it 'has sparked a wide-ranging and timely online conversation about how obsessive and predatory male behavior passes for romance in too much of our pop culture'. He suggests that '[a]t their best, mash-up videos can serve as a form of critical media literacy, exposing myths and messages embedded in media typically masked by glossy Hollywood productions'. But he also cautions against a too-celebratory reading of the success of his remix. In his own words: 'Ultimately, Buffy's triumph over Edward is only one small part of [a] much larger story: the story of our collective journey towards a world of gender equity and empowerment.'[54] GO HIM! But if the sexual politics animating *Buffy vs Edward* are fairly straightforward (stalking is not sexy!), the ways in which this message is produced reward further scrutiny. In what follows I want to consider how the rhetorical mode of metalepsis informs the logic of this video mash-up, and how the strategies of narrative metalepsis – what Gerard Genette has termed metaleptic transgression – might help to illuminate some of the less obvious workings of fan creative practice and viewing pleasure, particularly as they relate to *Buffy*.[55]

Most studies of metalepsis in contemporary cultural studies (and, despite the obscure terminology, these *are* growing) take their cue from Genette's 1972 work, *Narrative Discourse: An Essay in Method*. Genette explains the phenomenon as 'a transgression of the boundary between narrative levels or narrative worlds; the transgressed boundary is that between, for example diegesis and hypodiegesis (story and embedded story) or diegesis and extradiegesis (story and discourse)'. As Tisha Turk points out, according to Genette 'these narrative levels are, by definition, intratextual; reality – which includes the flesh-and-blood author and reader – is extratextual'.[56] Thus while metalepsis as defined by Genette has been useful in studying narrative texts like Defoe's *Robinson Crusoe* and Sterne's *Tristram Shandy* (works that involve a text within a text, or a frame story that features the rhetorical act of storytelling), Genette's definition is bound by the assumptions that: 1) the borders of the text are stable; and 2) that the author (or the author's proxy in the form of the narrator) controls the metalepsis. As Turk alerts us:

> These assumptions make sense in discussions of traditional media and established genres [...] which are generally understood as self-contained texts with impermeable borders. But they do not necessarily make sense for fan works, which redefine both the boundaries of texts and the relationship between creators and audiences.[57]

In Turk's succinct summation:

> If metalepsis is 'the transgression between the real world and the fictional world', the traditional understanding of the term is always intratextual in that the 'real' world is in fact fictional: diegesis and hypodiegesis are both contained within the borders of the text. As we shall see, the metalepses in fan fiction and fan vids are extratextual: they employ the actual real world, not just a representation of it.[58]

For 'fans who produce and consume fan works, the boundaries of the source text's fictional world are not fixed; rather they are infinitely expandable'.[59] In their study of online media fan practices, Katrina Busse and Karen Hellekson invoke Roland Barthes idea of 'the writerly text' as one most appropriate to fan appropriation.[60] The readerly text, Barthes writes, is a mere product; it can be read but not written and it is characterised by what Barthes calls 'the pitiless divorce between the producer of the text and its user, between its owner and its customer, between its author and its reader'. The writerly text, in contrast, encourages the reader to be 'no longer a consumer, but a producer of the text'.[61] Tisha Turk adds that 'the most significant boundary that is crossed in fan works is not the border of the fictional world but the border of the text itself; the boundary that separates creator and flesh-and-blood [...] audience'.[62] The metaleptic transgressions of fan works are thus different from those in conventional texts. Turk states:

> If conventional metalepsis appears to destabilize the boundary between reality and fiction, fan works effectively destabilize the boundary between audience and creator. Fan works, then, are always metaleptic in the sense that they represent an imposition of extradiegetic desires upon the fictional world and the transformation of a text in the service of those desires.[63]

How does this admittedly somewhat abstruse analysis relate to the mash-up *Buffy vs Edward*? McIntosh's remix is not a piece of fan fiction nor, he assures us, is it technically a vid, but it shares some features in common with the fan vid, particularly the meta vid, which in Francesca Coppa's words, can also be understood as 'a visual essay that stages an argument':[64] 'it represents a vidder's collection of evidence, for a particular interpretation of a visual text and her attempt, whether implicit or explicit, to persuade the vidwatcher to share that interpretation'.[65]

Intratextually, or within the text, *Buffy vs Edward* uses metalepsis to mash together two wildly different political and ethical registers, those from the world of the Slayer and the Sparkly Vampire. For viewers staunchly on the side of the Slayer, the ludic pleasure of the video stems from the collision of a smug, self-regarding yet still-creepy stalker and a strong feminist heroine who refuses to put up with his shit. The recurring visual trope of Edward stymied and walking sulkily away from confrontation with Buffy is repeatedly set up by a series of Edward's ostensibly engaging conversational gambits:

1. Hello. I'm Edward Cullen.
2. I'm sorry, I'm just trying to figure you out.
3. You know, I'm on a special diet.
4. Hi!
5. I like watching you sleep.
6. You're like my own personal brand of heroin.[66]

There have been some excellent feminist critiques of *Twilight*'s sexual politics, and moments like these have led many critics to view Edward's relationship with Bella as variously infantilising, destructive, abusive and heteronormatively patriarchal, and the series itself as pro-life, romanticising violence against women, upholding the myths of rape culture and, my personal 'fave', as 'abstinence porn'.[67] Others see such feminist critiques themselves as elitist, doctrinal and out of touch with fan sensibilities. One commentator writes: 'I know of many girls who will acknowledge Edward's abusive tendencies but will immediately defend him, "Yes he's abusive and he does a lot of bad things, but he does it because he loves her!"'[68] Can you imagine a similar defence of a female stalker, say Glenn Close's character in *Fatal Attraction*? But she really loves him! And that bunny will be all the better for a little boiling …

The deftness of McIntosh's visual critique is that it is pitched as a battle between equals (rather than, say, between a hypothetical snarky feminist scholar and an imaginary innocent teenage fan) and Buffy's responses to Edward produce satisfying metaleptic collisions:

1. Hello. I'm Edward Cullen.

   [Mystified disbelief. Ignores him.]

2. I'm sorry, I'm just trying to figure you out.

   I'm the Slayer. Slay–er. The Chosen One. Look it up.

3. You know, I'm on a special diet.

   What are you doing? Here – at this table? Talking to me like we are some kind of talking buddies?

Figure 17: *Buffy vs Edward*, Jonathan McIntosh

4. Hi!

   Stop trying to see me. And stop calling me.

5. I like watching you sleep.

   Get out! Get out or I will drop you out – head first.

6. You're like my own personal brand of heroin.

   Oh my god – are you 12?[69]

The extratextual metalepsis of *Buffy vs Edward* stems from its status as fan work and from its self-conscious reference to itself as such. When Buffy asks Edward whether he is perhaps suffering from delusions of grandeur, because she has met 'more than one pimply teenaged fanboy who called himself Lestat', the mash-up belittles, through bathos, the purported beauty of the *Twilight* protagonist; it positions Pattinson as a pushy, but very pathetic, reader of popular culture, and it situates the *Twilight* franchise as a showy but substandard, even silly, spin off.[70] At the same time it positions the *Buffy* fan, through her proxy Jonathan McIntosh, in the role of author, a reconfiguration of writerly and readerly roles that extends the metaleptic mode of *Buffy vs Edward* significantly beyond that envisaged by Genette. As Turk encapsulates:

> Because a fandom is a community, or rather a series of interlinked and overlapping communities, it is not just the individual vidder or writer who participates in this metaleptical move; all fans are implicated by virtue of their imaginative work – the work of staging fan fiction and interpreting vids, of manipulating and extending the textual world. Genette locates the responsibility for metalepsis with authors; fan works show us that it can also be taken up by audiences.[71]

If the *Twilight* franchise is arguably, and despite some alluring critiques to the contrary, a particularly viral form of post-feminist backlash, then what *Buffy vs Edward* does is highlight that fact by subjecting Edward's unacceptable behaviour to the challenge of a feisty feminist heroine and her emancipated gender worldview. I see *Twilight* as post-feminist in the way Angela McRobbie describes this phenomenon in *The Aftermath of Feminism* – as 'an undoing or dismantling of feminism [...] a process which says feminism is no longer needed, it is now common sense, and as such it is something young women can do without'.[72] McRobbie sees elements of popular culture (and I would count *Twilight* among them) as 'perniciously effective in this undoing of feminism, while simultaneously appearing to be engaging in a well-informed and even well-intended response to feminism'.[73] Nina Power is even more forthright in her condemnation: 'Contemporary cinema is profoundly conservative in this regard; and the fact that it both reflects and dictates modes of current behaviour is depressingly effective, and effectively depressing.'[74] Similar *Buffy vs Edward* fan work that Jill Smo has posted on Facebook juxtaposes Edward and Bella's post-feminist power dynamic with Buffy and Angel's more egalitarian alternative.

What McIntosh's *Buffy vs Edward* does is similar cultural work – exposing the romantic valorisation of Edward's predatory antics and resituating

Figure 18: 'Lessons from Twilight'

his regressive worldview firmly in a *post*-post-feminist world. While some critics see the fan practices of Generation Mash-Up as avowedly apolitical (and with remixes of Nirvana and Destiny's Child like 'Smells like teen booty' they may have a point), McIntosh's mash-up *repoliticises* the sexual politics of contemporary popular culture, inviting us to share in Buffy's disdain – and dusting – of her outdated post-feminist nemesis.[75]

As we have already noted, *Buffy* is a series that deliberately encourages fan interaction and engages with those interactions in an unusually dialogic way. A brief return to Season 7's 'Storyteller' is useful in illustrating the distinctive feedback loops fostered by the show's innovative creator–fan relationships. Andrew's documentary, 'Buffy, Slayer of the Vampyres' is in several senses a fan vid – it involves the creative reconstruction of canonical events, live documentary footage and some wonderfully idiosyncratic directorial interpretation in terms of voice-over and narration. It also involves the cutting, splicing and arranging of film that Francesca Coppa sees as one of the chief pleasures of fan vidding. Coppa characterises fan vidding as a fetishistic act, highlighting its artistic emphasis on editing, 'slicing visual texts into pieces before putting them together again, fetishizing not only body parts and visual tropes, but the frame, the filmic moment, that they pull out of otherwise coherent wholes'.[76] The fan vid editing process involves cutting and segmenting individual moments, details and gestures from a narrative that is presented to fans as 'unified and complete'; it is a process of 'selective seeing, or seeing in parts'.[77] Fan vidders collect segmented parts of a larger narrative and 'reassemble them into coherent wholes of their own devising'.[78]

Despite claiming to be a 'detached journalist, recording with a neutral eye', Andrew is involved in this fannish process of cutting and segmenting parts of a narrative whole, and ascribing to them an alternative meaning in his own narrative. Conducting a tour of the Summers' house, he creeps into the living room, speaking to his audience: 'here's something I think you're going to be interested in, gentle viewers'. Through his camera lens we see Willow and Kennedy sharing a quiet reprieve on the couch; this private moment offers potential appeal for many fan viewers of 'Buffy, Slayer of the Vampyres': however, it is not part of Andrew's narrative. The camera zooms in to focus on the window behind them: 'Look at the fine work Xander did on replacing that window sash. You can't even tell it's new, it blends in so well!' We then see our narrator, nodding his head with a faint smile. 'He's extraordinary!'

Later, seated opposite Xander's excellent window sash with his camera and a notepad, Andrew takes on the dual role of celebrity reporter and therapist to conduct an interview with Xander and Anya: 'I understand that exactly one year ago today you left Anya at the altar. Any comment on that?' He frames and justifies his personal questions by referring to his audience: 'I just think people will be interested.' Taking notes, looking to his interviewees and nodding, Andrew murmurs: 'Interesting. I feel like we're getting to something here … Is that true, Xander? Do you still love her?' Later, we are privy to Andrew playing back footage he secretly filmed of Xander and Anya's relationship exposé that he had instigated in his interview. Concentrating intensely as he dramatically performs Anya's side of the conversation alongside her, Andrew places himself in the romantic female role, with Xander as his male lead. In scenes that recall Coppa's insistence that rewatching is a crucial part of fannish viewing and vidding, Andrew rewinds and replays the footage,

Figure 19: Andrew as Documentary Maker, 'Storyteller', 7.16

sighing gustily and clearly relishing his illicit inclusion in the drama of his captured moment.[79]

In one sense, Andrew might be seen here to democratise and queer the male gaze – in Laura Mulvey's original sense of that phrase – that men look and women are to be looked at.[80] But a more expansive understanding of the male gaze would see Andrew's sublimated homoerotic desire for Xander in these scenes not as an anomaly to the gaze's conventional structures of desire but as a constitutive part of it. The openly out romance of Willow and Kennedy holds no allure for Andrew and his camera. Indeed, the audience's potential desire for the 'gay' exposé promised by Andrew's close-up is stymied by his zooming in on Xander's superlative handiwork. The overtly gay narrative is thus jettisoned for what is an arguably queerer reading of the Scoobies' domestic dynamics, and the slash desires of the fan vidder (Andrew) are upheld over the canonical text's focus on Willow and Kennedy. If queering the Slayer text has usually been seen as the province of slash fan fiction writers, here Whedon and Co. recuperate that process as part of the mainstream narrative, elevating and celebrating fan practices of production and consumption as canonical.

8

'Where Do We Go From Here?': Trajectories in *Buffy* Studies

In late 2013 the '*Buffy* Studies' entry on Wikipedia – that suspect but indispensable research tool – stated: 'Emerson College recently debuted the first Bachelors of Art Degree in *Buffy* Studies.' The claim was immediately followed by the ubiquitous proviso: '[*citation needed*]'.[1] By the time I was editing this book, this intriguing factoid had been deleted from the website, and remains difficult to retrace. Regardless of the verity of its information (and its substantiation is largely irrelevant to my argument), this is an astonishing claim. Whether we are being punk'd or not, the author clearly believes (or believed at the end of 2013) that there are enough people 'out there' who will accept or at least notice this information, and I for one am happy to notice it.[2] Overall, the Wikipedia entry on *Buffy* studies is adequately referenced and approaches balance in its inclusion of commentators supportive and derisive of the phenomenon. But how, I ask you, have we reached a situation today where the very thought of a BA degree in *Buffy* studies is understood enough to be a joke or indeed a reality?[3]

The term '*Buffy* studies' is now, as its Wikipedia entry suggests, common parlance, at least among those who study and teach it, though whether it is treated by those outside the field as a reality, a joke or an abomination is still open to question. As my last chapter indicates, *Buffy* is currently the most written about popular culture text of all time, and as its academic popularity increases, it becomes harder to map the scope of the field. In his 2002 bibliography, Derik A. Badman lists almost 160 *Buffy*-related articles in various journals and anthologies,[4] whilst in 2012 *Slate* magazine stopped counting *Buffy*-related academic works once they passed 200.[5] The MLA International Bibliography lists at this writing 150 articles under '*Buffy the Vampire Slayer*', including student dissertations and theses; however, searches under the series' full title are necessarily limited. The number of *Buffy* papers and articles listed by *Slayage: The Online International Journal of Buffy Studies*, which includes unpublished and proposed papers from conferences, is closer to 500.[6] The webpage *Whedonology: An Academic Whedon Studies Bibliography*, a continually updated list of Whedon articles and essays in several different languages (from popular articles and discussion/analysis, to rigorous academic papers, to conference papers made available online, to all known master's and PhD dissertations and theses), lists somewhere around 1,300 currently published and available works on the *Buffy the Vampire Slayer* television series.[7] Helene Frohard-Dourlent, one of the local organisers of the 2012 *Slayage* conference on the Whedonverses in Vancouver, Canada, cites the number of works devoted to *Buffy* as 1,500.[8]

These figures do not even include the myriad works on the *Angel* spin-off series, the original *Buffy* film, the comic book or video game series or other Whedon texts. According to David Lavery, no recent television creator or author has 'generated more critical and scholarly discussion or acquired as devoted a cult following as Joss Whedon',[9] and with the box office success of Marvel's *The Avengers* (2012) and the tie-in television series *Agents of S.H.I.E.L.D.* (2013–), interest continues in Whedon's work – from *Buffy* to more recent ventures such as *The Cabin in the Woods* (2012), *Much Ado About Nothing* (2013) and *Avengers: Age of Ultron* (2015).[10] After the first *Slayage* conference in 2004, the Buffy Studies Association changed its name to the Whedon Studies Association and subsequent *Slayage* conferences have increasingly incorporated scholarship on the extended Whedon canon. In the face of these developments, in fact, the retention of '*Buffy* studies' as a name is somewhat surprising: even though *Buffy* studies has been officially taken under the wing of Whedon studies, it continues to operate as a distinct and independent academic specialisation.

Perhaps this is due to the sheer bulk of the work devoted to *Buffy*. At the time of writing, there are at least 19 published and available books dedicated to *Buffy* studies – excluding anthologies that include other television, science fiction or Whedon works, and excluding also popular non-academic fan guides. It is difficult to definitively count every single individual academic or popular critical essay on *Buffy*, as many of these essays are published in more generalised anthologies or reside in unexpected fields of study, from music, business, theology, political science, linguistics and criminal justice studies.[11] Many of these publications were initially presented at one of 14 conferences on the Whedonverses, held in the UK, USA, Canada, Australia, Turkey and France.[12] The sixth biennial *Slayage* Conference on the Whedonverses (SCW6) was held on the campus of California State University, Sacramento, California on 19–22 June 2014, marking the tenth anniversary of the first *Slayage* Conference.[13] The online journal *Slayage* has had a continued academic presence since 2001 and has been supplemented by *Watcher Junior*, a journal publishing undergraduate student scholarship on Whedon since 2005.[14]

Joss Whedon has responded positively to the scholarly reaction to Buffy:

> I think it's great that the academic community has taken an interest in the show. I think it's always important for academics to study popular culture, even if the thing they are studying is idiotic. If it's successful or made a dent in culture, then it is worthy of study to find out why. *Buffy*, on the other hand is, I hope, not idiotic. We think very carefully about what we're trying to say emotionally, politically, and even philosophically while we're writing it [...] it really is, apart from being a pop-culture phenomenon, something that is deeply layered textually episode by episode.[15]

This scholarly attention has also, inevitably, had its critics. For instance, in the US, Mary Graber was unimpressed with the growing presence of *Buffy* in universities, protesting that 'most parents who send their children off to college have no idea of what is being taught in the humanities classes: pornography appreciation, analysis of the clothing of transvestites, Native American scalp dances, *Buffy the Vampire Slayer*.'[16] In Australia,

Buffy became something of a byword for pop-culture infringement on the secondary English curriculum, with Yuko Narushima reporting favourably in 2008 on a refocus on Shakespeare, Dickens and Austen and away from texts such as *Buffy*, *Clueless* and *Star Wars*.[17] Performance studies scholar Jason Winslade notes that 'teaching *Buffy* itself requires an awkward dance between experiential viewing pleasures and thoughtful analysis',[18] and Jes Battis, author of *Blood Relations in Buffy and Angel*, admits that study of the Buffyverse 'invokes an uneasy combination of enthusiasm and ire' and meets 'a certain amount of disdain from within the halls of the academy'.[19]

'Once more, with feeling'

The central event in the *Buffy* studies calendar is undoubtedly the biennial *Slayage* conference. The fifth of these, SCW5, took place on 12–15 July 2012 in Vancouver, BC, Canada. Central conveners David Lavery, Rhonda V. Wilcox and Tanya Cochran moved the conference 'north' and, under the aegis of local organisers Helene Frohard-Dourlent, Sharon Sutherland and Sarah Swan, *Slayage* was international in location for the first time.[20] SCW5 embraced the broad sweep of Joss Whedon's *oeuvre*, with papers on the flagship *Buffy*, the 'spin-off with a soul', *Angel*,[21] the unjustly abbreviated *Firefly* and its big-screen adaptation *Serenity*. There were also sessions devoted to *Dollhouse* (2009–10), *Cabin in the Woods* (2012) and comics from the Whedon canon, such as *Astonishing X-Men* and *Dr Horrible's Sing-Along Blog* (2008). Thoroughly multidisciplinary in scope, the conference brought together academics and independent scholars working in the fields not only of literary, film and television studies but also of sociology, psychology, religious studies, media studies, American studies, mathematics, philosophy, law, music, art, performance studies, women's and gender studies, linguistics, bibliography, rhetoric and pedagogy. The range of methodologies adopted by individual papers and panels was equally eclectic; in addition to traditional analyses of character, genre, narrative and symbolism, presenters also explored the influence of intertexts as diverse as fairy tales, pseudo documentary, Jean-Paul Sartre, Deleuze and Guattari and Paul de Man. Several panels examined the ever-expanding worlds of Whedon fandom, providing ethnographies of fan communities and reports on various fandom projects. Papers explored the 'disability narrative' in

Whedon's works, the translation of *Buffy* into French, Italian and Spanish, and asked the question: 'Is Buffy clinically depressed?'[22] Others considered questions of morality and ethics, citizenship and belonging, consumption and containment, race, class, gender, sexuality, science, geography and ecology. To that vexing question (a question I admit to asking myself from time to time) 'is there really anything new to say about *Buffy*?', the conference provided a resounding 'duh!' To sceptics questioning the longevity and relevance of *Buffy* studies, the *Slayage* conferences moreover offer ample evidence of the ongoing importance of Whedon's texts to an international scholarly community.

'Going through the motions?'

'I was always brave, and kind of righteous. Now I find I'm wavering': thus sang Buffy in the self-consciously Disney 'I want' song at the beginning of Season 6's musical, 'Once More, with Feeling' (6.7). In the time that I have been working on this book, I have sometimes found myself in a similar frame of mind. If not brave, exactly, I *have* always been kind of righteous about defending the scholarly legitimacy of *Buffy the Vampire Slayer*, which I started writing about for undergraduate literature classes with the release of the Twentieth Century Fox film in 1992. It has become *de rigueur* in *Buffy* studies to bemoan the shortcomings of this early incarnation and, following Joss Whedon's lead, to deem it infinitely inferior to the final product. I can only say that making the female lead's 'secret weapon' PMS was a masterstroke for which I remain profoundly grateful, and reiterate that Joss Whedon is only one – albeit it an important one – of the many readers of the texts he helps to produce. But 20 years later (eek!), a healthy swathe of international conferences and many a monograph later, there have certainly been points at which I have felt decidedly less sanguine about the radical potential of Buffy in general and *Buffy* studies in particular.

At the first *Slayage* conference in Nashville, some scholars and fans were already betraying an incipient impatience with the state of Buffy scholarship. 'It's a relief to hear papers that don't go on about feminism' is a rough paraphrase of a comment I heard in a panel on colonialism – a remark that sets up an unfortunate mutual exclusivity. In her Mr Pointy award-winning keynote address, '"Not just another Buffy paper": towards an aesthetics of television', Sue Turnbull offered a wittily self-reflexive account of her struggles to justify her own Buffy scholarship to her colleagues ('Why I sometimes wish I was studying orthodonture') and to do something different with the Slayer text ('a new aesthetics of television study').[23] A year previously, in their now somewhat notorious 2003 essay, 'Feeling for Buffy: The girl next door', Michael P. Levine and Steven Jay Schneider had offered a scathing critique of the state of *Buffy* scholarship, writing that:

> The irony here is that, in attempting to bring scholarship or serious discussion to bear on BtVS, the scholars in question evince their own lack of understanding of, and insight into, the show, and perhaps more importantly, into the kinds of tasks, purposes, and methods that cultural theorists and others who engage with popular culture set for themselves and employ.[24]

Levine and Schneider went on to say, not without some justification, that:

> there has been much less of the kind of self-reflective work about the nature of BtVS scholarship – what it is about and what it is trying to accomplish versus what it should or could be about – than there should be, or than there in fact is within various disciplines in the humanities generally as regards their objects of study. It is BtVS scholarship that warrants study and this point, not BtVS itself.[25]

What are the chances – today – that *Buffy* studies can do more than go 'through the motions', that our scholarship can move through, beyond or even more deeply into these problems – the purported redundancy of content ('not more feminism!'), the search for new approaches, the lack of reflexivity?

'The same old trips – why should we care?'

One answer is that, in a very basic sense, *Buffy* studies has just about the same chance as any other academic specialisation of unearthing new content, unveiling new approaches and being self-conscious about the state of the field. I feel sure that I am not alone when I say that during several presentations and even entire panels at *Buffy* conferences I have been haunted by a sense of déjà vu. Why does it feel as if people are just telling us what we already know? Is the alternative to papers that assume too much insider knowledge simply presentations that include a lot of plot or character synopsis? How do we make a series we know so well new again to an informed audience? What *can* we assume about our audience? The regular conventions of paper presentations don't seem to hold here – or do they? Admittedly, what I hear as 'mostly filler' others will hear as a 'break-away pop hit' or favourite 'book number'. What's new to me might be old to someone else, and vice versa. I am not arguing here for the priority of my sense of what is new and important in *Buffy* scholarship, but simply pointing out that that standard itself is an ineluctably subjective one.

However, one difference, I suspect, between the experience of attending the biennial *Slayage* conference and, say, the annual Shakespeare Association of America conference is that the beloved object of study is also a maligned and imperilled object of study, so perhaps we *care* more when what we hear is substandard, even if we know that 'substandard' inevitably means different things to different people. Having been asked to write a report of the second *Slayage* conference in Barnesville, Georgia, I know that I was morbidly preoccupied with what I perceived as 'filler' papers until a fellow attendee made the candid observation that when she attended an academic conference in her primary field, she was satisfied if she heard one good paper over the course of the conference. Having just heard five great papers in the space of a single day, and holding similarly low expectations of academic conferences in general, this contrast gave me pause. Do we hold higher hopes (and greater dread?) of *Buffy* scholarship than we do of other scholarship because, following Sue Turnbull, the study of *Buffy* is clearly such a joke to some of our colleagues? Does what Rhonda Wilcox has recently called the 'demonisation' of television studies within the wider academy influence the nature of our critical and emotional investments in the series and in the scholarly paratexts (books, conferences, journals) with which the study of *Buffy* endeavours to legitimise itself?[26] And how does the embattled nature of the field impact the quality of community and conversation and, perhaps more importantly, the possibilities for disagreement and dissent, when large numbers of *Buffy* scholars congregate en masse?

'What can't we face if we're together?'

With *Buffy* scholarship expanding so rapidly, it makes sense that conferences devoted to the series and Whedon's works in general involve people from many levels of the academy and beyond – distinguished professors, common or garden professors, undergraduates, graduate students grappling with different stages of their master's or doctoral programmes, independent scholars, professional writers, struggling writers and loyal fans. Levels of familiarity with Whedon's texts and with the existing scholarship differ markedly as well, without necessarily corresponding closely with individuals' professional development. This is in no way a bad thing. In fact, it is one of those egalitarian, perhaps even utopian, features of this field that Rhonda Wilcox and David Lavery, as the first conference coordinators and editors of *Slayage*, have deliberately fostered and promoted. *Buffy* studies is unusual in its inclusivity, in the deliberate efforts it makes to welcome scholars and students with different levels of expertise. As Rhys Edwards explains, the 'convivial nature of *Slayage* merges high and low culture and creates an openness that might attract students who are otherwise alienated by the formality of academic conferences'.[27] Particularly at a gathering like *Slayage*, those who write about *Buffy* are justifiably proud that – as scholars, fans, academics and students (and often more than one of these simultaneously) – they are 'in this thing together'.

'Something to sing about'

In the wider world of *Buffy* scholarship several areas of recent expansion seem noteworthy trajectories: the emerging literature on *Buffy* pedagogy, the move from *Buffy* studies to Whedon studies (and the associated work of comparison) and the legacy left by *Buffy* in contemporary popular culture.

Jodie A. Krieder and Meghan K. Winchell, editors of the collection *Buffy in the Classroom: Essays on Teaching with the Vampire Slayer*, highlight the breadth and depth of this flexible text about a vampire slayer and her 'Scooby gang', which can be decoded as a historical context, an exploration about myth and power, ethics and a reimagining of classic themes – to name only some of the avenues of pedagogical approach.[28] In this volume, the role of intertextuality throughout *Buffy the Vampire Slayer* is explored by Kristopher Woofter, whose examination of fairy tale to revisionist tale allows students to consider the ways in which the fairy tale has been 'transformed, from a parody of form (and formula) to serious critical engagement' when they view 'Buffy vs Dracula' (5.1) towards the conclusion of the course.[29] Barry Morris considers the function of archetypical characters (such as the 'Chosen One', the 'Mentor' or the 'Rogue') in *Buffy* studies and relates this to the way in which the study of popular culture and further examination of Whedon's work allows us to see how such characters are continually reused and reimagined throughout the Whedonverse.[30] Meghan K. Winchell examines how *Buffy* succeeds in taking the 'scary' out of 'feminism' in her first-year course 'Decoding *Buffy the Vampire Slayer*', where course material covers a broad spectrum from Puritan New England to Victorianism, before tracing popular culture and *Buffy*'s place as a feminist text.[31]

Many of the topics covered in *Buffy* pedagogy, such as narrative complexity, media and popular culture, gender studies, censorship, identity and archetypal characters, are reworked or reimagined in Whedon's newer texts and are beginning to be addressed in research devoted to those texts. Morris argues that, as they did in *Buffy*, the character types and plots that Whedon brings to the screen or page 'embody popular stereotypes, then negotiate, exaggerate and eviscerate them'.[32] As Whedon's body of work continues to grow, scholarly investigation will no doubt continue to develop into the other 'verses' that have been created since the series concluded its run on television. Of course, with the potential for countless 'seasons' to continue in comic format, *Buffy* studies itself is by no means over, but it has – in many respects – been merged under the Whedon studies umbrella. Since the global success of *The Avengers*, Whedon's status has shifted somewhat from 'cult' to 'popular' – perhaps even mainstream – director.[33] Naturally, the 'old' Whedon fans can proudly boast of having been part of the original *Slayage* guard, and *Buffy* remains the flagship for many Whedon scholars. My own decision to concentrate on *Buffy* for this book in some ways resists the trend to consider Whedon's work as an *oeuvre*, but is motivated by a desire to consider the series itself as a discrete text with its distinctive feminist rhetorical strategies, coupled with concerns about the efficacy of auteur-based approaches, discussed in more detail below.

Another new direction for *Buffy* studies that does not seem to have attracted significant scholarly attention as yet is the Slayer's legacy in popular culture. Wikipedia, that font of all wisdom, lists an astonishing number of texts that refer directly to the cult series.[34] Since concluding its television run, *Buffy the Vampire Slayer* has continued to feature on various 'Top' lists relating to popular television, including: Bravo's 2004 '100 Greatest TV Characters', *Empire* magazine's '50 Greatest TV Shows of all Time' (2008) and *TV Guide*'s list (30 May 2004 issue) of the '25 Top Cult Shows Ever!'[35] The series is also frequently referenced in various other televisual texts and these references are not limited to any particular genre. Of course, there are obvious examples in 'supernatural' television shows, such as: *Xena: Warrior Princess*: 'I hear "Buffus the Bacchae Slayer" is playing next door';[36] *Charmed*: 'where's Buffy when you need her?'; *The Vampire Diaries*: 'C'mon, Buffy!'; and *True Blood*: 'You know who I really wish would come to Marthaville? Huh? Buffy. Or Blade.'[37] Examples outside the realm of the supernatural include the animated works *The Simpsons* (Marge mentions a restaurant named 'Buffet the Hunger Slayer'), *Daria* (Quinn states that they'll be 'home in time for Buffy') and *Family Guy* (regularly spoofing Seth Green's role as Oz on the show).[38] Comedy shows also reference the Vampire Slayer, including *Friends* (Phoebe's twin, Ursula, starred in a porn film named 'Buffay the Vampire Layer'), *Will & Grace* ('Oh, my God. I love TV. Buffy is my life') and *How I Met Your Mother*, starring Alyson Hannigan, which contains several Buffy references (such as suggesting 'Tara' for a baby name).[39] Buffy is also referenced in *Dawson's Creek*[40] (Pacey suggests Capeside would become a Hellmouth if he acted on his feelings) and *Bones*, starring David Boreanaz, sees a character remark, 'WWBD?' (Daisy: 'You know, every time I get stuck on my dissertation, I think to myself, "WWBD"', with WWBD being known to stand for 'What Would Buffy Do?').[41] These are only a few examples and do not touch on those allusions that feature in film, comics and other media. What they reveal, though, is that *Buffy* – like other cult shows before it (for example, *Star Trek*) – has cemented itself in the popular culture psyche and, as a result, is not only genre compatible but relevant now. For example, as 'vampire' texts – generally adapted from novel form – continue to make their way to the big and small screen (*Vampire Diaries*, *True Blood*, *Twilight*, NBC's *Dracula*), an inevitable comparison with *Buffy* is waiting to be drawn – both in popular culture and academic scholarship.

If the above examples illustrate new content and new approaches in scholarship on *Buffy*, a question arguably remains about the capacity of the field for self-reflection. Scholarship that answers the 'so what?' question ('So why should what you have to say be of interest to anyone not already interested?') provides a particularly important contribution to *Buffy* scholarship at this stage of its development. For *Buffy* studies to develop beyond its cultish counter-canonical cache (admittedly part of its appeal), it needs to explicitly demonstrate the kinds of contribution it can make to the disparate disciplines its exponents engage with. Michael Adams' linguistic analysis of *Buffy* has done this for his field in *Slayer Slang*; Erin B. Waggoner's edited collection, *Sexual Rhetoric in the Works of Joss Whedon*, succeeds in doing this for the fields of both sexuality studies and rhetoric; and Allison McCracken's marvellous essay, 'At stake: Angel's body, fantasy masculinity, and queer desire in teen television' promises to do this for studies of girlhood and queer spectatorship.[42]

'I'm just worried that this whole session's going to turn into some training montage from an '80s movie'

With the plethora of excellent scholarship on offer, it might seem churlish to probe what I see as some of the more problematic aspects of the field, yet this is also part this chapter's purpose. At the first *Slayage* conference in 2004, I voiced the concern that while original and informative papers abounded, Buffy scholars seemed surprisingly reluctant to critique the show, and that when such critiques were offered, they were often perceived as arresting rather than furthering scholarly dialogue. I am most familiar with this tendency in feminist scholarship. The last decade has produced a wealth of exciting feminist criticism of *Buffy*, but with significant exceptions, there is a tendency to focus on the series' transgressive play with gender at the expense of considering other, less obviously liberatory aspects of the show. In this context, as we saw in Chapter 4, critical scrutiny of, say, Buffy's post-colonial or racial politics is seen by some to wilfully undermine or detract from the series' feminist credentials, and perhaps by implication from the work of scholars who have celebrated it. A critique of Buffy's less progressive politics becomes a treacherous act of double-crossing. And if feminist scholars see a critique of Buffy's racial politics as an attack on *Buffy* studies itself, then this separation will solidify by degrees. In Nashville I suggested that it is a poor reflection on *Buffy* studies if serious-minded critique of the show is somehow seen as an inappropriate response to the text.

This tension is not unique to feminist scholarship of *Buffy*; indeed similar, sometimes unspoken conflicts might be discerned in discussions about the putative 'success' of Season 7 and the respective merits of formal (often deemed 'aesthetic') and ideological (often termed 'sociological') criticism in *Buffy* studies.[43] Far from endangering its development, I believe such tensions indicate some of the field's most promising avenues of exploration – but only if they are explored deliberately and self-consciously. This will require that new scholarship will sometimes take issue with existing scholarship, and such disagreements should not be seen as a threat to the field but rather as an important source of its strength. Cynthea Masson's SC2 paper offers a wonderful example of work that engages usefully with existing *Buffy* scholarship and departs from it in several pertinent respects to produce a vigorous new reading of a familiar text. Masson argues that in 'Once More, with Feeling' (6.7) 'Buffy's words of confidence – her apparent truth of faith in togetherness – is not so confident or truthful when viewed rhetorically'. Instead, Masson suggests, 'she asks rhetorical questions that overtly imply togetherness, while covertly gesturing toward her ongoing separation from the group'. In a different but nonetheless related way, some attendees at SC2 expressed discomfort with the fact that when they asked questions that were perceived as critical – of the series itself, of the conference papers in question – they were essentially shut down in a sort of default collective strategy that discouraged dissension. In analysing a series as invested in the slippage between text and subtext as *Buffy*, we should be equally wary of misreading rhetorical questions as we are of mistaking genuine questions for a species of assault. The flipside to the inclusive sense of community that the *Slayage* conferences foster is the sense that any critical take on *Buffy* – its politics, its narrative strategies, Spike (!) – can be misread as an attack on that community itself – a community that is necessarily (and thankfully) less unified than its own rhetoric might suggest.

In 'Once More, with Feeling', Buffy's anthem 'What Can't We Face' celebrates the sense of community that is a celebrated feature of the show. But as several critics have noted, this song is a wishful affirmation of unity in the face of decided differences and, I would suggest, the state of *Buffy* scholarship is no different.[44] Similarly, when Buffy warns Giles, 'I'm just worried that this whole session's going to turn into some training montage from an '80s movie', she voices a fear that the discipline and rigour of their training is about to be cheapened by caricature, portrayed with a sentimentality that drains it of significance. The extraordinary goodwill and intellectual generosity that inform the *Slayage* conferences should not blind us to the fact that the field of *Buffy* studies unwittingly courts trivialisation if it pursues critical consensus at the expense of a dynamic discussion of differences. In this spirit, I want briefly to consider two developments in *Buffy* scholarship that I believe warrant further scrutiny.

'It's getting eerie. What's this cheery singing all about?'

The level of affective response elicited by *Buffy* is demonstrably and designedly powerful. We know that Whedon developed the series with this aim in mind: 'I designed the show to create that strong reaction. I designed Buffy to be an icon, to be an emotional experience, to be loved in a way that other shows can't be loved.'[45] One of the most unusual moments I have experienced at any conference occurred at 11 am on a Sunday morning at SC2 when Claudia Rollins' careful analysis of Anya's response to Joyce's death in 'The Body' (5.16) left half of the audience unexpectedly blinking back tears. We do not generally expect to be moved this viscerally by a television show, still less by an academic presentation, although perhaps we should be more often. Participation in the *Slayage* conferences often blurs the boundaries between academic 'distance' and fannish 'immersion' in ways that help to dismantle this obdurate binary. The results can sometimes be exhilarating, as with Rollins' talk above. They can also be unnerving.

Vivien Burr, in her lucid account of the interplay between fan and academic identities at the first *Slayage* conference, testifies to the mixed feelings many experience when their personal and professional passions find a common object. She explores the 'tension and conflict implicit in the relationship between academic and fan identities, and the defensiveness and anxiety associated with trying to have a foot in both camps'.[46] Based on her own experiences in Nashville and the insights of 13 interviewees, Burr examines attendees' efforts to balance emotional engagement and academic rigour. One respondent, Ben, writes:

> I know that my engagement with the show is a peculiar combination of scholarly curiosity, appreciation, and deep emotional attachment [...] The best and most responsible critiques, I think, emerge from profound emotional engagements – but that emotional engagement needs to be invested with criticism and political interest, not simply taken up as an uncritical celebration.[47]

Given that *Slayage* 'quite clearly identified itself as an academic conference', Burr notes, 'it is not surprising [...] that it was almost exclusively the more fannish aspects of the activities that sometimes felt problematic'.[48]

The fannish aspects of *Buffy* conferences that feel most problematic to me are the recurring use of two words: 'Joss' and 'genius'. In academic circles we call Dante simply by his first name but even this is a mistake of literary history. When I'm talking to my friends, or discussing my struggles with writing this book to colleagues, I will refer to the creator of *Buffy* as 'Joss'. But this doesn't mean it's good practice. I want to make the puny, pedantic plea that in academic conference papers we refer to Whedon by his full or last name. The problem is compounded when 'Joss' becomes synonymous with 'genius' and the two are collapsed in a way that forestalls conversation. 'Joss' is a 'genius', 'Joss' 'wrote' this episode, therefore, this episode is 'genius'. If there is a case to be made for Whedon's 'genius', then that case needs to *established*, and not just assumed. I suppose one of the pleasures of conferences such as *Slayage* is precisely the fellow fannish feeling that allows such assumptions to be made, but the fact remains that we are all fan-scholars and scholar-fans with different political and theoretical investments. 'Genius' is a particularly loaded term in literary criticism, with a history that harkens back to Romantic notions of individual creativity and transcendence, and which was responsible in part for the exclusion of women and other minorities from the canon of English literature for several centuries. The term 'genius' is certainly part of my fannish vocabulary for Whedon, but when we use it in academic contexts I suggest we need to be careful to define, and delimit, exactly what it is we are trying to say.

These admittedly anal comments are not intended to silence fan discourse on *Buffy* or to endorse any particularly rigid code of academic etiquette. As Alan, one of Vivien Burr's respondents, eloquently argues:

> I feel that fandom can certainly inform a scholar's work and adds to the playfulness that can make scholarly papers interesting. But a scholar needs to balance that with a more measured approach. I refrain from using the term 'objectivity', since that notion is as mythical as vampires are. But an academic writing on these topics needs to learn to coax his or her fandom into the service of scholarly inquiry.[49]

Nor do I mean, in voicing my beef with 'Joss' and 'genius', to reinforce a strict division between fan and academic identities. As Burr notes, following Matt Hills, these identities are performative, 'they are things that we *do*', not things that we, essentially, are.[50] And while turf struggles between fans and academics might seem potentially divisive of the inclusive community fostered by *Slayage*, the fact that the study of fan cultures has developed alongside *Buffy* studies and has from the outset constituted an important part of its literature suggests instead that the vagaries of academic/fan interaction within this community will continue to prove a particularly fertile field of research. In its energetic embrace of fan communities and fan idioms, *Buffy* studies has already gone a long way to answering the call Matt Hills makes at the end of *Fan Cultures* (and which David Lavery reiterates in his Mr Pointy award-winning paean to *Buffy* studies, '"I wrote my thesis on you": *Buffy* Studies as an academic cult'), the call for 'academic commitment [...] modeled on fan commitment', for 'affective reflexivity' and for '*impassioned thought* rather than the parroting of academic discursive mantras'.[51] I still think we should use his last name.

'I've got a theory'

Closely related to the celebration of 'Joss' as 'genius' has been the swift rise of auteur theory as a model for Whedon's authorship. It is one thing to celebrate the ascendancy of a single television series at the height of its popularity – something the first *Slayage* conference did with gusto and good humour (well, OK, sometimes with really *bad* humour); it is another thing altogether to organise a decade's worth of conferences around the idea of 'the Whedonverses', a nomenclature that simultaneously signals the complex melding of fan and academic sensibilities informing this particular articulation of the field and the elevation of Joss Whedon himself to the role of auteur, of author function, invoked, whether ironically or unabashedly literally, as the veritable deity of an alternate universe. One recent and long-awaited publication that evokes Whedon as auteur is David Lavery's *Joss Whedon, A Creative Portrait: From* Buffy the Vampire Slayer *to* The Avengers.[52]

Lavery explains that his book modelled its methodology on John Livingston Lowes, *The Road to Xanadu: A Study in the Ways of the Imagination*, in which Lowes sought to

> systematically trace the origin of each and every image/symbol/metaphor in Coleridge's 'Kubla Khan' and 'Rime of the Ancient Mariner', to discover how the raw material that inspired the great British romantic's belief suspending words arrived in his imagination in the first place.[53]

Lavery hoped to 'scrutinize Whedon in much the same way Lowes investigated Coleridge', with one chapter of his book, 'Joss Whedon, Television Auteur' devoted to exploring how

> Whedon's signature writing and directing are elucidated through examination of such singular episodes as 'Hush' (4.10), 'Restless (4.22)', 'The Body (5.16)', 'Once More with Feeling' (6.7), 'Waiting in the Wings' (*Angel the Series*, 3.13), and 'Objects in Space' (*Firefly*, 1.14).[54]

Lavery claimed that he borrowed this approach from 'back in the good old days' when 'the discouraging words structuralism and deconstruction had not yet been heard'.[55] And, disarming self-deprecation aside, it is not without significance that one of the more recent proposals for *Buffy* scholarship, from an acknowledged leader of the field, draws its theoretical underpinning from a time before High Theory.

Auteur theory is useful for *Buffy* scholars for a number of reasons: it asserts by fiat the 'genius' of the object of analysis; it makes a polemic argument for reading those who produce television as seriously as those who produce film; it canonises Whedon as innovator and master of his craft at an important stage in the development of television studies; and it retrieves from the theoretical remains of the death of the author a single, self-conscious, self-evident author – all good grist for the New Critical mill. But it also begs the question of this scholarship's relationship to the critical theory that, over the last 40 years, has spawned the very fields – of feminism, film studies, cultural studies, etc. – that gave a home to *Buffy* studies to begin with. When I mentioned in the SC2 panel on Media/Television Studies that it was uncanny that auteur theory, itself the subject of fierce debate in film studies, should be resurrected in television studies 40 years after the death of the author, another audience member replied that she thought that the death of the author had been exaggerated. This moment exemplifies, as clearly as I think any can, the very different theoretical agenda that *Buffy* scholars bring to their work.[56] And again, I would like to make the pitch that I think these divisions can be potentially productive and powerful if they are brought out into the open.

In that spirit of constructive engagement, then, let me be a little less cryptic. I've already expressed my reservations about the use of the term 'genius': if it is defined in such a way as to *open up* our investigation into the nature of Whedon's artistry, then that is all to the good; if it is used simply to assert aesthetic value, then, like Buffy singing before Sweet at the conclusion to 'Once More, with Feeling', it 'needs back up'. Similarly, while the argument certainly needs to be made that television shows are as worthy of scholarly scrutiny as film texts or literature, it seems counter-intuitive to make this claim using the *same* values of 'quality' and 'excellence' that have kept television from being taken seriously in the first place. The mechanism of canonisation is, in some ways, inimical to the progressive politics that the *Buffy* series and many *Buffy* scholars uphold. Moreover, while auteur theory was, in its heyday, certainly a polemic movement, it was also, as Bill Nichols notes – citing John Hess in his commentary on Truffaut's watershed essay, 'A certain tendency of the French cinema' – 'a justification couched in aesthetic terms, of a culturally conservative, politically reactionary attempt to remove film from the realm of social and political concern'.[57] While auteur theory has developed in decidedly different directions since then (in the distinctive styles of Andrew Sarris, Peter Wollen and Robin Wood, for instance),[58] it seems important for *Buffy* scholars today to carefully historicise the theory they employ, to identify which strain of this theory speaks most to their concerns and to unpack the theoretical baggage that travels with the label 'auteur', not least of which is its gendering (like the label 'genius' before it) as precocious masculine talent.

Finally, I want to glance briefly at the solidification of the author function that attends *Buffy* studies' adoption of auteur theory. While it makes sense for the immediate promotion of the field, the elevation of Joss Whedon to auteur, to single-author status, also comes at a time when *Buffy* studies might contribute meaningfully to broader, cross-disciplinary interests in the nature of collective authorship, intellectual property, the dynamics of television production and the mythology of the author function as it relates to media studies more generally. No TV episode, still less a TV series, is a single-authored work, and to proceed as if it were seems to me to jettison one of the most compelling contributions the study of *Buffy* might have to offer the wider academic community. I am not arguing here for the wholesale rejection of auteur theory but merely for a more specific and nuanced exploration of its applicability. A critical analysis of the ways in which Whedon's authorship confirms *and resists* various strains of auteur theory might be able to take in new directions not just *Buffy* studies but auteur theory as well.

'Where do we go from here?'

Buffy studies in its present incarnation offers unique opportunities to explore the peculiarities and problematics of television 'authorship'. Whether approached via auteur theory or from a more deconstructive position, *Buffy* has much to offer. *Buffy* studies also offers fertile fields for the study of fan cultures and, more particularly, for the interrogation of the fan/scholar continuum. It continues to foster provocative scholarship in feminism and has branched out in many other exciting directions. As the ongoing expansion of scholarship attests, *Buffy* will continue to elicit challenging responses from both the formalist and post-structuralist sides of the critical divide. The trick will be to bring the two into conversation. Academic interest in *Buffy the Vampire Slayer* has only increased in the ten plus years since the series' onscreen finale, and the diverse use of *Buffy* across dozens of academic fields, along with the prime position the series holds in science fiction, feminist and popular culture canons, shows no sign of waning. For *Buffy* fans and scholars, this represents a no-brainer. *Buffy* is a *Girl's Own* clarion call to keep fighting the good fight, and a poignant exploration of how to stay human in the process. As my epigraph from Joss Whedon indicates, this fight is an ongoing one, but *Buffy* shows us the pleasures of fighting it together.

Notes

Introduction: How to Do Things with *Buffy*

1 Patricia Pender, '"I'm Buffy and you're … history": The postmodern politics of *Buffy the Vampire Slayer*', in Rhonda Wilcox and David Lavery (eds), *Fighting the Forces: What's at Stake in Buffy the Vampire Slayer* (Lanham, MD: Rowman and Littlefield, 2002), pp. 35–44.
2 Patricia Pender, '"Kicking ass is comfort food": Buffy as third wave feminist icon', in Stacy Gillis, Gillian Howie and Rebecca Munford (eds), *Third Wave Feminism: A Critical Exploration* (New York: Palgrave Macmillan, 2004), pp. 164–74, reprinted in Stacy Gillis, Gillian Howie and Rebecca Munford (eds), *Third-Wave Feminism: A Critical Exploration*, 2nd edn (Houndmills: Palgrave Macmillan, 2007), pp. 224–36.
3 Jonathan McIntosh, 'Buffy vs Edward (Twilight remixed)', *Rebellious Pixels*, 20 June 2009. Available at http://www.rebelliouspixels.com/page/11 (accessed 20 June 2012).

Chapter 1: 'I'm Buffy and You're … History': *Buffy* Baffles the Binaries

1 Alyssa Katz, 'Buffy the Vampire Slayer', *Nation*, 6 April 1998, pp. 35–6, p. 35.
2 Anamika Samanta and Erin Franzman, 'Women in action', *HUES: Hear Us Emerging Sisters* 4/3 (1998), pp. 28–31, p. 28.
3 Rachel Fudge, 'The Buffy effect: Or, a tale of cleavage and marketing', *Bitch: Feminist Response to Pop Culture* 10 (1999). Available at http://bitchmagazine.org/article/buffy-effect (accessed 3 June 2012).
4 Lynette Lamb, 'Media criticism: The sad state of teen television', *New Moon Network: For Adults Who Care About Girls* 7/2 (1999), pp. 14–25, p. 14.
5 Jennifer L. Pozner, 'Thwack! Pow! Yikes! Not your mother's heroines', *Sojourner: The Women's Forum* 23/2 (1997):, pp. 12–13, p. 12.
6 Ibid.

7 Micol Ostow, 'Why I love Buffy', *Sojourner: The Women's Forum* 24.3 (1998), pp. 20–35, p. 20.
8 Ibid.
9 Ibid.
10 Ibid.
11 Fudge, 'The Buffy effect'.
12 Ibid.
13 Ostow, 'Why I love Buffy', p. 20.
14 Samanta and Franzman, 'Women in action', p. 28.
15 See especially Rachel Fudge, who says of Buffy that 'she's no scarred, deep-in-shit Tank Girl – this slayer's tank tops are pastel and pristine, revealing plenty of creamy, unmarred cleavage' and, on another occasion, that 'her ever present tank tops showcase her rack quite efficiently' (Fudge, 'The Buffy effect', p. 20). See also Anamika Samanta and Erin Franzman who maintain, somewhat confusingly, that '[n]o one notices that Buffy is the smartest, strongest (literally and figuratively) teen role model television has seen in ages. Instead the show gets attention for its Lolita-esque star's abundant cleavage. If more cleavage means more advertising dollars (which in turn means the show stays on the air), then hopefully more young women and girls will be able to see the show and appreciate the finer points of Buffy, such as they are. You have to take what you can get these days' (Samanta and Franzman, 'Women in action', p. 28).
16 Fudge, 'The Buffy effect'.
17 Ibid.
18 Jonathan Dollimore, *Sexual Dissidence: Augustine to Wilde, Freud to Foucault* (Oxford: Clarendon, 1991), p. 85.
19 Susan Sontag, 'Notes on Camp', in *Against Interpretation* (New York: Farrar and Strauss, 1996), pp. 275–92, p. 277.
20 Pamela Robertson, *Guilty Pleasures: Feminist Camp from Mae West to Madonna* (Durham, NC: Duke University Press, 1996), p. 10.
21 Ibid., p. 6.
22 Mark Dery, *The Pyrotechnic Insanitarium: American Culture on the Brink* (New York: Grove Press, 1999), p. 57.
23 Ibid., pp. 55–6.
24 Ibid., p. 36.
25 Ibid., p. 56.
26 Katz, 'Buffy the Vampire Slayer', p. 36.
27 A. Susan Owen, 'Vampires, postmodernity, and postfeminism: *Buffy the Vampire Slayer*', *Journal of Popular Film and Television* 27/2 (Summer 1999), pp. 24–31, p. 30.

28 Ibid., p. 31.
29 Fudge, 'The Buffy effect'.

Chapter 2: *Buffy* in History: Feminisms Pro and Faux, Post and Most

1 Rachel Fudge, 'The Buffy effect: Or, a tale of cleavage and marketing', *Bitch: Feminist Response to Pop Culture* 10 (1999), para. 2. Available at http://bitchmagazine.org/article/buffy-effect (accessed 3 June 2012); *Dawson's Creek*, created by Kevin Williamson (1998, The WB, prod. by Sony Pictures Television), television; *Felicity*, created by J. J. Abrams and Matt Reeves (1998, The WB, prod. by Touchstone Television and Imagine Television), television.
2 James L. Longworth, *TV Creators: Conversations with America's Top Producers of Television Drama*, vol. 2 (New York: Syracuse University Press, 2002), p. 211.
3 Michele Byers, '*Buffy the Vampire Slayer*: the next generation of television', in Rory Dicker and Alison Piepmeier (eds), *Catching a Wave: Reclaiming Feminism for the 21st Century* (Boston, MA: Northeastern University Press, 2003), pp. 171–87, p. 173.
4 Irene Karras, 'The third wave's final girl: Buffy the Vampire Slayer', *thirdspace* 1.2 (2002), para. 15. Available at http://journals.sfu.ca/thirdspace/index.php/journal/article/viewArticle/karras/50 (accessed 14 June 2012).
5 Fudge, 'The Buffy effect', para. 17.
6 Ginia Bellafante, 'Bewitching teen heroines', *Time*, 5 May 1997, p. 83; Mimi Marinucci, 'Feminism and the ethics of violence: Why Buffy kicks ass', in James B. South (ed.), *Buffy the Vampire Slayer and Philosophy: Fear and Trembling in Sunnydale* (Chicago, IL: Open Court, 2003), pp. 61–75; Elyce Rae Helford, '"My emotions give me power": The containment of girls' anger in Buffy', in Rhonda Wilcox and David Lavery (eds), *Fighting the Forces: What's at Stake in Buffy the Vampire Slayer* (Lanham, MD: Rowman and Littlefield, 2002), pp. 18–34, p. 24.
7 Zoe-Jane Playden, '"What you are, what's to come": Feminisms, citizenship and the divine', in Roz Kaveney (ed.), *Reading the Vampire Slayer: An Unofficial Critical Companion to Buffy and Angel* (London: I.B.Tauris, 2002), pp. 120–47, p. 143; Patricia Pender, '"I'm Buffy and you're … history": The postmodern politics of *Buffy the Vampire Slayer*', in Rhonda Wilcox and David Lavery (eds), *Fighting the Forces: What's at Stake in Buffy the Vampire Slayer* (Lanham, MD: Rowman and Littlefield, 2002), pp. 35–44, p. 43.

8 *Buffy the Vampire Slayer*, dir. Fran Rubel Kuzui, perf. Kristy Swanson, Donald Sutherland, Paul Reubens, Rutger Hauer, Luke Perry and Hilary Swank (1992, Twentieth Century Fox), film.

9 *Buffy the Vampire Slayer*, created by Joss Whedon (1997, The WB and UPN, prod. by Mutant Enemy, Kuzui Enterprises, Sandollar Television, and Twentieth Century Fox Television), television. Originally aired from 10 March 1997 until 20 May 2003.

10 *Shortchanging Girls, Shortchanging America: A Call to Action* (American Association of University Women, 1994); Lynn Phillips (prod.), *The Girls Report: What We Know & Need to Know About Growing Up Female* (National Council for Research on Women, USA, 1998).

11 Mary Pipher, *Reviving Ophelia: Saving the Selves of Adolescent Girls* (New York: Ballantine Books, 2001).

12 Ibid., p. 12.

13 Lyn Mikel Brown, *Raising their Voices: The Politics of Girls' Anger* (Cambridge, Mass.: Harvard University Press, 1999).

14 Ibid., p. vii (emphasis in original).

15 Ibid.

16 Kathleen Rowe Karlyn, '*Scream*, popular culture, and feminism's third wave: "I'm not my mother"', *Genders* 38 (2003), para. 1. Available at http://www.genders.org/g38/g38_rowe_karlyn.html (accessed 13 June 2012).

17 Angela McRobbie, *Feminism and Youth Culture: From 'Jackie' to 'Just Seventeen'* (Boston, MA: Unwin Hyman, 1991).

18 Angela McRobbie, *The Aftermath of Feminism: Gender, Culture and Social Change* (London: Sage, 2009), p. 4.

19 Ibid., p. 5.

20 Ibid.

21 Ibid.

22 Valerie Walkerdine, *Daddy's Girl: Young Girls and Popular Culture* (Cambridge, MA: Harvard University Press, 1997); Valerie Walkerdine, Helen Lucey and June Melody, *Growing Up Girl: Psychosocial Explorations of Gender and Class* (New York: New York University Press, 2001); Bonnie J. Ross Leadbeater and Niobe Way (eds), *Urban Girls: Resisting Stereotypes, Creating Identities* (New York: New York University Press, 1996); Bonnie J. Ross Leadbeater and Niobe Way (eds), *Urban Girls Revisited: Building Strengths* (New York: New York University Press, 2007).

23 Sherrie A. Inness (ed.), *Delinquents and Debutantes: Twentieth-Century American Girls' Cultures* (New York: New York University Press, 1998); Catherine Driscoll, *Girls: Feminine Adolescence in Popular Culture*

and Cultural Theory (New York: Columbia University Press, 2002); Anita Harris, *Future Girl: Young Women in the Twenty-First Century* (New York: Routledge, 2004); Anita Harris (ed.), *All About the Girl: Culture, Power, and Identity* (New York: Routledge, 2004).

24 Susan Douglas, *Where the Girls Are: Growing Up Female with the Mass Media* (London: Penguin, 1994); Joan Smith, *Different for Girls: How Culture Creates Women* (London: Vintage, 1998); Emily White, *Fast Girls: Teenage Tribes and the Myth of the Slut* (New York: Simon and Schuster, 2002).

25 Frances K. Gateward and Murray Pomerance (eds), *Sugar, Spice, and Everything Nice: Cinemas of Girlhood* (Detroit, MI: Wayne State University Press, 2002); Murray Pomerance and Frances K. Gateward (eds), *Where the Boys Are: Cinemas of Masculinity and Youth* (Detroit, MI: Wayne State University Press, 2005); Mary Celeste Kearney, *Girls Make Media* (New York: Routledge, 2006).

26 Yvonne Tasker and Diane Negra (eds), *Interrogating Postfeminism: Gender and the Politics of Popular Culture* (Durham, NC: Duke University Press, 2007).

27 Yvonne Tasker and Diane Negra, 'Introduction: Feminist politics and postfeminist culture', in Tasker and Negra, *Interrogating Postfeminism*, pp. 1–25, p. 18.

28 Rebecca C. Hains, *Growing Up With Girl Power: Girlhood On Screen and in Everyday Life* (New York: Peter Lang, 2012).

29 Emilie Zaslow, *Feminism, Inc.: Coming of Age in Girl Power Media Culture* (New York: Palgrave Macmillan, 2009), p. 9.

30 Ibid., p. 138.

31 *Beetlejuice*, dir. Tim Burton, perf. Alec Baldwin, Geena Davis, Michael Keaton, and Winona Ryder (1988, Warner Bros), film; *Beverly Hills, 90210*, created by Darren Star (1990, Fox, prod. by 90210 Productions, Fair Dinkum Productions, Spelling Television and Torand Productions), television.

32 *Heathers*, dir. Michael Lehmann, perf. Winona Ryder, Christian Slater and Shannen Doherty (1988, New World Pictures), film; 'Fifty best high school movies', *Entertainment Weekly*, 22 September 2012. Available at http://www.ew.com/gallery/50-best-high-school-movies-0 (accessed 26 February 2014); 'The 500 greatest movies of all time', *Empire*, n.d. Available at http://www.empireonline.com/500/17.asp (accessed 26 February 2014); 'Box office/business for *Heathers*', Internet Movie Database (IMDb), n.d. Available at http://www.imdb.com/title/tt0097493/business (accessed 26 February 2014).

33 *Freeway*, dir. Matthew Bright, perf. Kiefer Sutherland, Reese Witherspoon and Brooke Shields (1996, Republic Pictures), film; *Just Another Girl on the IRT*, dir. Leslie Harris, perf. Ariyan A. Johnson. (1992, Miramax Films), film; *Mi Vida Loca*, dir. Allison Anders, perf. Angel Aviles, Seidy Lopez and Jacob Vargas (1992, Sony Pictures Classics), film; *GirlFight*, dir. Karyn Kusama, perf. Michelle Rodriguez, Santiago Douglas and Jaime Tirelli (2000, Screen Gems), film; *All Over Me*, dir. Alex Sichel, perf. Alison Folland, Tara Subkoff and Cole Hauser (1997, Alliance and Fine Line Features), film; *Boys Don't Cry*, dir. Kimberly Peirce, perf. Hilary Swank, Chloë Sevigny and Peter Sarsgaard (1999, Fox Searchlight Pictures), film; *Girl, Interrupted*, dir. James Mangold, perf. Winona Ryder, Angelina Jolie, and Brittany Murphy (1999, Columbia Pictures), film; *Foxfire*, dir. Annette Haywood-Carter, perf. Hedy Burress, Angelina Jolie and Jenny Lewis (1996, The Samuel Goldwyn Company), film; *Girls Town*, dir. Jim McKay, perf. Lili Taylor, Bruklin Harris and Anna Grace (1996, October Films), film. See Leslie Heywood, 'Film, third-wave', in *The Women's Movement Today: An Encyclopedia of Third-Wave Feminism*, vol. 1 (Westport, CT: Greenwood Publishing Co., 2006), pp. 148–54.

34 Kimberley Roberts, 'Pleasures and Problems of the "Angry Girl"' in *Sugar, Spice, and Everything Nice: Cinemas of Girlhood*, ed. Frances Gateward and Murray Pomerance (Detroit: Wayne State University Press, 2002), p. 217.

35 Ibid.

36 Ibid., p. 219.

37 Ibid., p. 217.

38 *Clueless*, dir. Amy Heckerling, perf. Alicia Silverstone, Stacey Dash, and Brittany Murph (1995, Paramount Pictures), film; *Spice World*, dir. Bob Spiers, perf. Melanie Brown, Emma Bunton, Melanie Chisholm, Geri Halliwell and Victoria Beckham (1997, PolyGram Filmed Entertainment and Columbia Pictures), film; *Election*, dir. Alexander Payne, perf. Matthew Broderick, Reese Witherspoon and Chris Klein (1999, Paramount Pictures), film; *Legally Blonde*, dir. Robert Luketic, perf. Reese Witherspoon, Luke Wilson, and Selma Blair (2001, Metro-Goldwyn-Mayer), film; *The Incredibly True Adventure of Two Girls in Love*, dir. Maria Maggenti, perf. Laurel Holloman, Nicole Ari Parker and Maggie Moore (1995, New Line Cinema, 1995), film; *But I'm a Cheerleader*, dir. Jamie Babbit, perf. Natasha Lyonne, Clea DuVall and Michelle Williams (1999, Lionsgate), film; *10 Things I Hate About You*, dir. Gil Junger, perf. Heath Ledger, Julia Stiles, Joseph Gordon-Levitt and

Larisa Oleynik (1999, Buena Vista Pictures), film; *She's the Man*, dir. Andy Fickman, perf. Amanda Bynes, Laura Ramsey and Channing Tatum (2006, DreamWorks), film.

39 Timothy Shary, 'The nerdy girl and her beautiful sister', in Gateward and Pomerance, *Sugar, Spice*, p. 249 n. 4.

40 *Dawson's Creek*; *Roswell*, created by Jonathon Dukes, developed by Jason Katims (1999, The WB, prod. by Jason Katims Productions, Regency Television and Twentieth Century Fox Television), television; *Felicity*; *Charmed*, created by Constance M. Burge (1998, The WB, prod. by Spelling Television), television; *7th Heaven*, created by Brenda Hampton (1996, The WB, prod. by Spelling Television and CBS Paramount Network Television), television; *Star Trek: Voyager*, created by Rick Berman, Michael Piller and Jeri Taylor (1995, UPN, prod. by Paramount Network Television), television; *Star Trek: Enterprise*, created by Rick Berman and Brannon Braga (2001, UPN, prod. by Paramount Network Television), television; *The Twilight Zone*, created by Rod Serling (2001, UPN, prod. by Paramount Network Television), television.

41 Elyce Rae Helford (ed.), *Fantasy Girls: Gender in the New Universe of Science Fiction and Fantasy Television* (Lanham, MD: Rowman & Littlefield, 2000); Sherrie A. Inness (ed.), *Action Chicks: New Images of Tough Women in Popular Culture* (New York: Palgrave Macmillan, 2004).

42 Charlotte Brunsdon, Julie D'Acci and Lynn Spigel (eds), *Feminist Television Criticism: A Reader* (Oxford: Clarendon Press, 1997), p. 5.

43 Bonnie J. Dow, *Prime-Time Feminism: Television, Media Culture, and the Women's Movement Since 1970* (Philadelphia, PA: University of Pennsylvania Press, 1996), p. 207.

44 Ibid., p. 214.

45 Janet McCabe and Kim Akass, 'Feminist television criticism: Notes and queries', *Critical Studies in Television* 1/1 (2006), pp. 108–20, p. 111.

46 Moorti, Sujata and Karen Ross, 'Reality television: Fairy tale or feminist nightmare?', *Feminist Media Studies* 4/2 (2004), pp. 203–31.

47 McCabe and Akass, 'Feminist television criticism', p. 115.

48 Jennifer Maher, 'The post-feminist mystique', *College Literature* 34/3 (2007), pp. 193–201, p. 200.

49 McCabe and Akass, 'Feminist television criticism', p. 114.

50 Ibid., p. 110.

51 Ibid., p. 114.

52 Ibid.

53 Merri Lisa Johnson, 'Introduction: Ladies love your box: The rhetoric of pleasure and danger in feminist television studies', in *Third Wave Feminism and Television: Jane Puts It in a Box* (London: I.B.Tauris, 2007), pp. 1–27.
54 John Fiske, *Understanding Popular Culture* (London: Routledge, 1989), p. 56. Cited in Johnson, p. 4.
55 Terry Eagleton, 'The ideology of the aesthetic', in Stephen Regan (ed.), *The Politics of Pleasure: Aesthetics and Cultural Theory* (Milton Keynes: Open University Press, 1992), pp. 17–31, 21. Cited in Johnson, pp. 7–8.
56 Johnson, 'Introduction', p. 6.
57 Ibid., p. 8 (emphasis in original).
58 Ibid.
59 Like McRobbie above, Mulvey has reflected on her earlier assumptions about cinematic viewing pleasure in her 1981 essay 'Afterthoughts on "Visual Pleasure and Narrative Cinema" inspired by King Vidor's *Duel in the Sun* (1946)', included in her collection, *Visual and Other Pleasures* (Bloomington, IN: Indiana University Press, 1989), pp. 32–3.
60 Johnson, 'Introduction', p. 19.
61 Ibid.
62 Ibid., p. 16.
63 Ibid., p. 8.
64 Karras, 'The third wave's final girl'.
65 Ibid.
66 Byers, '*Buffy the Vampire Slayer*', p. 175.
67 Ibid., p. 178.
68 Karras, 'The third wave's final girl'.
69 Byers, '*Buffy the Vampire Slayer*', p. 177.
70 Ibid., pp. 172–3.
71 Karras, 'The third wave's final girl'.
72 Byers, '*Buffy the Vampire Slayer*', p. 179.
73 Ibid., p. 182.
74 Ibid., p. 179.
75 Ibid., p. 184–5.
76 Karras, 'The third wave's final girl'; Byers, '*Buffy the Vampire Slayer*', p. 171.
77 Karras, 'The third wave's final girl'.
78 Byers, '*Buffy the Vampire Slayer*', p. 172.
79 Karras, 'The third wave's final girl'.
80 McRobbie, pp. 5, 8.
81 Ibid., p. 6.

82 Ibid., p. 10.
83 Ibid., p. 11.
84 Ibid., p. 60.
85 Ibid., p. 6.
86 Tasker and Negra, 'Introduction', p. 19.
87 Ibid., p. 2.
88 Ibid., pp. 2–3.
89 Diane Negra, *What a Girl Wants? Fantasizing the Reclamation of Self in Postfeminism* (London and New York: Routledge, 2009), p. 2.
90 Ibid., p. 6.
91 Linda Williams, 'Why I did not want to write this essay', *Signs* 30/1: *Beyond the Gaze: Recent Approaches to Film Feminisms* (Autumn 2004), pp. 1264–72, p. 1264. Cited in Johnson, p. 11.
92 Ibid., pp. 1266–7. Cited in Johnson, p. 11.
93 Gayle Wald, 'Clueless in the neocolonial world order', in Gateward and Pomerance, *Sugar, Spice*, pp. 103–23.
94 Gayle Wald, '"I want it that way": teenybopper music and the girling of boy bands', *Genders* 35 (2002). Available at http://www.genders.org/g35/g35_wald.html (accessed 3 June 2012).

Chapter 3: 'Kicking Ass is Comfort Food': Buffy as Third-Wave Feminist Icon

1 Joss Whedon, qtd in Mim Udovitch, 'What makes Buffy slay?', *Rolling Stone,* July 2000, pp. 40–1.
2 Rebecca Munford, '"Wake up and smell the lipgloss": Gender, generation and the (a)politics of girl power', in Stacy Gillis, Gillian Howie and Rebecca Munford (eds), *Third Wave Feminism: A Critical Exploration* (New York: Palgrave Macmillan, 2004), pp. 142–53, pp. 144–5.
3 Ednie Kaeh Garrison, 'US feminism-grrrl style! Youth (sub)cultures and the technologics of the third wave', *Feminist Studies* 26/1 (2000), pp. 141–70, p. 145.
4 Ibid., p. 143.
5 Ibid., p. 142.
6 Munford, '"Wake up and smell the lipgloss"', p. 144.
7 Rebecca Walker (ed.), *To Be Real: Telling the Truth and Changing the Face of Feminism* (New York: Anchor Books, 1995); Barbara Findlen (ed.), *Listen Up: Voices from the Next Feminist Generation* (Emeryville, CA: Seal Press, 2001);

Jason Schultz, 'Getting off on feminism', in Walker, *To Be Real*, pp. 107–26; Rebecca Walker, interview with Veronica Webb, 'How does a supermodel do feminism?' in Walker, *To Be Real*, pp. 209–18; Anastasia Higginbotham, 'Chicks goin' at it', in Findlen, *Listen Up*, pp. 11–18.

8 R. Claire Snyder, 'What is third-wave feminism? A new directions essay', *Signs* 34/1 (2008), pp. 175–96, pp. 177–8.

9 Rebecca Walker, '"Becoming the third wave", from *Ms* magazine', in Leslie Heywood (ed.), *The Women's Movement Today: An Encyclopedia of Third-Wave Feminism*, vol. 2 (Westport, CT: Greenwood Publishing Co., 2006), pp. 3–5, p. 4.

10 Ibid.

11 Ibid., p. 5.

12 Ibid., pp. 4–5.

13 Ibid., p. 5.

14 Ibid.

15 Ibid.

16 Ibid.

17 Ibid.

18 Jennifer Baumgardner and Amy Richards, *Manifesta: Young Women, Feminism, and the Future* (New York: Farrar, Straus and Giroux, 2000).

19 Marcelle Karp and Debbie Stoller (eds), *The BUST Guide to the New Girl Order* (New York: Penguin, 1999); Lisa Jervis and Andi Zeisler (eds), *bitchfest: Ten Years of Cultural Criticism from the Pages of Bitch Magazine* (New York: Farrar, Straus & Giroux, 2006).

20 *Bitch Media*, 'Our history', n.d. Available at http://bitchmagazine.org/history (accessed 9 September 2013).

21 Snyder, 'What is third-wave feminism?', p. 181.

22 Leslie Heywood and Jennifer Drake (eds), *Third Wave Agenda: Being Feminist, Doing Feminism* (Minneapolis: University of Minnesota Press, 1997); Leslie Heywood (ed.), *The Women's Movement Today: An Encyclopedia of Third-Wave Feminism*, vols 1 and 2 (Westport, CT: Greenwood Publishing Co., 2006); Stacy Gillis, Gillian Howie and Rebecca Munford (eds), *Third Wave Feminism: A Critical Exploration* (Basingstoke: Palgrave Macmillan, 2004).

23 Angela McRobbie, 'Postfeminism and popular culture', *Feminist Media Studies* 4/3 (2004), pp. 255–64, p. 255.

24 Ibid., p. 259.

25 Ibid., pp. 258–9.

26 Munford, '"Wake up and smell the lipgloss"', p. 143.

27 Ibid.

28 Snyder, 'What is third-wave feminism?', p. 192.
29 Amber E. Kinser, 'Negotiating spaces for/through third-wave feminism', *NWSA Journal* 16/3 (2004), pp. 124–53.
30 Garrison, 'US feminism-grrrl style!', p. 165, n. 3.; Stephanie Gilmore, 'Looking back, thinking ahead: Third wave feminism in the United States', *Journal of Women's History* 12/4 (2001), pp. 215–21, p. 218.
31 Rory Cooke Dicker and Alison Piepmeier, 'Introduction', in Rory Cooke Dicker and Alison Piepmeier (eds), *Catching a Wave: Reclaiming Feminism for the Twenty-first Century* (Boston, MA: Northeastern University Press, 2003), pp. 3–28, p. 5.
32 Rachel Fudge, 'The Buffy effect: Or, a tale of cleavage and marketing', *Bitch: Feminist Response to Pop Culture* 10 (1999), para. 8. Available at http://bitchmagazine.org/article/buffy-effect (accessed 3 June 2012).
33 Irene Karras, 'The third wave's final girl: Buffy the Vampire Slayer', *thirdspace* 1.2 (2002), para. 15. Available at http://journals.sfu.ca/thirdspace/index.php/journal/article/viewArticle/karras/50 (accessed 14 June 2012).
34 Michele Byers, '*Buffy the Vampire Slayer*: The next generation of television', in Dicker and Piepmeier, *Catching a Wave*, pp. 171–87, pp. 171–2.
35 Sophie Levy, '"You still my girl?": Adolescent femininity as resistance in *Buffy the Vampire Slayer*', *Reconstruction* 3/1 (2003), para. 3. Available at http://reconstruction.eserver.org/Issues/031/levy.htm (accessed 11 June 2012).
36 Elyce Rae Helford, '"My emotions give me power": The containment of girls' anger in Buffy', in Rhonda Wilcox and David Lavery (eds), *Fighting the Forces: What's at Stake in* Buffy the Vampire Slayer (Lanham, MD: Rowman and Littlefield, 2002), pp. 18–34, p. 24.
37 Ginia Bellafante, 'Is feminism dead?', *Time*, 29 June 1998, pp. 53–60, p. 54.
38 Rita Panahi, 'Reaction to Margaret Thatcher's passing proves feminism is about politics, not equality', *Herald Sun*, 10 April 2013. Available at http://www.heraldsun.com.au/news/opinion/reaction-to-margaret-thatchers-passing-proves-feminism-is-about-politics-not-equality/story-e6frfhqf-1226616184704 (accessed 17 June 2013); Cathy Young, 'Margaret Thatcher and feminism', *Real Clear Politics*, 18 April 2013. Available at http://www.realclearpolitics.com/articles/2013/04/18/margaret_thatcher_and_feminism_118018.html (accessed 17 June 2013).
39 Amanda Foreman, 'Why the Iron Lady was the ultimate women's libber', *Mail Online*, 3 February 2013. Available at http://www.dailymail.co.uk/femail/article-2085368/Margaret-Thatcher-The-Iron-Lady-ultimate-womens-libber.html (accessed 17 June 2013).

40 Panahi, 'Reaction to Margaret Thatcher's passing'; Emma Barnett, 'Margaret Thatcher: ultimate feminist icon – whether she liked it or not', *The Telegraph*, 8 April 2013. Available at http://www.telegraph.co.uk/women/womens-politics/9979076/Margaret-Thatcher-ultimate-feminist-icon-whether-she-liked-it-or-not.html (accessed 17 June 2013).

41 Ibid.

42 Lionel Shriver, 'Thatcher was a real feminist', *The Sydney Morning Herald*, 9 April 2013. Available at http://www.smh.com.au/comment/thatcher-was-a-real-feminist-20130409-2hibr.html (accessed 17 June 2013).

43 Hadley Freeman, 'Margaret Thatcher was no feminist', *The Guardian*, 10 April 2013. Available at http://www.guardian.co.uk/commentisfree/2013/apr/09/margaret-thatcher-no-feminist (accessed 17 June 2013).

44 Ibid.

45 Jessica White, 'Is Margaret Thatcher really worth redeeming?', *Al Jazeera*, 20 April 2013. Available at http://www.aljazeera.com/indepth/opinion/2013/04/201341882140384449.html (accessed 15 June 2013).

46 Freeman, 'Margaret Thatcher was no feminist'; Clara Fischer, 'Iron Lady was a self-serving anti-feminist', *The Irish Times*, 12 April 2013. Available at http://www.irishtimes.com/news/social-affairs/iron-lady-was-a-self-serving-anti-feminist-1.1357706 (accessed 17 June 2013).

47 Freeman, 'Margaret Thatcher was no feminist'.

48 White, 'Is Margaret Thatcher really worth redeeming?'.

49 Ibid.

50 Ibid.

51 Ibid.

52 Rachel Roberts, '"Feminists should weep" at the death of Margaret Thatcher – and why would that be, exactly?', *The Independent*, 10 April 2013. Available at http://www.independent.co.uk/voices/comment/feminists-should-weep-at-the-death-of-margaret-thatcher–and-why-would-that-be-exactly-8567202.html (accessed 15 June 2013).

53 Rhonda V. Wilcox, '"Show me your world": Exiting the text and the globalization of *Buffy*', keynote address to the *Staking a Claim: Global Buffy, Local Identities*, 22 July 2003, University of South Australia, Adelaide.

54 Leslie Heywood and Jennifer Drake, 'We learn America like a script: Activism in the third wave; or, enough phantoms of nothing', in Heywood and Drake, *Third Wave Agenda*, pp. 40–54, p. 47.

55 Baumgardner and Richards, *Manifesta*, p. 85.

56 Ibid.

57 Garrison, 'US feminism-grrrl style!'.
58 Ibid., p. 149.
59 Baumgardner and Richards, *Manifesta*, p. 77.
60 Heywood and Drake, 'We learn America like a script', p. 49.
61 Leslie Heywood and Jennifer Drake, 'Introduction' in Heywood and Drake, *Third Wave Agenda*, pp. 1–20, p. 13.
62 Stacy Gillis and Rebecca Munford, 'Introduction: Harvesting our strengths: Third wave feminism and Women's Studies', *Journal of International Women's Studies* 4/2 (2003), pp. 1–6, pp. 3–4.
63 Rebecca L. Clark Mane, 'Transmuting grammars of whiteness in third-wave feminism: Interrogating postrace histories, postmodern abstraction, and the proliferation of difference in third-wave texts', *Signs* 38/1 (2012), pp. 71–98, p. 72.
64 Kimberly Springer, 'Third Wave Black Feminism?', *Signs* 27/4 (2002), pp. 1061–2.
65 Sherin Saadallah, 'Muslim feminism in the third wave: A reflective inquiry', in Gillis, Howie and Munford, *Third Wave Feminism*, pp. 216–26, p. 216.
66 Winnie Woodhull, 'Global feminisms, transnational political economies, third world cultural production', *Journal of International Women's Studies* 4/3 (2003), pp. 76–90, p. 78.
67 Ibid.
68 Wilcox, 'Show me your world', p. 95.
69 Kathleen Rowe Karlyn, '*Scream*, popular culture, and feminism's third wave: "I'm not my mother"', *Genders* 38 (2003), para. 21. Available at http://www.genders.org/g38/g38_rowe_karlyn.html (accessed 13 June 2012).
70 Ibid.
71 Snyder, 'What is third-wave feminism?', p. 186.
72 Leslie Heywood, 'Postmodern theory', in *The Women's Movement Today: An Encyclopedia of Third-Wave Feminism*, vol. 1 (Westport, CT: Greenwood Publishing Co., 2006), pp. 257–8.
73 R. Claire Snyder-Hall, 'Third-wave feminism and the defense of "choice"', *Perspectives on Politics* 8/1 (2010), pp. 255–61, p. 259.
74 Snyder, 'What is third-wave feminism?', p. 183.
75 Leslie Heywood, 'Transgender', in *The Women's Movement*, vol. 2, p. 326.
76 Snyder, 'What is third-wave feminism?', pp. 187–8.
77 Ibid., p. 187.
78 Ibid., p. 183.
79 Fudge, 'The Buffy effect', para. 17.

Chapter 4: Whose Revolution Has Been Televised?: Race, Whiteness and 'Transnational' Slayer Suffrage

1 Kent A. Ono, 'To be a vampire on *Buffy the Vampire Slayer*: Race and ("Other") socially marginalized positions on horror TV', in Elyce Rae Helford (ed.), *Fantasy Girls: Gender in the New Universe of Science Fiction and Fantasy Television* (New York: Rowman & Littlefield, 2000), pp. 163–86, p. 163.

2 Ibid., pp. 164–70.

3 Ibid., p. 168 (emphasis in original).

4 Vivian Chin, 'Buffy? She's like me, she's not like me – she's rad', in Frances Early and Kathleen Kennedy (eds), *Athena's Daughters: Television's New Women Warriors* (Syracuse, NY: Syracuse University Press, 2003), pp. 92–102, p. 93.

5 Ibid.

6 Ibid., p. 94.

7 Ewan Kirkland, 'The Caucasian persuasion of *Buffy the Vampire Slayer*', *Slayage: The Journal of the Whedon Studies Association* 5/1 (2005). Available at http://slayageonline.com/PDF/kirkland.pdf (accessed 5 August 2013).

8 Naomi Alderman and Annette Seidel-Arpaci, 'Imaginary para-sites of the soul: Vampires and representations of 'Blackness' and 'Jewishness' in the Buffy/Angelverse', *Slayage: The Journal of the Whedon Studies Association* 3/2 (2003). Available at http://slayageonline.com/PDF/alderman_seidel-arpaci.pdf (accessed 5 August 2013).

9 Elyce Rae Helford, '"My emotions give me power": The containment of girls' anger in Buffy', in Rhonda Wilcox and David Lavery (eds), *Fighting the Forces: What's at Stake in Buffy the Vampire Slayer* (Lanham, MD: Rowman and Littlefield, 2002), pp. 18–34, pp. 26–30.

10 Lynne Edwards, 'Slaying in Black and White: Kendra as tragic mulatta in *Buffy*', ibid., pp. 85–97, p. 87.

11 Jessica Hautsch, 'Staking her colonial claim: Colonial discourses, assimilation, soul-making, and ass-kicking in *Buffy the Vampire Slayer*', *Slayage: The Journal of the Whedon Studies Association* 9/1 (2011). Available at http://slayageonline.com/essays/slayage33/Hautsch.pdf (accessed 5 August 2013).

12 Ono, 'To be a vampire', pp. 168–9.

13 Neal King, 'Brownskirts: Fascism, Christianity, and the eternal demon', in James B. South (ed.), Buffy the Vampire Slayer *and Philosophy: Fear and*

Trembling in Sunnydale (Chicago, IL: Open Court, 2003), pp. 197–211, p. 198.

14 Cynthia Fuchs, 'Did anyone ever explain to you what "secret identity" means?': Race and displacement in *Buffy* and *Dark Angel*', in Elana Levine and Lisa Parks (eds), *Undead TV: Essays on* Buffy the Vampire Slayer (Durham, NC and London: Duke University Press, 2007), pp. 96–115, p. 101.

15 Ibid., p. 101.

16 Ibid., p. 102 (emphasis in original).

17 Ibid.

18 Ibid., p. 105.

19 Ibid., pp. 106–7.

20 Arwen Spicer, '"It's bloody brilliant!" The undermining of metanarrative feminism in the Season Seven arc narrative of *Buffy*', *Slayage: The Journal of the Whedon Studies Association* 4/3 (2004). Available at http://slayageonline.com/PDF/spicer2.pdf (accessed 4 June 2012).

21 For examples, see James South, 'On the philosophical consistency of Season Seven: Or, "It's not about right, not about wrong…"', *Slayage: The Journal of the Whedon Studies Association* 4/3 [15] (2004). Available at http://slayageonline.com/PDF/south.pdf (accessed 7 June 2012); Michael J. Richardson and J. Douglas Rabb, *The Existential Joss Whedon: Evil and Human Freedom in* Buffy the Vampire Slayer, Angel, Firefly *and* Serenity (Jefferson, NC: McFarland, 2007); Gregory Stevenson, *Televised Morality: The Case of* Buffy the Vampire Slayer (Lanham, MD: Hamilton Books, 2004); and James B. South, 'Kiss kiss, stake stake: Storytelling and the philosophical pleasures of Season Seven', in Lynne Y. Edwards, Elizabeth L. Rambo and James B. South (eds), *Buffy Goes Dark: Essays on the Final Two Seasons of* Buffy the Vampire Slayer *on Television* (Jefferson, NC: McFarland, 2009), pp. 198–210.

22 Kevin K. Durand, 'The battle against the patriarchal forces of darkness', in his *Buffy Meets the Academy: Essays on the Episodes and Scripts as Texts* (Jefferson, NC: McFarland, 2009), pp. 176–84, p. 176.

23 Christine Hoffman, 'Happiness is a warm scythe: The evolution of villainy and weaponry in the Buffyverse', *Slayage: The Journal of the Whedon Studies Association* 7/3 (2009), para. 31. Available at http://slayageonline.com/essays/slayage27/Hoffmann.htm (accessed 7 August 2013).

24 Paul Hawkins, 'Season Six and the supreme ordeal', in Edwards, Rambo and South, *Buffy Goes Dark*, pp. 183–97, p. 184.

25 Gregory Erickson and Jennifer Lemberg, 'Bodies and narrative in crisis: Figures of rupture and chaos in Seasons Six and Seven', in Edwards, Rambo and South, *Buffy Goes Dark*, pp. 114–29, pp. 114–17.
26 Rhonda V. Wilcox, '"Set on this earth like a bubble": Word as flesh in the dark seasons', in Edwards, Rambo and South, *Buffy Goes Dark*, pp. 95–113, pp. 95–6.
27 Michael Adams, 'Buffy and the death of style', in Edwards, Rambo and South, *Buffy Goes Dark*, pp. 83–94, p. 83.
28 Lynne Y. Edwards and Carly Haines, 'Reality bites: Buffy in the UPN years', in Edwards, Rambo and South, *Buffy Goes Dark*, pp. 130–42, pp. 135–9.
29 Trish Salah, 'Of activist fandoms, auteur pedagogy and imperial feminism: from *Buffy the Vampire Slayer* to *I am Du'a Khalil*', in Lisa Taylor and Jasmin Zine (eds), *Muslim Women, Transnational Feminism and the Ethics of Pedagogy: Contested Imaginaries in post-9/11 Cultural Practice* (New York: Routledge, 2014), pp. 152–74, 158–9.
30 Ibid., p. 159.
31 David Solomon and Joss Whedon, *Buffy the Vampire Slayer: The Complete Seventh Season, 'Lessons'*, perf. Sarah Michelle Gellar, Nicholas Brendon and Emma Caulfield (Twentieth Century Fox, 2004), DVD audio commentary.
32 Ibid.
33 Ibid.
34 Gayatri Spivak, 'Three women's texts and the critique of imperialism', *Critical Inquiry* 12/1 (1985), pp. 243–61.
35 Ibid., p. 251.
36 Ibid., p. 243.
37 Ibid., p. 244.
38 *Run Lola Run*, dir. Tom Tykwer, perf. Franka Potente and Moritz Bleibtreu (1999, Sony Pictures Classics), film.
39 *Blade Runner*, dir. Ridley Scott, perf. Harrison Ford, Rutger Hauer and Sean Young (1982, Warner Bros), film.
40 My thanks to Ellen McGeoch for drawing this episode to my attention and for sharing her insights on Chao Ahn's characterisation.
41 I am grateful to Stacey Abbott for clarification on this point. The World Series was initially named after the New York *World* newspaper.
42 This is not restricted to criticisms of race; in many cases people feel it necessary to apologise for any critique of *Buffy*.
43 Gayle Wald, 'Just a girl? Rock music, feminism, and the cultural construction of female youth', *Signs: Journal of Women in Culture and Society* 23/3 (1998), pp. 585–610.

44 Samuel A. Chambers and Daniel Williford, 'Anti-imperialism in the Buffy-verse: Challenging the mythos of Bush as vampire slayer', *Poroi* 3/2 (December 2004), pp. 109–29, p. 123. Available at http://ir.uiowa.edu/cgi/viewcontent.cgi?article=1040&context=poroi (accessed 5 August 2013).
45 Jeffrey L. Pasley, 'You can't pin a good Slayer down: The politics, if any, of *Buffy the Vampire Slayer* and *Angel*', *Pasley Brothers*, 2003. Available at http://www.pasleybrothers.com/jeff/writings/buffy.htm (accessed 6 March 2014); Jeffrey L. Pasley, 'Old familiar vampires: The politics of the Buffyverse', in South, Buffy the Vampire Slayer *and Philosophy*, pp. 254–67.
46 Helen Graham, 'Post-pleasure: representations, ideologies and affects of a newly post-9/11 "feminist icon"', *Feminist Media Studies* 7/1 (2007), pp. 1–15, p. 3.
47 Dennis Showalter, 'Buffy goes to war: Military themes and images in *Buffy the Vampire Slayer*', paper presented to The *Slayage* Conference on *Buffy the Vampire Slayer*, Nashville, TN, 28–30 May 2004. Available at http://slayageonline.com/SCBtVS_Archive/Talks/Showalter.pdf (accessed 5 August 2013).
48 King, 'Brownskirts', pp. 203–5.
49 Jonah Goldberg, 'Buffy, the UN slayer', *TownHall*, 26 September 2002. Available at http://townhall.com/columnists/jonahgoldberg/2002/09/26/buffy,_the_un_slayer (accessed 5 August 2013).
50 Anthony H. Cordesman, 'Biological warfare and the "Buffy paradigm"', Centre for Strategic and International Studies, 29 September 2001. p. 3. Available at http://csis.org/files/media/csis/pubs/buffy012902[1].pdf (accessed 5 March 2014).
51 Ensley F. Guffey, '"We just declared war": Buffy as general', *Watcher Junior* 5/1 (2011). Available at http://www.watcherjunior.tv/06/guffey.php (accessed 5 August 2013).
52 Martin Buinicki and Anthony Enns, 'Buffy the vampire disciplinarian: Institutional excess, spiritual technologies, and the new economy of power', *Slayage: The Journal of the Whedon Studies Association* 1/4 (2001). Available at http://slayageonline.com/PDF/buinicki_enns.pdf (accessed 5 August 2013).
53 Kim Kirkpatrick, 'Scoobies and Potentials: the Slayer community as hero in *Buffy the Vampire Slayer*', *MP JOURNAL* 1/4 (2006). Available at http://academinist.org/wp-content/uploads/2010/06/kirkpatrick.pdf (accessed 5 August 2013).
54 Laura Bush, 'The Taliban's war against women', radio address to the nation, Crawford, Texas, 17 November 2001. Available at http://2001–2009.state.gov/g/drl/rls/rm/2001/6206.htm (accessed 7 June 2013).

55 See Purnima Bose, 'From humanitarian intervention to the beautifying mission: Afghan women and beauty without borders', *Genders* 51 (2010). Available at http://www.genders.org/g51/g51_bose.html (accessed 5 August 2013).
56 Christina Ho, 'Responding to Orientalist feminism: Women's rights and the War on Terror', *Australian Feminist Studies* 25/66 (2010), pp. 433–9, p. 433.
57 Ibid., p. 434.
58 Sharon Smith, 'Using women's rights to sell Washington's war', *International Socialist Review* 21 (2002). Available at http://isreview.org/issues/21/afghan_women.shtml (accessed 5 August 2013).
59 Ibid.
60 Carol A. Stabile and Deepa Kumar, 'Unveiling imperialism: media, gender and the war on Afghanistan', *Media, Culture and Society* 27/5 (2005), pp. 765–82, p. 765.
61 Ibid., p. 766.
62 Ibid., p. 769.
63 Ibid., p. 770.
64 Ho, 'Responding to Orientalist feminism', p. 433.
65 Stabile and Kumar, 'Unveiling imperialism', p. 770.
66 '"Joss Whedon Answers 100 questions", *SFX* Magazine/2002. From *SFX*, Future Publishing, 2002', in David Lavery and Cynthia Burkhead (eds), *Joss Whedon: Conversations* (Jackson, MS: University of Mississippi Press, 2011), pp. 34–41, p. 39.
67 Salah, 'Of activist fandoms', pp. 160–1.
68 Spivak, 'Three women's texts', p. 244.

Chapter 5: Becoming Worthy of Buffy: Performing Masculinity in a Patriarchal World

1 An enormous amount of scholarship has been published on Angel and Spike. As particularly powerful 'gateway drugs', see Stacey Abbott (ed.), *Reading* Angel*: The TV Spin-off with a Soul* (London: I.B.Tauris, 2005); Allison McCracken, 'At stake: Angel's body, fantasy masculinity, and queer desire in teen television', in Elana Levine and Lisa Parks (eds), *Undead TV: Essays on Buffy the Vampire Slayer* (Durham, NC: Duke University Press, 2007), pp. 116–44; Gwyn Symonds, '"Bollocks!": Spike fans and reception of *Buffy the Vampire Slayer*, *Refractory: A Journal*

of Entertainment Media, 18 March 2003. Available at http://refractory.unimelb.edu.au/2003/03/18/bollocks-spike-fans-and-reception-of-buffy-the-vampire-slayer-gwyn-symonds/ (accessed 4 June 2012); Arwen Spicer, 'Love's bitch but man enough to admit it': Spike's hybridized gender', *Slayage: The Online International Journal* 2/3 (December 2002).

2 I am grateful to Stacey Abbott for directing me to this connection.

3 Other examples include the 'retinal scan' used to access Initiative headquarters (which Xander mishears as 'rectal scan' in 'The "I" in Team' (4.13), the monitored elevator that Xander refers to as a 'man-sized microwave' in the same episode', images of Spike as the 'lab rat', 'Hostile 17' in 'The Initiative' (4.7) and Buffy's dream about kissing Riley in front of her psychology class at the beginning of 'Hush' (4.10).

4 Lorna Jowett, *Sex and the Slayer: A Gender Studies Primer for the Buffy Fan* (Middletown, CT: Wesleyan University Press, 2005), p. 104.

5 See Frances Early, 'Staking her claim: Buffy the Vampire Slayer as transgressive woman warrior', *Journal of Popular Culture* 35/3 (Winter 2001), pp. 11–27.

6 Douglas Petrie, *Buffy the Vampire Slayer: The Complete Fourth Season, 'The Initiative'*, perf. Sarah Michelle Gellar, Nicholas Brendon and Alyson Hannigan (Twentieth Century Fox, 2002), DVD audio commentary; Stevie Simkin, '"Who died and made you John Wayne?": Anxious masculinity in *Buffy the Vampire Slayer*', *Slayage: The Online International Journal* 3/3–4 (2004). Available at http://slayageonline.com/PDF/simkin_wayne.pdf (accessed 5 June 2012), cited by Jowett, *Sex and the Slayer*, pp. 103, 104.

7 As Michelle Sagara West puts it: 'The Scoobies were misfits. They managed to be cute without projecting *cute* […] Alyson Hannigan was the nerd's nerd. Nicholas Brendan's Xander was the witty pop culture guru who couldn't get a date with something that wasn't trying to eat him or his friends, and Sarah Michelle Gellar's Buffy, although beautiful was considered too weird for words […] Riley Finn was parachuted into the archetypal Buffy landscape when he clearly had no such outsider archetype to anchor himself to' ('For the love of Riley', in Glenn Yeffeth (ed.), *Seven Seasons of Buffy: Science Fiction and Fantasy Authors Discuss Their Favorite Television Show* (Dallas, TX: BenBella Books, 2003), pp. 65–71, p. 66.

8 Robert W. Connell, *Masculinities*, 2nd edn (Crows Nest, NSW: Allen and Unwin, 2005), p. xii.

9 Rachel Adams and David Savran (eds), *The Masculinity Studies Reader* (Malden, MA: Blackwell Publishing, 2002), p. 5.

10 Tim Carrigan, Bob Connell and John Lee, 'Toward a new sociology of masculinity', *Theory and Society* 14/5 (1985), pp. 561–604.
11 Robert W. Connell, *Masculinities* (St Leonards, NSW: Allen & Unwin, 1995) and *Masculinities*, 2nd edn, p. xiii.
12 David Buchbinder, *Studying Men and Masculinities* (Oxford: Routledge, 2013), p. 90.
13 Robert W. Connell and James W. Messerschmidt, 'Hegemonic masculinity: rethinking the concept', *Gender and Society* 19/6 (2005), pp. 829–59, p. 832 (emphasis in original).
14 John Hartley, 'Hegemony' in Tim O'Sullivan, John Hartley, Danny Saunders, Martin Montgomery and John Fiske (eds), *Key Concepts in Communication and Cultural Studies*, 2nd edn (London: Routledge, 1994), p. 135.
15 Michael S. Kimmel, 'Masculinity as homophobia: Fear, shame, and silence in the construction of gender identity', in Stephen M. Whitehead and Frank J. Barrett (eds), *The Masculinities Reader* (Cambridge: Polity, 2001), pp. 266–87.
16 Buchbinder, *Studying Men and Masculinities*, p. 94 (emphasis in original).
17 Ibid. (emphasis in original).
18 Ibid., p. 79.
19 Michel Foucault, *Discipline and Punish: The Birth of the Prison*, trans. Alan Sheridan (New York: Pantheon Books, 1977).
20 Ibid., p. 201.
21 Buchbinder, *Studying Men and Masculinities*, p. 81.
22 Ibid., pp. 80–1 (emphasis in original).
23 See West, 'For the love of Riley'.
24 Eve Sedgwick, 'Introduction', in her *Between Men: English Literature and Male Homosocial Desire* (New York: Columbia University Press, 1985), p. 1, cited in Buchbinder, *Studying Men and Masculinities*, pp. 82–3.
25 Kimmel, 'Masculinity as homophobia', pp. 266–87 (emphasis added).
26 Buchbinder, *Studying Men and Masculinities*, p. 101 (emphasis in original).
27 Brenton J. Malin, *American Masculinity Under Clinton: Popular Media and the Nineties' Crisis of Masculinity* (New York: Peter Lang, 2005), p. 149.
28 Ibid., p. 150.
29 Frank J. Barrett, 'The organisation of hegemonic masculinity: the case of the US Navy', in Adams and Savran, *The Masculinities Studies Reader*, pp. 77–99, pp. 80–1.
30 William Arkin and Lynne R. Dobrofsky, 'Military socialization and masculinity', *Journal of Social Issues* 34 (1978), pp. 151–68, cited by Barrett, The organisation of hegemonic masculinity', p. 77.

31 Richard Dyer, 'The white man's muscles', in Adams and Savran, *The Masculinities Studies Reader*, pp. 262–73.
32 Ibid., p. 265.
33 Ibid.
34 Buffy in conversation with Angel, 'Sanctuary' (1.19), *Angel the Series*, 2000.
35 Steve Rogers became 'Captain America' after volunteering for Operation: Rebirth, a project intended to enhance US soldiers to the height of physical perfection via 'Super Solider Serum'. The process successfully altered his physiology from its frail state to the maximum of human efficiency, including greatly enhanced musculature and reflexes; Marvel Universe Wiki, 'Captain America (Steve Rogers)'. Available at http://marvel.com/universe/Captain_America_(Steve_Rogers) (accessed 6 March 2014).

Chapter 6: 'From Beneath You It Devours': Andrew and the Homoerotics of Evil

1 On Willow and Tara, see: Farah Mendelsohn, 'Surpassing the love of vampires; or why (and how) a queer reading of Buffy/Willow is denied', in Rhonda V. Wilcox and David Lavery (eds), *Fighting the Forces: What's at Stake in* Buffy the Vampire Slayer (Lanham, MD: Rowman & Littlefield, 2002), pp. 45–60; Jes Battis, *Blood Relations: Chosen Families in* Buffy the Vampire Slayer *and* Angel (Jefferson, NC: McFarland, 2005); Rebecca Beirne, 'Queering the Slayer-text: Reading possibilities in *Buffy the Vampire Slayer*', *Refractory: A Journal of Entertainment Media* 5 (2004). Available at http://blogs.arts.unimelb.edu.au/refractory/category/browse-past-volumes/volume-5/ (accessed 18 February 2009); and Em McAvan, '"I think I'm kinda gay": Willow Rosenberg and the absent/present bisexual in *Buffy the Vampire Slayer*', *Slayage: The Online International Journal of Buffy Studies* 6/4 (2007). Available at http://slayageonline.com/Numbers/slayage24.htm (accessed 18 February 2009). For other studies which analyse ostensibly straight male characters see: Stevie Simkin, '"Who died and made you John Wayne?": Anxious masculinity in *Buffy the Vampire Slayer*', *Slayage: The Online International Journal* 3/3–4 (2004), para. 12 and fn 5. Available at http://slayageonline.com/PDF/simkin_wayne.pdf (accessed 18 February 2009); Battis, *Blood Relations*; Lorna Jowett, *Sex and the Slayer: A Gender Studies Primer for the Buffy Fan* (Middletown, CT: Wesleyan University Press, 2005); Marc Camron, 'The importance of being the Zeppo: Xander, gender identity and hybridity in *Buffy the Vampire Slayer*', *Slayage: The Online International Journal of Buffy Studies*

6/3 (2007). Available at http://slayageonline.com/Numbers/slayage23.htm (accessed 18 February 2009); Allison McCracken, 'At stake: Angel's body, fantasy masculinity, and queer desire in teen television', in Elana Levine and Lisa Parks (eds), *Undead TV: Essays on Buffy the Vampire Slayer* (Durham, NC: Duke University Press, 2007), pp. 116–44; and Cynthea Masson and Marni Stanley, 'Queer eye of that vampire guy: Spike and the aesthetics of camp', *Slayage: The Online International Journal of Buffy Studies* 6/2 (2006). Available at http://slayageonline.com/Numbers/slayage_22.htm (accessed 18 February 2009).

2 B. Ruby Rich, 'New Queer Cinema', *Sight and Sound* 2/5 (September 1992), pp. 31–4.

3 Michele Aaron, 'New Queer Cinema: An Introduction', in Michele Aaron (ed.), *New Queer Cinema: A Critical Reader* (Edinburgh: Edinburgh University Press, 2004), pp. 3–14, pp. 3–4.

4 Ibid., p. 5.

5 Ibid. (emphasis added).

6 Ibid., p. 7.

7 Ibid., p. 10.

8 Mendelsohn, 'Surpassing the love of vampires'.

9 McCracken, 'At stake', p. 118.

10 Ibid., pp. 118–19.

11 Patricia Pender, '"Why can't you just masturbate like the rest of us?" Andrew and the erotics of fandom in "Storyteller"', paper presented to the Slayage Conference on Whedonverses, 26–28 May 2006, Gordon College, Georgia.

12 Quoted in Stevie Simkin, 'The wit and wisdom of Joss Whedon', *Slayage: The Online International Journal of Buffy Studies*. Available at http://slayageonline.com/pages/Wit_Wisdom_Joss_Whedon.pdf (accessed 3 March 2014).

13 Simkin, "Who died and made you John Wayne?".

14 Ibid., para. 12.

15 Ibid., para. 28.

16 Jowett, *Sex and the Slayer*, p. 26.

17 Ron Becker, 'Guy love: a queer straight masculinity for a post-closet era?', in Glyn Davis and Gary Needhan (eds), *Queer TV: Theories, Histories, Politics* (Oxford: Routledge, 2009), pp. 121–40, p. 132.

18 Stevie Simkin, '"You hold your gun like a sissy girl": Firearms and anxious masculinity in *Buffy the Vampire Slayer*', *Slayage: The Online International Journal of Buffy Studies* 3/3–4, para. 21. Available at http://slayageonline.com/essays/slayage11_12/Simkin_Gun.htm (accessed 18 February 2009).

19 Ibid.

20 Ibid., fn 20.

21 See Aaron, 'New Queer Cinema'.
22 Becker, 'Guy love', p. 127.
23 Harry M. Benshoff, 'Reception of a queer mainstream film', in Aaron, *New Queer Cinema*, pp. 172–86, p. 174.
24 Ibid.
25 Ellis Hanson, 'Introduction: Out takes', in Ellis Hanson (ed.), *Out Takes: Essays on Queer Theory and Film* (Durham, NC and London: Duke University Press, 2005), pp. 1–19, p. 17.
26 Thomas Peele, 'Introduction: popular culture, queer culture', in Thomas Peele (ed.), *Queer Popular Culture: Literature, Media, Film, and Television* (London: Palgrave Macmillan, 2007), pp. 1–8, p. 2.
27 Battis, *Blood Relations*, p. 54.
28 See in particular Justine Larbalestier, '*Buffy's* Mary Sue is Jonathan: *Buffy* acknowledges the fans', in Rhonda V. Wilcox and David Lavery (eds), *Fighting the Forces: What's at Stake in Buffy the Vampire Slayer* (Lanham, MD: Rowman & Littlefield, 2002), pp. 227–38 and Esther Saxey, 'Staking a claim: The series and slash fan-fiction', in Roz Kaveney (ed.), *Reading The Vampire Slayer: An Unofficial Critical Companion to* Buffy *and* Angel, 2nd edn (New York: I.B.Tauris, 2001), pp. 187–210.
29 Quoted in Simkin, 'The wit and wisdom of Joss Whedon'.
30 Ibid.
31 Hanson, 'Introduction', pp. 5 and 10.
32 McCracken, 'At stake', p. 125.
33 Alexander Doty, *Making Things Perfectly Queer: Interpreting Mass Culture* (Minneapolis, MN and London: University of Minneapolis Press, 1993), p. 15 (emphasis in original).
34 Ibid.

Chapter 7: 'Why Can't You Just Masturbate Like the Rest of Us?': The Erotics and Politics of *Buffy* Fandom

1 Daniel Lametti, Aisha Harris, Natasha Geiling and Natalie Matthews-Ramo, 'Which pop culture property do academics study the most?', *Slate (Brow Beat: Slate's Culture Blog)*, 11 June 2012. Available at http://www.slate.com/blogs/browbeat/2012/06/11/pop_culture_studies_why_do_academics_study_buffy_the_vampire_slayer_more_than_the_wire_the_matrix_alien_and_the_simpsons_.html (accessed 12 December 2013).

2 For representative scholarship on *Lost*, see Roberta E. Pearson (ed.), *Reading Lost: Perspectives on a Hit Television Show* (London: I.B.Tauris, 2009); Randy Laist (ed.), *Looking for Lost: Critical Essays on the Enigmatic Series* (Jefferson, NC: McFarland & Co., 2011); Jonathan Gray and Jason Mittell, 'Speculation on spoilers: *Lost* fandom, narrative consumption and rethinking textuality', *Particip@tions* 4/1 (May 2007). Available at http://www.participations.org/Volume%204/Issue%201/4_01_graymittell.htm (accessed 12 December 2013); Jon Lachonis and Amy Johnston, *Lost Ate My Life: The Inside Story of a Fandom Like No Other* (Toronto: ECW Press, 2008); on *Mad Men*, see Scott Frederick Stoddart (ed.), *Analyzing Mad Men: Critical Essays on the Television Series* (Jefferson, NC: McFarland & Co., 2011); Gary R. Edgerton (ed.), *Mad Men: Dream Come True TV* (London: I.B.Tauris, 2010); J.M. Tyree, 'No fun: debunking the 1960s in *Mad Men* and *A Serious Man*', *Film Quarterly* 63/4 (Summer 2010), pp. 33–9; Heather Havrilesky, 'Will the truth set Don Draper free?', *Salon*, 24 June 2013. Available at http://www.salon.com/2013/06/24/will_the_truth_set_don_draper_free/ (accessed 12 December 2013); on *The Wire*, see Tiffany Potter and C.W. Marshall (eds), *The Wire: Urban Decay and American Television* (New York: Continuum, 2009); Helena Sheehan and Sheamus Sweeney, '*The Wire* and the world: Narrative and metanarrative', *Jump Cut: A Review of Contemporary Media* 51 (2009). Available at http://www.ejumpcut.org/archive/jc51.2009/Wire/ (accessed 12 December 2013); Joe Palazzolo, 'Want to learn criminal law and procedure? Watch *The Wire*', *The Wall Street Journal (Law Blog)*, 10 December 2013. Available at http://blogs.wsj.com/law/2013/12/10/want-to-learn-criminal-law-and-procedure-watch-the-wire/ (accessed 12 December 2013).

3 See Catherine Johnson's *Telefantasy* (London: British Film Institute, 2005), which covers a great deal of material about why *Buffy* was the right show at the right time in terms of changes to broadcast television.

4 Jonathan Gray, Cornel Sandvoss and C. Lee Harrington, 'Introduction: Why study fans?' in Jonathan Gray, Cornel Sandvoss and C. Lee Harrington (eds), *Fandom: Identities and Communities in a Mediated World* (New York: New York University Press, 2007), pp. 1–16, p. 5.

5 Ibid., p. 4.

6 Mark Duffett, *Understanding Fandom: An Introduction to the Study of Media Fan Culture* (New York: Bloomsbury, 2013), p. 2.

7 Ibid., p. 19.

8 Roberta E. Pearson, 'Bachies, Bardies, Trekkies, and Sherlockians', in Gray, Sandvoss and Harrington, *Fandom*, pp. 98–109.

9 Nancy Reagin and Anne Rubenstein, '"I'm Buffy, and you're history": Putting fan studies into history', *Transformative Works and Cultures* 6 (2011). Available at http://journal.transformativeworks.org/index.php/twc/article/view/272/200 (accessed 12 December 2013).

10 Gray, Sandvoss and Harrington, 'Introduction', p. 5.

11 Lynn Zubernis and Katherine Larsen, *Fandom at the Crossroads: Celebration, Shame and Fan/Producer Relationship* (Newcastle upon Tyne: Cambridge Scholars Publishing, 2012), p. 9.

12 Nick Couldry, 'On the set of *The Sopranos*: "inside" a fan's construction of nearness', in Gray, Sandvoss and Harrington, *Fandom*, pp. 139–48; Will Brooker, 'A sort of homecoming: Fan viewing and symbolic pilgrimage', in Zubernis and Larsen, *Fandom at the Crossroads*, pp. 149–64; Katherine Larsen and Lynn S. Zubernis, *Fangasm: Supernatural Fangirls* (Iowa City, IA: University of Iowa Press, 2013).

13 For more on online fandom, see Paul Booth, *Digital Fandom: New Media Studies* (New York: Peter Lang, 2010); Karen Hellekson and Kristina Busse (eds), *Fan Fiction and Fan Communities in the Age of the Internet* (Jefferson, NC: MacFarland, 2006); Duffett, *Understanding Fandom*, pp. 168–70.

14 Henry Jenkins, *Convergence Culture: Where Old and New Media Collide* (New York: New York University Press, 2006).

15 Zubernis and Larsen, *Fandom at the Crossroads*, p. 1.

16 For further discussion, see essays by Lynn Zubernis and Katherine Larsen, ibid.

17 Ibid., p. 20.

18 Ibid., p. 10.

19 Ibid., p. 53.

20 Henry Jenkins, *Textual Poachers: Television Fans and Participatory Culture* (New York and London: Routledge, 1992).

21 Ibid., p. 2.

22 Ibid., p. 23.

23 Ibid., pp. 26–7.

24 Matt Hills, *Fan Cultures* (London and New York: Routledge, 2002).

25 Ibid., pp. 8–10.

26 Ibid., p. 30.

27 Ibid., pp. 8–11.

28 Ibid.

29 For example, Jenkins, *Convergence Culture.*

30 Camille Bacon-Smith, *Enterprising Women: Television Fandom and the Creation of Popular Myth* (Philadelphia, PA: University of Pennsylvania Press, 1992).
31 Hills, *Fan Cultures*, pp. 40–1.
32 David Bleich, 'Gender interests in reading and language', in Elizabeth A. Flynn and Patrocinio P. Schweickart (eds), *Gender and Reading: Essays on Readers, Texts, and Contexts* (Baltimore, MD: Johns Hopkins University Press, 1986), pp. 234–66.
33 For example, Mary Kirby-Diaz, 'So, what's the story? Story-oriented and series-oriented fans: a complex of behaviors', in Mary Kirby-Diaz (ed.), *Buffy and Angel Conquer the Internet: Essays on Online Fandom* (Jefferson, NC: MacFarland, 2009), pp. 62–86.
34 Hills, *Fan Cultures*, pp. 37–8.
35 Ibid., p. 38.
36 Alexis Lothian, Kristina Busse and Robin Anne Reid, '"Yearning void and infinite potential": Online slash fandom as queer female space', *English Language Notes* 45/2 (2007), pp. 103–11.
37 Ibid., p. 107.
38 Ibid., p. 109.
39 Rhonda V. Wilcox and David Lavery (eds), *Fighting the Forces: What's at Stake in* Buffy the Vampire Slayer (Lanham, MD: Rowman & Littlefield, 2002).
40 Justine Larbalestier, '*Buffy*'s Mary Sue is Jonathon: *Buffy* acknowledges the fans', in Rhonda V. Wilcox and David Lavery (eds), *Fighting the Forces: What's at Stake in* Buffy the Vampire Slayer (Lanham, MD: Rowman & Littlefield, 2002), pp. 227–38; Katrina Busse, 'Crossing the final taboo: Family, sexuality, and incest in Buffyverse fan fiction', in Wilcox and Lavery, *Fighting the Forces*, pp. 207–17; S. Renee Dechert, '"My boyfriend's in the band!" *Buffy* and the rhetoric of music', ibid., pp. 218–26; Amanda Zweerink and Sarah N. Gatson, 'www.buffy.com: cliques, boundaries, and hierarchies in an internet community', ibid., pp. 239–49.
41 For example, see the following texts on Faith, Buffy and Spike and Tara and Willow respectively: Sue Tjardes, '"If you're not enjoying it, you're doing something wrong": Textual and viewer constructions of Faith, the Vampire Slayer' in Frances Early and Kathleen Kennedy (eds), *Athena's Daughters: Television's New Women Warriors* (Syracuse, NY: Syracuse University Press, 2003), pp. 66–77; Dawn Heinecken, 'Fan readings of sex and violence on *Buffy the Vampire Slayer*', *Slayage: The Journal of the Whedon Studies Association* 3/3–4 (2004). Available at

http://slayageonline.com/PDF/heinecken.pdf (accessed 6 November 2013); Judith L. Tabron, 'Girl on girl politics: Willow/Tara and new approaches to media fandom', *Slayage: The Journal of the Whedon Studies Association* 4/1–2 (2004). Available at http://slayageonline.com/PDF/tabron.pdf (accessed 12 December 2013).

42 Wendy A.F.G. Stengel, 'Synergy and smut: The brand in official and unofficial *Buffy the Vampire Slayer* communities of interest', *Slayage: The Journal of the Whedon Studies Association* 1/4 (2001). Available at http://slayageonline.com/PDF/stengel.pdf (accessed 12 December 2013); Katrina Blasingame, '"I can't believe I'm saying it twice in the same century ... but 'duh' ...": The evolution of *Buffy the Vampire Slayer* sub-culture language through the medium of fanfiction', *Slayage: The Journal of the Whedon Studies Association* 5/4 (20) (2006). Available at http://slayageonline.com/PDF/Blasingame.pdf (accessed 12 December 2013); Kirby-Diaz, *Buffy and Angel Conquer the Internet*.

43 '*The Encyclopedia of* Buffy *Studies: Buffy* Studies by discipline/method/approach', *Slayage: The Journal of the Whedon Studies Association*, n.d. Available at http://slayageonline.com/EBS/buffy_studies/buffy_studies_by_discipline.htm (accessed 16 December 2013).

44 Roland Barthes, *The Pleasure of the Text*, trans. Richard Miller (New York: Hill and Wang, 1975).

45 'Jonathan McIntosh', *Rebellious Pixels*, n.d. Available at http://www.rebelliouspixels.com/jonathan-mcintosh (accessed 16 December 2013); Rebellious Pixels, 'Buffy vs Edward: *Twilight* remixed – [original version]', *YouTube*, uploaded 19 June 2009. Available at http://www.youtube.com/watch?v=RZwM3GvaTRM (accessed 16 December 2013).

46 Jonathan McIntosh, 'Buffy vs Edward remix unfairly removed by Lionsgate', *Rebellious Pixels*, 9 January 2013. Available at http://www.rebelliouspixels.com/2013/buffy-vs-edward-remix-unfairly-removed-by-lionsgate (accessed 16 December 2013).

47 The Short Mr Pointy Award is awarded annually by the Whedon Studies Association for the best essay on an aspect of Whedon's output published the previous year. See 'The sixth annual Mr Pointy Award for Buffy Studies Scholarship (2010)', *Slayage: The Journal of the Whedon Studies Association*, n.d. Available at http://slayageonline.com/Mr_Pointy/mrpointy_winners_2010.htm (accessed 21 February 2014).

48 McIntosh, '*Buffy vs Edward* remix unfairly removed'.

49 For a more detailed account, see ibid.

50 Ibid.

51 Jonathan McIntosh, 'What would Buffy do?: Notes on dusting Edward Cullen', *WIMN's Voices* (2009). Available at http://www.wimnonline.org/WIMNsVoicesBlog/?p=1272 (accessed 12 December 2013).
52 Ibid.
53 Ibid.
54 Ibid.
55 Gerard Genette, *Narrative Discourse: An Essay in Method*, trans. Jane E. Lewin (Ithaca, NY: Cornell University Press, 1983).
56 Tisha Turk, 'Metalepsis in fan vids and fan fiction', in Karin Kukkonen and Sonja Klimek (eds), *Metalepsis in Popular Culture* (New York: De Gruyter, 2011), pp. 83–103, p. 86.
57 Ibid., p. 87.
58 Ibid.
59 Ibid., p. 88.
60 Kristina Busse and Karen Hellekson, 'Introduction: work in progress', in Karen Hellekson and Kristina Busse (eds), *Fan Fiction and Fan Communities in the Age of the Internet: New Essays* (Jefferson, NC: McFarland, 2006), pp. 5–32, p. 6.
61 Roland Barthes, *S/Z*, trans. Richard Miller (New York: Hill and Wang, 1974), p. 4.
62 Turk, 'Metalepsis in fan vids', p. 90.
63 Ibid.
64 Francesca Coppa, 'Women, *Star Trek*, and the early development of fannish vidding', *Transformative Works and Cultures* 1 (2008). Available at http://journal.transformativeworks.org/index.php/twc/article/view/44/64 (accessed 12 December 2013); cited in Turk, 'Metalepsis in fan vids', p. 91.
65 Ibid. For more on the move within film studies to incorporate audiovisual essays as a means of constructing a critical argument, see Catherine Grant's Film Studies for Free website (http://filmstudiesforfree.blogspot.co.uk/) and REFRAMe which is involved in multimedia publishing (http://reframe.sussex.ac.uk/). I am grateful to Stacey Abbott for drawing my attention to these sites.
66 Rebellious Pixels, 'Buffy vs Edward: *Twilight* Remixed – [original version]'.
67 Christine Seifert, 'Bite me! (or don't)', *Bitch Media*, n.d. Available at http://bitchmagazine.org/article/bite-me-or-dont (accessed 20 February 2014).
68 Anne Torkelson, 'Violence, agency, and the women of *Twilight*', in Maggie Parke and Natalie Wilson (eds), *Theorising Twilight: Critical Essays on What's at Stake in a Post-Vampire World* (Jefferson, NC: McFarland and Co., 2011), pp. 209–23, p. 220.

69 Rebellious Pixels, 'Buffy vs Edward: *Twilight* Remixed – [original version]'.
70 Ibid.
71 Turk, 'Metalepsis in fan vids', p. 100.
72 Angela McRobbie, *The Aftermath of Feminism: Gender, Culture and Social Change* (London: Sage, 2009), p. 8.
73 Ibid., p. 11.
74 Nina Power, *One Dimensional Woman* (Winchester: O Books, 2009), p. 42.
75 On the Nirvana/Destiny's Child mash-up, see Michael Serazio, 'The apolitical irony of Generation Mash-Up: A cultural case study in popular music', *Popular Music and Society* 31/1 (2008), pp. 79–94, p. 83.
76 Francesca Coppa, 'A fannish taxonomy of hotness', *Cinema Journal* 48/4 (2009), pp. 107–13, p. 107.
77 Ibid., pp. 109–10.
78 Ibid., p. 110.
79 Ibid.
80 Laura Mulvey, 'Visual pleasure and narrative cinema', in her *Visual and Other Pleasures*, 2nd edn (London: Palgrave Macmillan, 2009), pp. 14–31, p. 19.

Chapter 8: 'Where Do We Go From Here?': Trajectories in *Buffy* Studies

1 '*Buffy* Studies', *Wikipedia*. Available at http://en.wikipedia.org/wiki/Buffy_studies (accessed 4 December 2013).
2 Ibid. In fact, the initial statement seems to have confused the semester-long *Buffy* course taught by David Kociemba at Emerson College with a Buffy Bachelor of Arts Degree. See David Kociemba, 'To spoil or not to spoil: Teaching television's narrative complexity', in Jodie A. Kreider and Meghan K. Winchell (eds), Buffy *in the Classroom: Essays on Teaching with the Vampire Slayer* (Jefferson, NC: McFarland, 2010), pp. 7–21.
3 See David Kociemba, 'Teaching with *Buffy*', *Watcher Junior: The Undergraduate Journal of Whedon Studies*, 7 September 2010. Available at http://blog.watcherjunior.tv/2010/09/teaching-with-buffy.html (accessed 3 March 2014).
4 Derik A. Badman, 'Academic *Buffy* bibliography', *Slayage: The Journal of the Whedon Studies Association* 2/3 (2002). Available at http://slayageonline.com/PDF/badman.pdf (accessed 4 March 2014).
5 Daniel Lametti, Aisha Harris, Natasha Geiling and Natalie Matthews-Ramo, 'Which pop culture property do academics study the most?', *Slate (Brow Beat:*

Slate's Culture Blog), 11 June 2012. Available at http://www.slate.com/blogs/browbeat/2012/06/11/pop_culture_studies_why_do_academics_study_buffy_the_vampire_slayer_more_than_the_wire_the_matrix_alien_and_the_simpsons_.html (accessed 12 December 2013).

6 '*The Encyclopedia of* Buffy *Studies*: *Buffy* Studies by discipline/method/approach', *Slayage: The Journal of the Whedon Studies Association*. Available at http://slayageonline.com/EBS/buffy_studies/buffy_studies_by_discipline.htm (accessed 16 December 2013).

7 Alysa Hornick, 'Whedonology: An academic Whedon Studies bibliography'. Available at http://www.alysa316.com/Whedonology/ (accessed 3 March 2014). This page was last updated in 2014 and is trustworthy and well-regarded by the Whedon Studies Association.

8 Quoted in interview with Rhys Edwards, 'Staking out a place in academia: UBC hosts fifth Joss Whedon conference', *The Ubyssey*, 10 July 2012. Available at http://ubyssey.ca/culture/slayage-conference687 (accessed 3 March 2014).

9 David Lavery and Cynthia Burkhead, 'Introduction', in David Lavery and Cynthia Burkhead (eds), *Joss Whedon: Conversations* (Jackson, MI: University Press of Mississippi, 2011), pp. vii–xii, p. vii.

10 Adam Chitwood, 'Joss Whedon talks the imperfections of *The Avengers*, his plans for *The Avengers: Age of Ultron*, and *Agents of S.H.I.E.L.D.*', *Collider*, 26 September 2013. Available at http://collider.com/avengers-age-of-ultron-news-joss-whedon-agents-of-shield/ (accessed 3 March 2014).

11 See, for example, Anthony H. Cordesman, 'Biological warfare and the "Buffy paradigm"', Centre for Strategic and International Studies, 29 September 2001. Available at http://csis.org/files/media/csis/pubs/buffy012902[1].pdf (accessed 5 March 2014).

12 'Conferences on the Whedonverses'. Available at http://slayageonline.com/Conferences_on_the_Whedonverses (accessed 5 March 2014).

13 'Call for papers: *Slayage* conference on the Whedonverses, California State University-Sacramento Sacramento, CA – June 19–22, 2014'. Available at http://slayageonline.com/SC6/WSA_SCW6_CFP.pdf (accessed 3 March 2014).

14 *Watcher Junior: The Undergraduate Journal of Whedon Studies*. Home page http://www.whedonstudies.tv/watcher-junior-the-undergraduate-journal-of-whedon-studies.html.

15 'Joss Whedon', *International New York Times*, 16 May 2003. Available at http://www.nytimes.com/2003/05/16/readersopinions/16WHED.html (accessed 3 March 2014).

16 Mary Graber, 'Colleges open minds close door on sense', *MaryGraber.com*. Available at http://www.marygrabar.com/grabar_new/index.php/local-media/82-articles-and-columns/104-colleges-open-minds-close-door-on-sense (accessed 3 March 2014). First published in *The Atlanta Journal-Constitution*, 4 August 2006.

17 Yuko Narushima, 'Back to basics proposal for English pupils', *Sydney Morning Herald*, 17 October 2008. Available at http://www.smh.com.au/news/national/back-to-basics-proposal-for-english-pupils/2008/10/16/1223750232631.html (accessed 15 January 2015).

18 Jason Winslade, '"Have you tried not being a Slayer?": Performing Buffy fandom in the classroom', in Jodie A. Kreider and Meghan K. Winchell (eds), *Buffy in the Classroom: Essays on Teaching with the Vampire Slayer* (Jefferson, NC: McFarland, 2010), pp. 22–34, p. 23.

19 Jes Battis, *Blood Relations: Chosen Families in* Buffy the Vampire Slayer *and* Angel (Jefferson, NC: McFarland, 2005), p. 9.

20 Rhonda V. Wilcox and David Lavery, 'Welcome', Fifth Biennial *Slayage* Conference on the Whedonverses (2012). Available at http://www.slayageonline.com/SC5/SCW5_Program_Final.pdf (accessed 3 March 2014). The organisation itself is international in scope and membership (although heavily North American). However, the conferences were historically American and the move to Canada in 2010 (and plans for future conferences) was part of a move to ensure the conferences are international as well.

21 The phrase comes from Stacey Abbott's edited collection of essays, *Reading* Angel: *The TV Spin-off With a Soul* (London: I.B.Tauris, 2005).

22 Wilcox and Lavery, Fifth Biennial *Slayage* Conference.

23 Sue Turnbull, '"Not just another Buffy paper": Towards an aesthetics of television', *Slayage: The Journal of the Whedon Studies Association* 4/1–2 (2004). Available at http://slayageonline.com/PDF/turnbull.pdf (accessed 3 March 2014).

24 Michael P. Levine and Steven Jay Schneider, 'Feeling for Buffy: The girl next door', in James B. South (ed.), Buffy the Vampire Slayer *and Philiosophy: Fear and Trembling in Sunnydale* (Chicago, IL: Open Court, 2003), pp. 294–308, p. 299.

25 Ibid., p. 301. I disagree with most of Levine and Schneider's assessments, both about the *Buffy* series and *Buffy* studies, but the charge that there is not enough self-reflexive analysis of the field does have some merit. Significant exceptions are provided by Vivien Burr's 'Scholars/'shippers and Spikeaholics', *European Journal of Cultural Studies* 8/3 (2005), pp. 375–83,

Rhonda Wilcox's 'In "the demon section of the card catalogue"', *Critical Studies in Television* 1/1 (April 2006), pp. 37–48 and David Lavery's '"I wrote my thesis on you": *Buffy* Studies as an academic cult', *Slayage: The Online International Journal of Buffy Studies* 4/1–2 (October 2004). Available at http://slayageonline.com/PDF/lavery4.pdf (accessed 3 March 2014).

26 Wilcox, 'In "the demon section of the card catalogue"', p. 37.

27 Edwards, 'Staking out a place in academia'.

28 Jodie A. Krieder and Meghan K. Winchell, 'Introduction: "let's have a lesson then"', in Jodie A. Kreider and Meghan K. Winchell (eds), Buffy *in the Classroom: Essays on Teaching with the Vampire Slayer* (Jefferson, NC: McFarland, 2010), pp. 1–6.

29 Kristopher Karl Woofter, 'Little Red Riding … Buffy? "Buffy vs. Dracula" in explorations of intertextuality in Introduction to College English', ibid., pp. 169–85.

30 Barry Morris, 'Round up the usable suspects: archetypal characters in the study of popular culture', ibid., pp. 46–60. *Angel the Series*, *Fray*, *Firefly* and *Serenity* all utilise the archetypal character types, as does Whedon's cinematic work, such as *The Avengers*.

31 Meghan K. Winchell, 'Whedon takes "the scary" out of feminism', ibid., pp. 73–82.

32 Morris, 'Round up the usable suspects', p. 49.

33 *The Avengers* grossed over US$1.5 billion worldwide, placing it third on 'All Time World Wide Grosses' on the *Box Office Mojo* website, http://www.boxofficemojo.com /alltime/world/.

34 http://en.wikipedia.org/wiki/Buffy_the_Vampire_Slayer_in_popular_culture.

35 Buffy Summers is no. 13 on Bravo's '100 Greatest TV Characters', ranked no. 2 on *Empire* magazine's '50 Greatest TV Shows of all Time' (2008), and listed as no. 3 on *TV Guide*'s list of '25 Best Cult TV Shows from the Past 25 Years': '*Buffy the Vampire* Slayer trivia', Internet Movie Database (IMDb). Available at http://www.imdb.com/title/tt0118276/trivia?tr=tr0688963 (accessed 6 March 2014).

36 In the Buffy episode 'Halloween', Willow asks: 'She [Buffy] couldn't have dressed as Xena?' when people take on the personas of their costumes – in Buffy's case, a damsel in distress.

37 'The Play's the Thing', *Xena: Warrior Princess* (1999); 'The Power of Two', *Charmed* (1999); 'Smells Like Teen Spirit', *The Vampire Diaries* (2011); 'Mine', *True Blood* (2008).

38 'The Homer of Seville', *The Simpsons* (2007); 'Speedtrapped', *Daria* (1999); 'It's A Trap!', *Family Guy* (2011).
39 'The One Where Chandler Can't Cry', *Friends* (2000); 'Love Plus One', *Will & Grace* (2000); 'Baby Talk', *How I Met Your Mother* (2010).
40 In the Buffy episode, 'Chosen', Buffy asks Angel: 'Are you just going to come here and go all Dawson on me every time I have a boyfriend?'
41 'Valentine's Day Massacre', *Dawson's Creek* (2000); 'The Cinderella in the Cardboard', *Bones* (2009).
42 Erin B. Waggoner (ed.), *Sexual Rhetoric in the Works of Joss Whedon* (Jefferson, NC: McFarland, 2010); Allison McCracken, 'At stake: Angel's body, fantasy masculinity, and queer desire in teen television', in Elana Levine and Lisa Parks (eds), *Undead TV: Essays on Buffy the Vampire Slayer* (Durham, NC: Duke University Press, 2007), pp. 116–44.
43 For one take on the 'aesthetic' versus 'sociological' debate, see Wilcox, 'In "the demon section of the card catalogue"'.
44 See especially Wilcox's chapter, 'Song: Singing and dancing and burning and dying', in Ronda Wilcox (ed.), *Why Buffy Matters: The Art of* Buffy the Vampire Slayer (London: I.B.Tauris, 2005), pp. 191–205.
45 Tasha Robinson, 'The Onion AV Club interview with Joss Whedon (1)', in David Lavery and Cynthia Burkhead (eds), *Joss Whedon: Conversations* (Jackson, MI: University Press of Mississippi, 2011), pp. 23–33.
46 Burr, 'Scholars/'shippers and Spikeaholics', pp. 375–6.
47 Ibid., p. 379.
48 Ibid., pp. 376–7.
49 Ibid., p. 379.
50 Ibid., p. 376.
51 Matt Hills, *Fan Cultures* (London: Routledge, 2002), p. 184.
52 David Lavery, *Joss Whedon, A Creative Portrait: From* Buffy the Vampire Slayer *to* The Avengers (London: I.B.Tauris, 2013).
53 David Lavery, 'Joss Whedon, wonder boy', featured paper at SC2: The *Slayage* Conference on the Whedonverses, 25–28 May 2006, Gordon College, Georgia.
54 Lavery and Burkhead, 'Introduction', p. viii.
55 Lavery, 'Joss Whedon, wonder boy'.
56 For work on Angel that challenges the notion of the auteur in relation to Whedon see Abbott, *Reading* Angel, in which she explores the collective creativity of the writers room and consider the collection of voices that contribute to the work.

57 Bill Nichols (ed.), *Movies and Methods*, vol. I (Berkeley, CA: University of California Press, 1976), p. 224 and François Truffaut, 'A certain tendency of the French cinema', *Cahiers du Cinéma* in English 1. Originally published in French in *Cahiers du Cinéma* 31 (1954).

58 Andrew Sarris, 'Notes on the auteur theory in 1962', *Film Culture* 27 (Winter 1962/3), pp. 1–8; Robin Wood, 'Ideology, genre, auteur', in his *Hitchcock's Films Revisited* (New York: Columbia University Press, 1989), pp. 288–302; Peter Wollen, 'The *auteur* theory', in his *Signs and Meaning in the Cinema* (Bloomington, IN: Indiana University Press, 1973), pp. 74–115.

Bibliography

7th Heaven, created by Brenda Hampton (1996, The WB, prod. by Spelling Television and CBS Paramount Network Television), television.

10 Things I Hate About You, dir. Gil Junger, perf. Heath Ledger, Julia Stiles, Joseph Gordon-Levitt and Larisa Oleynik (1999, Buena Vista Pictures), film.

'50 best high school movies', *Entertainment Weekly*, 22 September 2012. Available at http://www.ew.com/gallery/50-best-high-school-movies-0 (accessed 26 February 2014).

'The 500 greatest movies of all time', *Empire*, n.d. Available at http://www.empireonline.com/500/17.asp (accessed 26 February 2014).

Aaron, Michele (ed.), *New Queer Cinema: A Critical Reader* (Edinburgh: Edinburgh University Press, 2004).

Abbott, Stacey (ed.), *Reading* Angel: *The TV Spin-off With a Soul* (London: I.B.Tauris, 2005).

Adams, Michael, 'Buffy and the death of style', in Lynne Y. Edwards, Elizabeth L. Rambo and James B. South (eds), *Buffy Goes Dark: Essays on the Final Two Seasons of* Buffy the Vampire Slayer *on Television* (Jefferson, NC: McFarland, 2009), pp. 83–94.

Adams, Rachel and David Savran (eds), *The Masculinity Studies Reader* (Malden, MA: Blackwell Publishing, 2002).

Albright, Richard S., '"Breakaway pop hit or … book number?": "Once More, with Feeling" and genre', *Slayage: The Journal of the Whedon Studies Association* 5/1 (2005). Available at http://slayageonline.com/PDF/albright.pdf (accessed 12 June 2013).

Alderman, Naomi and Annette Seidel-Arpaci, 'Imaginary para-sites of the soul: Vampires and representations of "Blackness" and "Jewishness" in the Buffy/Angelverse', *Slayage: The Journal of the Whedon Studies Association* 3/2 (2003). Available at http://slayageonline.com/PDF/alderman_seidel-arpaci.pdf (accessed 5 August 2013).

All Over Me, dir. Alex Sichel, perf. Alison Folland, Tara Subkoff and Cole Hauser (1997, Alliance and Fine Line Features), film.

'All time world wide grosses', *Box Office Mojo*, n.d. Available at http://boxofficemojo.com /alltime/world/ (accessed 5 March 2014).

Arkin, William and Lynne R. Dobrofsky, 'Military socialization and masculinity', *Journal of Social Issues* 34 (1978), pp. 151–68.

Bacon-Smith, Camille, *Enterprising Women: Television Fandom and the Creation of Popular Myth* (Philadelphia, PA: University of Pennsylvania Press, 1992).

Badman, Derik A., 'Academic *Buffy* bibliography', *Slayage: The Journal of the Whedon Studies Association* 2/3 (2002). Available at http://slayageonline.com/PDF/badman.pdf (accessed 4 March 2014).

Barnett, Emma, 'Margaret Thatcher: ultimate feminist icon – whether she liked it or not', *The Telegraph*, 8 April 2013. Available at http://www.telegraph.co.uk/women/womens-politics/9979076/Margaret-Thatcher-ultimate-feminist-icon-whether-she-liked-it-or-not.html (accessed 17 June 2013).

Barrett, Frank J., 'The organisation of hegemonic masculinity: The case of the US Navy', in Rachel Adams and David Savran (eds), *The Masculinities Studies Reader* (Cambridge: Polity Press, 2001), pp. 77–99.

Barthes, Roland, *S/Z*, trans. Richard Miller (New York: Hill and Wang, 1974).

——, *The Pleasure of the Text*, trans. Richard Miller (New York: Hill and Wang, 1975).

Battis, Jes, *Blood Relations: Chosen Families in* Buffy the Vampire Slayer *and* Angel (Jefferson, NC: McFarland, 2005).

Baumgardner, Jennifer and Amy Richards, *Manifesta: Young Women, Feminism, and the Future* (New York: Farrar, Straus and Giroux, 2000).

——, 'Feminism and femininity: Or how we learned to stop worrying and love the thong', in Anita Harris (ed.), *All About the Girl: Culture, Power, and Identity* (New York: Routledge, 2004), pp. 59–67.

Becker, Ron, 'Guy love: A queer straight masculinity for a post-closet era?', in Glyn Davis and Gary Needhan (eds), *Queer TV: Theories, Histories, Politics* (Oxford: Routledge, 2009), pp. 121–40.

Beetlejuice, dir. Tim Burton, perf. Alec Baldwin, Geena Davis, Michael Keaton and Winona Ryder (1988, Warner Bros), film.

Beirne, Rebecca, 'Queering the Slayer-text: Reading possibilities in *Buffy the Vampire Slayer*', *Refractory: A Journal of Entertainment Media* 5 (2004). Available at http://blogs.arts.unimelb.edu.au/refractory/category/browse-past-volumes/volume-5/ (accessed 18 February 2009).

Bellafante, Ginia, 'Bewitching teen heroines', *Time*, 5 May 1997, pp. 82–5.

——, 'Is feminism dead?', *Time*, 29 June 1998, pp. 53–60.

Benshoff, Harry M., 'Reception of a queer mainstream film', in Michele Aaron (ed.), *New Queer Cinema: A Critical Reader* (Edinburgh: Edinburgh University Press, 2004), pp. 172–86.

Beverly Hills, 90210, created by Darren Star (1990, Fox, prod. by 90210 Productions, Fair Dinkum Productions, Spelling Television and Torand Productions), television.

Blade Runner, dir. Ridley Scott, perf. Harrison Ford, Rutger Hauer and Sean Young (1982, Warner Bros), film.

Blasingame, Katrina, '"I can't believe I'm saying it twice in the same century ... but 'duh' ...": The evolution of *Buffy the Vampire Slayer* sub-culture language through the medium of fanfiction', *Slayage: The Journal of the Whedon Studies Association* 5/4 (2006). Available at http://slayageonline.com/PDF/Blasingame.pdf (accessed 12 December 2013).

Bleich, David, 'Gender interests in reading and language', in Elizabeth A. Flynn and Patrocinio P. Schweickart (eds), *Gender and Reading: Essays on Readers, Texts, and Contexts* (Baltimore, MD: Johns Hopkins University Press, 1986), pp. 234–66.

Booth, Paul, *Digital Fandom: New Media Studies* (New York: Peter Lang, 2010).

Bose, Purnima, 'From humanitarian intervention to the beautifying mission: Afghan women and beauty without borders', *Genders* 51 (2010). Available at http://www.genders.org/g51/g51_bose.html (accessed 5 August 2013).

'Box office/business for *Heathers*', Internet Movie Database (IMDb), n.d. Available at http://www.imdb.com/title/tt0097493/business (accessed 26 February 2014).

Boys Don't Cry, dir. Kimberly Peirce, perf. Hilary Swank, Chloë Sevigny and Peter Sarsgaard (1999, Fox Searchlight Pictures), film.

Brooker, Will, 'A sort of homecoming: fan viewing and symbolic pilgrimage', in Lynn Zubernis and Katherine Larsen (eds), *Fandom at the Crossroads: Celebration, Shame and Fan/Producer Relationship* (Newcastle upon Tyne: Cambridge Scholars Publishing, 2012), pp. 149–64.

Brown, Lyn Mikel, *Raising their Voices: The Politics of Girls' Anger* (Cambridge, MA: Harvard University Press, 1999).

Buchbinder, David, *Studying Men and Masculinities* (Oxford: Routledge, 2013).

'*Buffy* Studies', *Wikipedia*. Available at http://en.wikipedia.org/wiki/Buffy_studies (accessed 4 December 2013).

Buffy the Vampire Slayer, dir. Fran Rubel Kuzui, perf. Kristy Swanson, Donald Sutherland, Paul Reubens, Rutger Hauer, Luke Perry and Hilary Swank (1992, Twentieth Century Fox), film.

Buffy the Vampire Slayer, created Joss Whedon (1997–2003, Twentieth Century Film Fox Corporation, produced by Mutant Enemy, Kuzui Enterprises, Sandollar Television), television.

'*Buffy the Vampire Slayer* in Popular Culture', *Wikipedia*, Available at http://en.wikipedia.org/wiki/Buffy_the_Vampire_Slayer_in_popular_culture (accessed 6 March 2014).

'*Buffy the Vampire* Slayer trivia', Internet Movie Database (IMDb). Available at http://www.imdb.com/title/tt0118276/trivia?tr=tr0688963 (accessed 6 March 2014).

Buinicki, Martin and Anthony Enns, 'Buffy the vampire disciplinarian: Institutional excess, spiritual technologies, and the new economy of power', *Slayage: The Journal of the Whedon Studies Association* 1/4 (2001). Available at http://slayageonline.com/PDF/buinicki_enns.pdf (accessed 5 August 2013).

Burr, Vivien, 'Scholars/'shippers and Spikeaholics', *European Journal of Cultural Studies* 8/3 (2005), pp. 375–83.

Bush, Laura, 'The Taliban's war against women', radio address to the nation, Crawford, Texas, 17 November 2001. Available at http://2001-2009.state.gov/g/drl/rls/rm/2001/6206.htm (accessed 7 June 2013).

Busse, Katrina, 'Crossing the final taboo: family, sexuality, and incest in Buffyverse fan fiction', in Rhonda V. Wilcox and David Lavery (eds), *Fighting the Forces: What's at Stake in* Buffy the Vampire Slayer (Lanham, MD: Rowman & Littlefield, 2002), pp. 207–17.

——, and Karen Hellekson (eds), *Fan Fiction and Fan Communities in the Age of the Internet: New Essays* (Jefferson, NC: McFarland, 2006).

But I'm a Cheerleader, dir. Jamie Babbit, perf. Natasha Lyonne, Clea DuVall and Michelle Williams (1999, Lionsgate), film.

Brunsdon, Charlotte, Julie D'Acci and Lynn Spigel (eds), *Feminist Television Criticism: A Reader* (Oxford: Clarendon Press, 1997).

Byers, Michele, '*Buffy the Vampire Slayer*: The next generation of television', in Rory Dicker and Alison Piepmeier (eds), *Catching a Wave: Reclaiming Feminism for the Twenty-first Century* (Boston, MA: Northeastern University Press, 2003), pp. 171–87.

'Call for papers: *Slayage* conference on the Whedonverses, California State University – Sacramento, CA – June 19–22, 2014'. Available at http://slayageonline.com/SC6/WSA_SCW6_CFP.pdf (accessed 3 March 2014).

Camron, Marc, 'The importance of being the Zeppo: Xander, gender identity and hybridity in *Buffy the Vampire Slayer*', *Slayage: The Online International Journal of Buffy Studies* 6/3 (2007). Available at http://slayageonline.com/Numbers/slayage23.htm (accessed 18 February 2009).

Carrigan, Tim, Bob Connell and John Lee, 'Toward a new sociology of masculinity', *Theory and Society* 14/5 (1985), pp. 561–604.

Chambers, Samuel A. and Daniel Williford, 'Anti-imperialism in the Buffy-verse: challenging the mythos of Bush as vampire slayer', *Poroi* 3/2 (December 2004), pp. 109–29, p. 123. Available at http://ir.uiowa.edu/cgi/viewcontent.cgi?article=1040&context=poroi (accessed 5 August 2013).

Charmed, created by Constance M. Burge (1998, The WB, prod. by Spelling Television), television.

Chin, Vivian, 'Buffy? She's like me, she's not like me – she's rad', in Frances Early and Kathleen Kennedy (eds), *Athena's Daughters: Television's New Women Warriors* (Syracuse, NY: Syracuse University Press, 2003), pp. 92–102.

Chitwood, Adam, 'Joss Whedon talks the imperfections of *The Avengers*, his plans for *The Avengers: Age of Ultron*, and *Agents of S.H.I.E.L.D.*', *Collider*, 26 September 2013. Available at http://collider.com/avengers-age-of-ultron-news-joss-whedon-agents-of-shield/ (accessed 3 March 2014).

Clueless, dir. Amy Heckerling, perf. Alicia Silverstone, Stacey Dash, and Brittany Murph (1995, Paramount Pictures), film.

Coker, Catherine, 'That girl: Bella, Buffy, and the feminist ethics of choice in *Twilight* and *Buffy the Vampire Slayer*', *Slayage: The Journal of the Whedon Studies Association* 8/4 [32] (2011). Available at http://slayageonline.com/essays/slayage32/Coker.pdf (accessed 12 June 2013).

'Conferences on the Whedonverses'. Available at http://slayageonline.com/Conferences_on_the_Whedonverses (accessed 5 March 2014).

Connell, Robert W., *Masculinities* (St Leonards, NSW: Allen & Unwin, 1995).

——, *Masculinities*, 2nd edn (Crows Nest, NSW: Allen and Unwin, 2005).

——, and James W. Messerschmidt, 'Hegemonic masculinity: Rethinking the concept', *Gender and Society* 19/6 (2005), pp. 829–59.

Coppa, Francesca, 'Women, *Star Trek*, and the early development of fannish vidding', *Transformative Works and Cultures* 1 (2008). Available at http://journal.transformativeworks.org/index.php/twc/article/view/44/64 (accessed 12 December 2013).

——, 'A fannish taxonomy of hotness', *Cinema Journal* 48/4 (2009), pp. 107–13.

Cordesman, Anthony H., 'Biological warfare and the "Buffy paradigm"', Centre for Strategic and International Studies, 29 September 2001. Available at http://csis.org/files/media/csis/pubs/buffy012902[1].pdf (accessed 5 March 2014).

Couldry, Nick, 'On the set of *The Sopranos*: "inside" a fan's construction of nearness', in Jonathan Gray, Cornel Sandvoss and C. Lee Harrington (eds), *Fandom: Identities and Communities in a Mediated World* (New York: New York University Press, 2007), pp. 139–48.

Craigo-Snell, Shannon, 'What would Buffy do? Feminist ethics and epistemic violence', *Jump Cut: A Review of Contemporary Media* 48 (2006). Available at http://www.ejumpcut.org/archive/jc48.2006/BuffyEthics/ (accessed 12 June 2013).

Crosby, Sara, 'The cruellest season: Female heroes snapped into sacrificial heroines', in Sherrie A. Inness (ed.), *Action Chicks: New Images of Tough Women in Popular Culture* (New York: Palgrave Macmillan, 2004), pp. 153–78.

Dawson's Creek, created by Kevin Williamson (1998, The WB, prod. by Sony Pictures Television), television.

Dechert, S. Renee, '"My boyfriend's in the band!" *Buffy* and the rhetoric of music', in Rhonda V. Wilcox and David Lavery (eds), *Fighting the Forces: What's at Stake in* Buffy the Vampire Slayer (Lanham, MD: Rowman & Littlefield, 2002), pp. 218–26.

Dery, Mark, *The Pyrotechnic Insanitarium: American Culture on the Brink* (New York: Grove Press, 1999).

Dicker, Rory Cooke and Alison Piepmeier (eds), *Catching a Wave: Reclaiming Feminism for the Twenty-first Century* (Boston, MA: Northeastern University Press, 2003).

Dollimore, Jonathan, *Sexual Dissidence: Augustine to Wilde, Freud to Foucault* (Oxford: Clarendon, 1991).

Donnelly, Ashley, 'Denial and salvation: The *Twilight Saga* and heteronormative patriarchy', in Maggie Parke and Natalie Wilson (eds), *Theorising Twilight: Critical Essays on What's at Stake in a Post-Vampire World* (Jefferson, NC: McFarland, 2011), pp. 178–93.

Doty, Alexander, *Making Things Perfectly Queer: Interpreting Mass Culture* (Minneapolis, MN and London: University of Minneapolis Press, 1993).

Douglas, Susan, *Where the Girls Are: Growing Up Female with the Mass Media* (London: Penguin, 1994).

Dow, Bonnie J., *Prime-Time Feminism: Television, Media Culture, and the Women's Movement Since 1970* (Philadelphia, PA: University of Pennsylvania Press, 1996).

Driscoll, Catherine, *Girls: Feminine Adolescence in Popular Culture and Cultural Theory* (New York: Columbia University Press, 2002).

Duffett, Mark, *Understanding Fandom: An Introduction to the Study of Media Fan Culture* (New York: Bloomsbury, 2013).

Durand, Kevin K. (ed.), *Buffy Meets the Academy: Essays on the Episodes and Scripts as Texts* (Jefferson, NC: McFarland, 2009).

Dyer, Richard. 'The white man's muscles', in Rachel Adams and David Savran (eds), *The Masculinity Studies Reader* (Malden, MA: Blackwell Publishing, 2002), pp. 262–73.

Eagleton, Terry, 'The ideology of the aesthetic', in Stephen Regan (ed.), *The Politics of Pleasure: Aesthetics and Cultural Theory* (Milton Keynes: Open University Press, 1992), pp. 17–31.

Early, Frances, 'Staking her claim: Buffy the Vampire Slayer as transgressive woman warrior', *Journal of Popular Culture* 35/3 (Winter 2001), pp. 11–27.

Early, Frances and Kathleen Kennedy (eds), *Athena's Daughters: Television's New Women* (Syracuse, NY: Syracuse University Press, 2003).

Edgerton, Gary R. (ed.), Mad Men: *Dream Come True TV* (London: I.B.Tauris, 2010).

Edwards, Lynne, 'Slaying in Black and White: Kendra as tragic mulatta in *Buffy*', in Rhonda V. Wilcox and David Lavery (eds), *Fighting the Forces: What's at Stake in* Buffy the Vampire Slayer (Lanham, MD: Rowman & Littlefield, 2002), pp. 85–97.

Edwards, Lynne and Carly Haines, 'Reality bites: Buffy in the UPN years', in Lynne Y. Edwards, Elizabeth L. Rambo and James B. South (eds), *Buffy Goes Dark: Essays on the Final Two Seasons of* Buffy the Vampire Slayer *on Television* (Jefferson, NC: McFarland, 2009), pp. 130–42.

Edwards, Rhys, 'Staking out a place in academia: UBC hosts fifth Joss Whedon conference', *The Ubyssey*, 10 July 2012. Available at http://ubyssey.ca/culture/slayage-conference687/ (accessed 3 March 2014).

Election, dir. Alexander Payne, perf. Matthew Broderick, Reese Witherspoon and Chris Klein (1999, Paramount Pictures), film.

'*The Encyclopedia of* Buffy *Studies: Buffy* Studies by discipline/method/approach', *Slayage: The Journal of the Whedon Studies Association*. Available at http://slayageonline.com/EBS/buffy_studies/buffy_studies_by_discipline.htm (accessed 16 December 2013).

Erickson, Gregory and Jennifer Lemberg, 'Bodies and narrative in crisis: figures of rupture and chaos in Seasons Six and Seven', in Lynne Y. Edwards, Elizabeth L. Rambo and James B. South (eds), *Buffy Goes Dark: Essays on the Final Two Seasons of* Buffy the Vampire Slayer *on Television* (Jefferson, NC: McFarland, 2009), pp. 114–29.

Felicity, created by J. J. Abrams and Matt Reeves (1998, The WB, prod. by Touchstone Television and Imagine Television), television.

Findlen, Barbara (ed.), *Listen Up: Voices from the Next Feminist Generation* (Emeryville, CA: Seal Press, 2001).

Fischer, Clara, 'Iron Lady was a self-serving anti-feminist', *The Irish Times*, 12 April 2013. Available at http://www.irishtimes.com/news/social-affairs/iron-lady-was-a-self-serving-anti-feminist-1.1357706 (accessed 17 June 2013).

Fiske, John, *Understanding Popular Culture* (London: Routledge, 1989).

Foreman, Amanda, 'Why the Iron Lady was the ultimate women's libber', *Mail Online*, 3 February 2013. Available at http://www.dailymail.co.uk/femail/article-2085368/Margaret-Thatcher-The-Iron-Lady-ultimate-womens-libber.html (accessed 17 June 2013).

Foucault, Michel, *Discipline and Punish: The Birth of the Prison*, trans. Alan Sheridan (New York: Pantheon Books, 1977).

Foxfire, dir. Annette Haywood-Carter, perf. Hedy Burress, Angelina Jolie and Jenny Lewis (1996, The Samuel Goldwyn Company), film.

Freeman, Hadley, 'Margaret Thatcher was no feminist', *The Guardian*, 10 April 2013. Available at http://www.guardian.co.uk/commentisfree/2013/apr/09/margaret-thatcher-no-feminist (accessed 17 June 2013).

Freeway, dir. Matthew Bright, perf. Kiefer Sutherland, Reese Witherspoon and Brooke Shields (1996, Republic Pictures), film.

Fuchs, Cynthia, '"Did anyone ever explain to you what 'secret identity' means?": Race and displacement in *Buffy* and *Dark Angel*', in Elana Levine and Lisa Parks (eds), *Undead TV: Essays on* Buffy the Vampire Slayer (Durham, NC and London: Duke University Press, 2007), pp. 96–115.

Fudge, Rachel, 'The Buffy effect: Or, a tale of cleavage and marketing', *Bitch: Feminist Response to Pop Culture* 10 (1999). Available at http://bitchmagazine.org/article/buffy-effect (accessed 3 June 2012).

Garrison, Ednie Kaeh, 'US feminism-grrrl style! Youth (sub)cultures and the technologics of the third wave', *Feminist Studies* 26/1 (2000), pp. 141–70.

——, 'Contests for the meaning of third wave feminism: Feminism and popular consciousness', in Stacy Gillis, Gillian Howie and Rebecca Munford (eds), *Third Wave Feminism: A Critical Exploration* (New York: Palgrave Macmillan, 2004), pp. 185–97.

Gateward, Frances K. and Murray Pomerance (eds), *Sugar, Spice, and Everything Nice: Cinemas of Girlhood* (Detroit, MI: Wayne State University Press, 2002).

Genette, Gerard, *Narrative Discourse: An Essay in Method*, trans. Jane E. Lewin (Ithaca, NY: Cornell University Press, 1983).

Gillis, Stacy, Gillian Howie and Rebecca Munford (eds), *Third Wave Feminism: A Critical Exploration* (Basingstoke: Palgrave Macmillan, 2004).

Gillis, Stacy and Rebecca Munford, 'Introduction: Harvesting our strengths: Third wave feminism and Women's Studies', *Journal of International Women's Studies* 4/2 (2003), pp. 1–6.

Gilmore, Stephanie, 'Looking back, thinking ahead: Third wave feminism in the United States', *Journal of Women's History* 12/4 (2001), pp. 215–21.

GirlFight, dir. Karyn Kusama, perf. Michelle Rodriguez, Santiago Douglas and Jaime Tirelli (2000, Screen Gems), film.

Girl, Interrupted, dir. James Mangold, perf. Winona Ryder, Angelina Jolie, and Brittany Murphy (1999, Columbia Pictures), film.

Girls Town, dir. Jim McKay, perf. Lili Taylor, Bruklin Harris and Anna Grace (1996, October Films), film.

Goldberg, Jonah, 'Buffy, the UN slayer', *TownHall*, 26 September 2002. Available at http://townhall.com/columnists/jonahgoldberg/2002/09/26/buffy,_the_un_slayer (accessed 5 August 2013).

Graber, Mary, 'Colleges open minds close door on sense', *MaryGraber.com*. Available at http://www.marygrabar.com/grabar_new/index.php/local-media/82-articles-and-columns/104-colleges-open-minds-close-door-on-sense (accessed 3 March 2014). First published in *The Atlanta Journal-Constitution*, 4 August 2006.

Graham, Helen, 'Post-pleasure: Representations, ideologies and affects of a newly post-9/11 "feminist icon"', *Feminist Media Studies* 7/1 (2007), pp. 1–15.

Gray, Jonathan and Jason Mittell, 'Speculation on spoilers: *Lost* fandom, narrative consumption and rethinking textuality', *Particip@tions* 4/1 (May 2007). Available at http://www.participations.org/Volume%204/Issue%20 1/4_01_graymittell.htm (accessed 12 December 2013).

Gray, Jonathan, Cornel Sandvoss and C. Lee Harrington (eds), *Fandom: Identities and Communities in a Mediated World* (New York: New York University Press, 2007).

Guffey, Ensley F., '"We just declared war": Buffy as general', *Watcher Junior* 5/1 (2011). Available at http://www.watcherjunior.tv/06/guffey.php (accessed 5 August 2013).

Hains, Rebecca C., *Growing Up With Girl Power: Girlhood On Screen and in Everyday Life* (New York: Peter Lang, 2012).

Halfyard, Janet K., 'Singing their hearts out: The problem of performance in *Buffy the Vampire Slayer* and *Angel*', *Slayage: The Journal of the Whedon Studies Association* 5/1 (2005). Available at http://slayageonline.com/PDF/halfyard2.pdf (accessed 12 December 2013).

Hanson, Ellis (ed.), *Out Takes: Essays on Queer Theory and Film* (Durham, NC and London: Duke University Press, 2005).

Harris, Anita (ed.), *All About the Girl: Culture, Power, and Identity* (New York: Routledge, 2004).

Harris, Anita, *Future Girl: Young Women in the Twenty-First Century* (New York: Routledge, 2004).

Hartley, John, 'Hegemony', in Tim O'Sullivan, John Hartley, Danny Saunders, Martin Montgomery and John Fiske (eds), *Key Concepts in Communication and Cultural Studies*, 2nd edn (London: Routledge, 1994), p. 135.

Hautsch, Jessica, 'Staking her colonial claim: Colonial discourses, assimilation, soul-making, and ass-kicking in *Buffy the Vampire Slayer*', *Slayage: The Journal of the Whedon Studies Association* 9/1 (2011). Available at http://slayageonline.com/essays/slayage33/Hautsch.pdf (accessed 5 August 2013).

Havrilesky, Heather, 'Will the truth set Don Draper free?', *Salon*, 24 June 2013. Available at http://www.salon.com/2013/06/24/will_the_truth_set_don_draper_free/ (accessed 12 December 2013).

Hawkins, Paul, 'Season Six and the supreme ordeal', in Lynne Y. Edwards, Elizabeth L. Rambo and James B. South (eds), *Buffy Goes Dark: Essays on the Final Two Seasons of* Buffy the Vampire Slayer *on Television* (Jefferson, NC: McFarland, 2009), pp. 183–97.

Heathers, dir. Michael Lehmann, perf. Winona Ryder, Christian Slater and Shannen Doherty (1988, New World Pictures), film.

Heinecken, Dawn, 'Fan readings of sex and violence on *Buffy the Vampire Slayer*', *Slayage: The Journal of the Whedon Studies Association* 3/3–4 (2004). Available at http://slayageonline.com/PDF/heinecken.pdf (accessed 6 November 2013).

Helford, Elyce Rae (ed.), *Fantasy Girls: Gender in the New Universe of Science Fiction and Fantasy Television* (Lanham, MD: Rowman & Littlefield, 2000).

Helford, Elyce Rae, '"My emotions give me power": The containment of girls' anger in Buffy', in Rhonda Wilcox and David Lavery (eds), *Fighting the Forces: What's at Stake in* Buffy the Vampire Slayer (Lanham, MD: Rowman and Littlefield, 2002), pp. 18–34.

Hellekson, Karen and Kristina Busse (eds), *Fan Fiction and Fan Communities in the Age of the Internet* (Jefferson, NC: MacFarland, 2006).

Heywood, Leslie, '"It's *all about the Benjamins*": Economic determinants of third wave feminism in the United States', in Stacy Gillis, Gillian Howie and Rebecca Munford (eds), *Third Wave Feminism: A Critical Exploration* (New York: Palgrave Macmillan, 2004), pp. 114–24.

—— (ed.), *The Women's Movement Today: An Encyclopedia of Third-Wave Feminism*, vols 1 and 2 (Westport, CT: Greenwood Publishing Co., 2006).

——, and Jennifer Drake (eds), *Third Wave Agenda: Being Feminist, Doing Feminism* (Minneapolis: University of Minnesota Press, 1997).

Higginbotham, Anastasia, 'Chicks goin' at it', in Barbara Findlen (ed.), *Listen Up: Voices from the Next Feminist Generation* (Emeryville, CA: Seal Press, 2001), pp. 11–8.

Hills, Matt, *Fan Cultures* (London and New York: Routledge, 2002).

Ho, Christina, 'Responding to Orientalist feminism: Women's rights and the War on Terror', *Australian Feminist Studies* 25/66 (2010), pp. 433–9.

Hoffman, Christine, 'Happiness is a warm scythe: The evolution of villainy and weaponry in the Buffyverse', *Slayage: The Journal of the Whedon Studies*

Association 7/3 (2009), para. 31. Available at http://slayageonline.com/essays/slayage27/Hoffmann.htm (accessed 7 August 2013).

Hornick, Alysa, 'Whedonology: an academic Whedon Studies bibliography'. Available at http://www.alysa316.com/Whedonology/ (accessed 3 March 2014).

Housel, Rebecca and J. Jeremy Wisnewski (eds), *Twilight and Philosophy: Vampires, Vegetarians, and the Pursuit of Immortality* (Hoboken, NJ: John Wiley & Sons, 2009).

The Incredibly True Adventure of Two Girls in Love, dir. Maria Maggenti, perf. Laurel Holloman, Nicole Ari Parker and Maggie Moore (1995, New Line Cinema, 1995), film.

Inness, Sherrie A. (ed.), *Delinquents and Debutantes: Twentieth-Century American Girls' Cultures* (New York: New York University Press, 1998).

—— (ed.), *Action Chicks: New Images of Tough Women in Popular Culture* (New York: Palgrave Macmillan, 2004).

Jenkins, Henry, *Textual Poachers: Television Fans and Participatory Culture* (New York and London: Routledge, 1992).

—— *Convergence Culture: Where Old and New Media Collide* (New York: New York University Press, 2006).

Jervis, Lisa and Andi Zeisler (eds), *bitchfest: Ten Years of Cultural Criticism from the Pages of Bitch Magazine* (New York: Farrar, Straus & Giroux, 2006).

Johnson, Catherine, *Telefantasy* (London: British Film Institute, 2005).

Johnson, Merri Lisa (ed.), *Third Wave Feminism and Television: Jane Puts It in a Box* (London: I.B.Tauris, 2007).

'Jonathan McIntosh', *Rebellious Pixels*, n.d. Available at http://www.rebelliouspixels.com/jonathan-mcintosh (accessed 16 December 2013).

'Joss Whedon', *International New York Times*, 16 May 2003. Available at http://www.nytimes.com/2003/05/16/readersopinions/16WHED.html (accessed 3 March 2014).

'"Joss Whedon answers 100 questions", *SFX* Magazine/2002. From *SFX*, Future Publishing, 2002', in David Lavery and Cynthia Burkhead (eds), *Joss Whedon: Conversations* (Jackson, MS: University of Mississippi Press, 2011), pp. 34–41.

Jowett, Lorna, *Sex and the Slayer: A Gender Studies Primer for the Buffy Fan* (Middletown, CT: Wesleyan University Press, 2005).

Just Another Girl on the IRT, dir. Leslie Harris, perf. Ariyan A. Johnson. (1992, Miramax Films), film.

Karlyn, Kathleen Rowe, '*Scream*, popular culture, and feminism's third wave: "I'm not my mother"', *Genders* 38 (2003), para. 1. Available at http://www.genders.org/g38/g38_rowe_karlyn.html (accessed 13 June 2012).

Karp, Marcelle and Debbie Stoller (eds), *The BUST Guide to the New Girl Order* (New York: Penguin, 1999).

Karras, Irene, 'The third wave's final girl: Buffy the Vampire Slayer', *thirdspace* 1.2 (2002). Available at http://journals.sfu.ca/thirdspace/index.php/journal/article/viewArticle/karras/50 (accessed 14 June 201).

Katz, Alyssa, 'Buffy the Vampire Slayer', *Nation*, 6 April 1998, pp. 35–6.

Kaveney, Roz (ed.), *Reading the Vampire Slayer: An Unofficial Critical Companion to* Buffy *and* Angel (London: I.B.Tauris, 2002).

Kearney, Mary Celeste, *Girls Make Media* (New York: Routledge, 2006).

Kelly, John D., 'Seeing red: Mao fetishism, Pax Americana, and the moral economy of war', in John D. Kelly, Beatrice Jauregui, Sean T. Mitchell and Jeremy Walton (eds), *Anthropology and Global Counterinsurgency* (Chicago, IL: University of Chicago Press, 2010), pp. 67–83.

Kimmel, Michael S., 'Masculinity as homophobia: Fear, shame, and silence in the construction of gender identity', in Stephen M. Whitehead and Frank J. Barrett (eds), *The Masculinities Reader* (Cambridge: Polity, 2001), pp. 266–87.

King, Neal, 'Brownskirts: Fascism, Christianity, and the eternal demon', in James B. South (ed.), Buffy the Vampire Slayer *and Philosophy: Fear and Trembling in Sunnydale* (Chicago, IL: Open Court, 2003), pp. 197–211.

Kinser, Amber E., 'Negotiating spaces for/through third-wave feminism', *NWSA Journal* 16/3 (2004), pp. 124–53.

Kirby-Diaz, Mary (ed.), *Buffy and Angel Conquer the Internet: Essays on Online Fandom* (Jefferson, NC: MacFarland, 2009).

Kirkland, Ewan, 'The Caucasian persuasion of *Buffy the Vampire Slayer*', *Slayage: The Journal of the Whedon Studies Association* 5/1 (2005). Available at http://slayageonline.com/PDF/kirkland.pdf (accessed 5 August 2013).

Kirkpatrick, Kim, 'Scoobies and Potentials: the Slayer community as hero in *Buffy the Vampire Slayer*', *MP JOURNAL* 1/4 (2006). Available at http://academinist.org/wp-content/uploads/2010/06/kirkpatrick.pdf (accessed 5 August 2013).

Kociemba, David, 'Teaching with *Buffy*', *Watcher Junior: the Undergraduate Journal of Whedon Studies*, 7 September 2010. Available at http://blog.watcherjunior.tv/2010/09/teaching-with-buffy.html (accessed 3 March 2014).

——, 'To spoil or not to spoil: Teaching television's narrative complexity', in Jodie A. Kreider and Meghan K. Winchell (eds), Buffy *in the Classroom: Essays on Teaching with the Vampire Slayer* (Jefferson, NC: McFarland, 2010), pp. 7–21.

Krieder, Jodie A. and Meghan K. Winchell (eds), Buffy *in the Classroom: Essays on Teaching with the Vampire Slayer* (Jefferson, NC: McFarland, 2010).

Lachonis, Jon and Amy Johnston, Lost *Ate My Life: The Inside Story of a Fandom Like No Other* (Toronto: ECW Press, 2008).

Laist, Randy (ed.), *Looking for* Lost: *Critical Essays on the Enigmatic Series* (Jefferson, NC: McFarland & Co., 2011).

Lamb, Lynette, 'Media criticism: The sad state of teen television', *New Moon Network: For Adults Who Care About Girls* 7/2 (1999), pp. 14–25.

Lametti, Daniel, Aisha Harris, Natasha Geiling and Natalie Matthews-Ramo, 'Which pop culture property do academics study the most?', *Slate (Brow Beat: Slate's Culture Blog)*, 11 June 2012. Available at http://www.slate.com/blogs/browbeat/2012/06/11/pop_culture_studies_why_do_academics_study_buffy_the_vampire_slayer_more_than_the_wire_the_matrix_alien_and_the_simpsons_.html (accessed 12 December 2013).

Larbalestier, Justine, '*Buffy*'s Mary Sue is Jonathon: *Buffy* acknowledges the fans', in Rhonda V. Wilcox and David Lavery (eds), *Fighting the Forces: What's at Stake in* Buffy the Vampire Slayer (Lanham, MD: Rowman & Littlefield, 2002), pp. 227–38.

Larsen, Katherine and Lynn S. Zubernis, *Fangasm: Supernatural Fangirls* (Iowa City, IA: University of Iowa Press, 2013).

Lavery, David, '"I wrote my thesis on you": *Buffy* Studies as an academic cult', *Slayage: The Online International Journal of Buffy Studies* 4/1–2 (October 2004). Available at http://slayageonline.com/PDF/lavery4.pdf (accessed 3 March 2014).

——, 'Joss Whedon, wonder boy', featured paper at SC2: The *Slayage* Conference on the Whedonverses, 25–28 May 2006, Gordon College, Georgia.

——, *Joss Whedon, A Creative Portrait: From* Buffy the Vampire Slayer *to* The Avengers (London: I.B.Tauris, 2013).

Lavery, David and Cynthia Burkhead (eds), *Joss Whedon: Conversations* (Jackson, MI: University Press of Mississippi, 2011).

Leadbeater, Bonnie J. Ross and Niobe Way (eds), *Urban Girls: Resisting Stereotypes, Creating Identities* (New York: New York University Press, 1996).

—— (eds), *Urban Girls Revisited: Building Strengths* (New York: New York University Press, 2007).

Legally Blonde, dir. Robert Luketic, perf. Reese Witherspoon, Luke Wilson, and Selma Blair (2001, Metro-Goldwyn-Mayer), film.

Levine, Elana and Lisa Parks (eds), *Undead TV: Essays on* Buffy the Vampire Slayer (Durham, NC: Duke University Press, 2007).

Levine, Michael P. and Steven Jay Schneider, 'Feeling for Buffy: The girl next door', in James B. South (ed.), Buffy the Vampire Slayer *and Philiosophy: Fear and Trembling in Sunnydale* (Chicago, IL: Open Court, 2003), pp. 294–308.

Levy, Sophie, '"You still my girl?": Adolescent femininity as resistance in *Buffy the Vampire Slayer*', *Reconstruction* 3/1 (2003), para. 3. Available at http://reconstruction.eserver.org/Issues/031/levy.htm (accessed 11 June 2012).

Longworth, James L., *TV Creators: Conversations with America's Top Producers of Television Drama*, vol. 2 (New York: Syracuse University Press, 2002).

Lothian, Alexis, Kristina Busse and Robin Anne Reid, '"Yearning void and infinite potential": Online slash fandom as queer female space', *English Language Notes* 45/2 (2007), pp. 103–11.

Maher, Jennifer, 'The post-feminist mystique', *College Literature* 34/3 (2007), pp. 193–201.

Malin, Brenton J., *American Masculinity Under Clinton: Popular Media and the Nineties' 'Crisis of Masculinity'* (New York: Peter Lang, 2005).

Mane, Rebecca L. Clark, 'Transmuting grammars of whiteness in third-wave feminism: Interrogating postrace histories, postmodern abstraction, and the proliferation of difference in third-wave texts', *Signs* 38/1 (2012), pp. 71–98.

Marinucci, Mimi, 'Feminism and the ethics of violence: Why Buffy kicks ass', in James B. South (ed.), Buffy the Vampire Slayer *and Philosophy: Fear and Trembling in Sunnydale* (Chicago, IL: Open Court, 2003), pp. 61–75.

Marvel Universe Wiki, 'Captain America (Steve Rogers)'. Available at http://marvel.com/universe/Captain_America_(Steve_Rogers) (accessed 6 March 2014).

Masson, Cynthea and Marni Stanley, 'Queer eye of that vampire guy: Spike and the aesthetics of camp', *Slayage: The Online International Journal of Buffy Studies* 6/2 (2006). Available at http://slayageonline.com/Numbers/slayage_22.htm (accessed 18 February 2009).

McAvan, Em, '"I think I'm kinda gay": Willow Rosenberg and the absent/present bisexual in *Buffy the Vampire Slayer*', *Slayage: The Online International Journal of Buffy Studies* 6/4 (2007). Available at http://slayageonline.com/Numbers/slayage24.htm (accessed 18 February 2009).

McCabe, Janet and Kim Akass, 'Feminist television criticism: notes and queries', *Critical Studies in Television* 1/1 (2006), pp. 108–20.

McCracken, Allison, 'At stake: Angel's body, fantasy masculinity, and queer desire in teen television', in Elana Levine and Lisa Parks (eds), *Undead TV: Essays on* Buffy the Vampire Slayer (Durham, NC: Duke University Press, 2007), pp. 116–44.

McIntosh, Jonathan, 'Buffy vs Edward (*Twilight* remixed)', *Rebellious Pixels*, 20 June 2009. Available at http://www.rebelliouspixels.com/page/11 (accessed 20 June 2012).

——, 'What would Buffy do?: notes on dusting Edward Cullen', *WIMN's Voices* (2009). Available at http://www.wimnonline.org/WIMNsVoicesBlog/?p=1272 (accessed 16 December 2013).

——, 'Buffy vs Edward remix unfairly removed by Lionsgate', *Rebellious Pixels*, 9 January 2013. Available at http://www.rebelliouspixels.com/2013/buffy-vs-edward-remix-unfairly-removed-by-lionsgate (accessed 16 December 2013).

McRobbie, Angela, *Feminism and Youth Culture: From 'Jackie' to 'Just Seventeen'* (Boston, MA: Unwin Hyman, 1991).

——, 'Postfeminism and popular culture', *Feminist Media Studies* 4/3 (2004), pp. 255–64.

——, *The Aftermath of Feminism: Gender, Culture and Social Change* (London: Sage, 2009).

Mendelsohn, Farah, 'Surpassing the love of vampires; Or why (and how) a queer reading of Buffy/Willow is denied', in Rhonda V. Wilcox and David Lavery (eds), *Fighting the Forces: What's at Stake in* Buffy the Vampire Slayer (Lanham, MD: Rowman & Littlefield, 2002), pp. 45–60.

Miller, Melissa, 'Maybe Edward is the most dangerous thing out there: The role of patriarchy', in Maggie Parke and Natalie Wilson (eds), *Theorising Twilight: Critical Essays on What's at Stake in a Post-Vampire World* (Jefferson, NC: McFarland and Co., 2011), pp. 165–77.

Mi Vida Loca, dir. Allison Anders, perf. Angel Aviles, Seidy Lopez and Jacob Vargas. (1992, Sony Pictures Classics), film.

Moorti, Sujata and Karen Ross, 'Reality television: Fairy tale or feminist nightmare?', *Feminist Media Studies* 4/2 (2004), pp. 203–31.

Morris, Barry, 'Round up the usable suspects: Archetypal characters in the study of popular culture', in Jodie A. Kreider and Meghan K. Winchell (eds), Buffy *in the Classroom: Essays on Teaching with the Vampire Slayer* (Jefferson, NC: McFarland, 2010), pp. 46–60.

Mulvey, Laura, *Visual and Other Pleasures* (Bloomington, IN: Indiana University Press, 1989).

——, *Visual and Other Pleasures*, 2nd edn (London: Palgrave Macmillan, 2009).

Munford, Rebecca, '"Wake up and smell the lipgloss": Gender, generation and the (a)politics of girl power', in Stacy Gillis, Gillian Howie and Rebecca Munford (eds), *Third Wave Feminism: A Critical Exploration* (New York: Palgrave Macmillan, 2004), pp. 142–53.

Narushima, Yuko, 'Back to basics proposal for English pupils', *Sydney Morning Herald*, 17 October 2008. Available at http://www.smh.com.au/news/national/back-to-basics-proposal-for-english-pupils/2008/10/16/1223750232631.html (accessed 15 January 2015).

Negra, Diane, *What a Girl Wants? Fantasizing the Reclamation of Self in Postfeminism* (London and New York: Routledge, 2009).

Nichols, Bill (ed.), *Movies and Methods*, vol. I (Berkeley, CA: University of California Press, 1976).

Ono, Kent A., 'To be a vampire on *Buffy the Vampire Slayer*: Race and ('Other') socially marginalized positions on horror TV', in Elyce Rae Helford (ed.), *Fantasy Girls: Gender in the New Universe of Science Fiction and Fantasy Television* (New York: Rowman & Littlefield, 2000), pp. 163–86.

Ostow, Micol, 'Why I love Buffy', *Sojourner: The Women's Forum* 24/3 (1998), pp. 20–35.

'Our history', *Bitch Media* n.d. Available at http://bitchmagazine.org/history (accessed 9 September 2013).

Owen, A. Susan, 'Vampires, postmodernity, and postfeminism: *Buffy the Vampire Slayer*', *Journal of Popular Film and Television* 27/2 (Summer 1999), pp. 24–31.

Palazzolo, Joe, 'Want to learn criminal law and procedure? Watch "The Wire"', *The Wall Street Journal (Law Blog)*, 10 December 2013. Available at http://blogs.wsj.com/law/2013/12/10/want-to-learn-criminal-law-and-procedure-watch-the-wire/ (accessed 12 December 2013).

Panahi, Rita, 'Reaction to Margaret Thatcher's passing proves feminism is about politics, not equality', *Herald Sun*, 10 April 2013. Available at http://www.heraldsun.com.au/news/opinion/reaction-to-margaret-thatchers-passing-proves-feminism-is-about-politics-not-equality/story-e6frfhqf-1226616184704 (accessed 17 June 2013).

Pasley, Jeffrey L., 'Old familiar vampires: The politics of the Buffyverse', in James B. South (ed.), Buffy the Vampire Slayer *and Philosophy: Fear and Trembling in Sunnydale* (Chicago, IL: Open Court, 2003), pp. 254–67.

——, 'You can't pin a good Slayer down: The politics, if any, of *Buffy the Vampire Slayer* and *Angel*', Pasley Brothers, 2003. Available at http://www.pasley-brothers.com/jeff/writings/buffy.htm (accessed 6 March 2014).

Pearson, Roberta. 'Bachies, Bardies, Trekkies, and Sherlockians', in Jonathan Gray, Cornel Sandvoss and C. Lee Harrington (eds), *Fandom: Identities and Communities in a Mediated World* (New York: New York University Press, 2007), pp. 98–109.

—— (ed.), *Reading Lost: Perspectives on a Hit Television Show* (London: I.B.Tauris, 2009).

Peele, Thomas (ed.), *Queer Popular Culture: Literature, Media, Film, and Television* (London: Palgrave Macmillan, 2007).

Pender, Patricia, '"I'm Buffy and you're … history": The postmodern politics of *Buffy the Vampire Slayer*', in Rhonda Wilcox and David Lavery (eds), *Fighting the Forces: What's at Stake in* Buffy the Vampire Slayer (Lanham, MD: Rowman and Littlefield 2002), pp. 35–44.

——, '"Why can't you just masturbate like the rest of us?" Andrew and the erotics of fandom in "Storyteller"', paper presented to the Slayage Conference on Whedonverses, 26–28 May 2006, Gordon College, Georgia.

——, '"Kicking ass is comfort food": Buffy as third wave feminist icon', in Stacy Gillis, Gillian Howie and Rebecca Munford (eds), *Third Wave Feminism: A Critical Exploration* (New York: Palgrave Macmillan, 2004), pp. 164–74.

Petrie, Douglas, DVD audio commentary, *Buffy the Vampire Slayer: The Complete Fourth Season, 'The Initiative'*, perf. Sarah Michelle Gellar, Nicholas Brendon and Alyson Hannigan (Twentieth Century Fox, 2002).

Phillips, Lynn (prod.), *The Girls Report: What We Know & Need to Know About Growing Up Female* (National Council for Research on Women, USA, 1998).

Pipher, Mary, *Reviving Ophelia: Saving the Selves of Adolescent Girls* (New York: Ballantine Books, 2001).

Playden, Zoe-Jane, '"What you are, what's to come": Feminisms, citizenship and the divine', in Roz Kaveney (ed.), *Reading the Vampire Slayer: An Unofficial Critical Companion to Buffy and Angel* (London: I.B.Tauris, 2002), pp. 120–47.

Pomerance, Murray and Frances K. Gateward (eds), *Where the Boys Are: Cinemas of Masculinity and Youth* (Detroit, MI: Wayne State University Press, 2005).

Potter, Tiffany and C. W. Marshall (eds), The Wire*: Urban Decay and American Television* (New York: Continuum, 2009).

Power, Nina, *One Dimensional Woman* (Winchester: O Books, 2009).

Pozner, Jennifer L., 'Thwack! Pow! Yikes! Not your mother's heroines', *Sojourner: The Women's Forum* 23/2 (1997), pp. 12–13.

Reagin, Nancy and Anne Rubenstein, '"I'm Buffy, and you're history": Putting fan studies into history', *Transformative Works and Cultures* 6 (2011). Available at http://journal.transformativeworks.org/index.php/twc/article/view/272/200 (accessed 12 December 2013).

Rebellious Pixels, 'Buffy vs Edward: *Twilight* remixed – [original version]', *YouTube*, uploaded 19 June 2009. Available at http://www.youtube.com/watch?v=RZwM3GvaTRM (accessed 16 December 2013).

Rich, B. Ruby, 'New Queer Cinema', *Sight and Sound* 2/5 (September 1992), pp. 31–4.

——, *New Queer Cinema* (Durham, NC: Duke University Press, 2013).

Richardson, Michael J. and J. Douglas Rabb, *The Existential Joss Whedon: Evil and Human Freedom in* Buffy the Vampire Slayer, Angel, Firefly *and* Serenity (Jefferson, NC: McFarland, 2007).

Roberts, Kimberley, 'Pleasures and problems of the "angry girl"', in Frances Gateward and Murray Pomerance (eds), *Sugar, Spice, and Everything Nice: Cinemas of Girlhood* (Detroit, MI: Wayne State University Press, 2002), pp. 217–33.

Roberts, Rachel, '"Feminists should weep" at the death of Margaret Thatcher – and why would that be, exactly?', *The Independent*, 10 April 2013. Available at http://www.independent.co.uk/voices/comment/feminists-should-weep-at-the-death-of-margaret-thatcher-and-why-would-that-be-exactly-8567202.html (accessed 15 June 2013).

Robertson, Pamela, *Guilty Pleasures: Feminist Camp from Mae West to Madonna* (Durham, NC: Duke University Press, 1996).

Robinson, Tasha, 'The Onion AV Club interview with Joss Whedon (1)', in David Lavery and Cynthia Burkhead (eds), *Joss Whedon: Conversations* (Jackson, MI: University Press of Mississippi, 2011), pp. 23–33.

Romayne, Douglas, 'Interview with Season 7 composer, Douglas Romayne', *Buffyfans.com*, 8 March 2009. Available at http://web.archive.org/web/*/http://buffyfans.com/exclusives.html (accessed 5 August 2013).

Roswell, created by Jonathon Dukes, developed by Jason Katims (1999, The WB, prod. by Jason Katims Productions, Regency Television and Twentieth Century Fox Television), television.

Run Lola Run, dir. Tom Tykwer, perf. Franka Potente and Moritz Bleibtreu (1999, Sony Pictures Classics), film.

Saadallah, Sherin, 'Muslim feminism in the third wave: a reflective inquiry', in Stacy Gillis, Gillian Howie and Rebecca Munford (eds), *Third Wave Feminism: A Critical Exploration* (New York: Palgrave Macmillan, 2004), pp. 216–26.

Salah, Trish, 'Of activist fandoms, auteur pedagogy and imperial feminism: From *Buffy the Vampire Slayer* to *I am Du'a Khalil*', in Lisa Taylor and Jasmin Zine (eds), *Muslim Women, Transnational Feminism and the Ethics of Pedagogy: Contested Imaginaries in Post-9/11 Cultural Practice* (New York: Routledge: 2014).

Samanta, Anamika, and Erin Franzman, 'Women in action', *HUES: Hear Us Emerging Sisters* 4/3 (1998), pp. 28–31.

Sarris, Andrew, 'Notes on the auteur theory in 1962', *Film Culture* 27 (Winter 1962/3), pp. 1–8.

Saxey, Esther, 'Staking a claim: The series and slash fan-fiction', in Roz Kaveney (ed.), *Reading The Vampire Slayer: An Unofficial Critical Companion to* Buffy *and* Angel, 2nd edn (New York: I.B.Tauris, 2001), pp. 187–210.

Schultz, Jason, 'Getting off on feminism', in Rebecca Walker (ed.), *To Be Real: Telling the Truth and Changing the Face of Feminism* (New York: Anchor Books, 1995), pp. 107–26.

Sedgwick, Eve, *Between Men: English Literature and Male Homosocial Desire* (New York: Columbia University Press, 1985).

Seifert, Christine, 'Bite me! (or don't)', *Bitch Media*, n.d. Available at http://bitchmagazine.org/article/bite-me-or-dont (accessed 20 February 2014).

Serazio, Michael, 'The apolitical irony of Generation Mash-Up: A cultural case study in popular music', *Popular Music and Society* 31/1 (2008), pp. 79–94.

Shachar, Hila, 'A post-feminist romance: Love, gender and intertextuality in Stephanie Meyer's saga', in Maggie Parke and Natalie Wilson (eds), *Theorising Twilight: Critical Essays on What's at Stake in a Post-Vampire World* (Jefferson, NC: McFarland and Co., 2011), pp. 147–61.

Shary, Timothy, 'The nerdy girl and her beautiful sister', in Frances Gateward and Murray Pomerance (eds), *Sugar, Spice, and Everything Nice: Cinemas of Girlhood* (Detroit, MI: Wayne State University Press, 2002), pp. 235–50.

Sheehan, Helena and Sheamus Sweeney, '*The Wire* and the world: Narrative and metanarrative', *Jump Cut: A Review of Contemporary Media* 51 (2009). Available at http://www.ejumpcut.org/archive/jc51.2009/Wire/ (accessed 12 December 2013).

She's the Man, dir. Andy Fickman, perf. Amanda Bynes, Laura Ramsey and Channing Tatum (2006, DreamWorks), film.

Shiga, John, 'Copy-and-persist: the logic of mash-up culture', *Critical Studies in Media Communication* 24/2 (2007), pp. 93–114.

Shortchanging Girls, Shortchanging America: A Call to Action (American Association of University Women, 1994). Available at http://www.aauw.org/files/2013/02/shortchanging-girls-shortchanging-america-executive-summary.pdf (accessed 5 August 2013).

Showalter, Dennis, 'Buffy goes to war: Military themes and images in *Buffy the Vampire Slayer*', paper presented to The *Slayage* Conference on *Buffy the Vampire Slayer*, Nashville, TN, 28–30 May 2004. Available at http://slayageonline.com/SCBtVS_Archive/Talks/Showalter.pdf (accessed 5 August 2013).

Shriver, Lionel, 'Thatcher was a real feminist', *The Sydney Morning Herald*, 9 April 2013. Available at http://www.smh.com.au/comment/thatcher-was-a-real-feminist-20130409-2hibr.html (accessed 17 June 2013).

Simkin, Stevie, '"Who died and made you John Wayne?": Anxious masculinity in *Buffy the Vampire Slayer*', *Slayage: The Online International Journal* 3/3–4 (2004). Available at http://slayageonline.com/PDF/simkin_wayne.pdf (accessed 5 June 2012).

——, '"You hold your gun like a sissy girl": Firearms and anxious masculinity in *Buffy the Vampire Slayer*', *Slayage: The Online International Journal of Buffy Studies* 3/3–4, para. 21. Available at http://slayageonline.com/essays/slayage11_12/Simkin_Gun.htm (accessed 18 February 2009).

——, 'The wit and wisdom of Joss Whedon', *Slayage: The Online International Journal of Buffy Studies*. Available at http://slayageonline.com/pages/Wit_Wisdom_Joss_Whedon.pdf (accessed 3 March 2014).

'The sixth annual Mr Pointy Award for Buffy Studies Scholarship (2010)', *Slayage: The Journal of the Whedon Studies Association*, n.d. Available at http://slayageonline.com/Mr_Pointy/mrpointy_winners_2010.htm (accessed 21 February 2014).

Smith, Joan, *Different for Girls: How Culture Creates Women* (London: Vintage, 1998).

Smith, Sharon, 'Using women's rights to sell Washington's war', *International Socialist Review* 21 (2002). Available at http://isreview.org/issues/21/afghan_women.shtml (accessed 5 August 2013).

Snyder, R. Claire, 'What is third-wave feminism? A new directions essay', *Signs* 34/1 (2008), pp. 175–96.

Snyder-Hall, R. Claire, 'Third-wave feminism and the defense of "choice"', *Perspectives on Politics* 8/1 (2010), pp. 255–61.

Solomon, David, and Joss Whedon, DVD audio commentary, *Buffy the Vampire Slayer: The Complete Seventh Season, 'Lessons'*, perf. Sarah Michelle Gellar, Nicholas Brendon and Emma Caulfield (Twentieth Century Fox, 2004).

Sontag, Susan, *Against Interpretation* (New York: Farrar and Strauss, 1996).

South, James B. (ed.), Buffy the Vampire Slayer *and Philosophy: Fear and Trembling in Sunnydale* (Chicago, IL: Open Court, 2003).

——, 'On the philosophical consistency of Season Seven: or, "It's not about right, not about wrong…"', *Slayage: The Journal of the Whedon Studies Association* 4/3 [15] (2004). Available at http://slayageonline.com/PDF/south.pdf (accessed 7 June 2012).

——, 'Kiss kiss, stake stake: Storytelling and the philosophical pleasures of Season Seven', in Lynne Y. Edwards, Elizabeth L. Rambo and James B. South (eds), *Buffy Goes Dark: Essays on the Final Two Seasons of* Buffy the Vampire Slayer *on Television* (Jefferson, NC: McFarland, 2009), pp. 198–210.

Spice World, dir. Bob Spiers, perf. Melanie Brown, Emma Bunton, Melanie Chisholm, Geri Halliwell and Victoria Beckham (1997, PolyGram Filmed Entertainment and Columbia Pictures), film.

Spicer, Arwen, '"Love's bitch but man enough to admit it": Spike's hybridized gender', *Slayage* 2/3 (December 2002).

——, '"It's bloody brilliant!" The undermining of metanarrative feminism in the Season Seven arc narrative of *Buffy*', *Slayage: The Journal of the Whedon Studies Association* 4/3 (2004). Available at http://slayageonline.com/PDF/spicer2.pdf (accessed 4 June 2012).

Spivak, Gayatri, 'Three women's texts and the critique of imperialism', *Critical Inquiry* 12/1 (1985), pp. 243–61.

Springer, Kimberly, 'Third Wave Black feminism?', *Signs* 27/4 (2002), pp. 1059–82.

Stabile, Carol A. and Deepa Kumar, 'Unveiling imperialism: Media, gender and the war on Afghanistan', *Media, Culture and Society* 27/5 (2005), pp. 765–82.

Star Trek: Enterprise, created by Rick Berman and Brannon Braga (2001, UPN, prod. by Paramount Network Television), television.

Star Trek: Voyager, created by Rick Berman, Michael Piller and Jeri Taylor (1995, UPN, prod. by Paramount Network Television), television.

Stengel, Wendy A.F.G., 'Synergy and smut: The brand in official and unofficial *Buffy the Vampire Slayer* communities of interest', *Slayage: The Journal of the Whedon Studies Association* 1/4 (2001). Available at http://slayageonline.com/PDF/stengel.pdf (accessed 12 December 2013).

Stevens, Kirsten, 'Meet the Cullens: Family, romance and female agency in *Buffy the Vampire Slayer* and *Twilight*'. *Slayage: The Journal of the Whedon Studies Association* 8/1 (2010). Available at http://slayageonline.com/PDF/Stevens.pdf (accessed 21 February 2014).

Stevenson, Gregory, *Televised Morality: The Case of* Buffy the Vampire Slayer (Lanham, MD: Hamilton Books, 2004).

Stoddart, Scott Frederick (ed.), *Analyzing* Mad Men*: Critical Essays on the Television Series* (Jefferson, NC: McFarland & Co., 2011).

Symonds, Gwyn, '"Bollocks!": Spike fans and reception of *Buffy the Vampire Slayer*–, *Refractory: A Journal of Entertainment Media*, 18 March 2003. Available at http://refractory.unimelb.edu.au/2003/03/18/bollocks-spike-fans-and-reception-of-buffy-the-vampire-slayer-gwyn-symonds/ (accessed 4 June 2012).

Tabron, Judith L., 'Girl on girl politics: Willow/Tara and new approaches to media fandom', *Slayage: The Journal of the Whedon Studies Association*

4/1–2 (2004). Available at http://slayageonline.com/PDF/tabron.pdf (accessed 12 December 2013).

Tasker, Yvonne and Diane Negra (eds), *Interrogating Postfeminism: Gender and the Politics of Popular Culture* (Durham, NC: Duke University Press, 2007).

Tjardes, Sue, '"If you're not enjoying it, you're doing something wrong": Textual and viewer constructions of Faith, the Vampire Slayer', in Frances Early and Kathleen Kennedy (eds), *Athena's Daughters: Television's New Women Warriors* (Syracuse, NY: Syracuse University Press, 2003), pp. 66–77.

Torkelson, Anne, 'Violence, agency, and the women of *Twilight*', in Maggie Parke and Natalie Wilson (eds), *Theorising Twilight: Critical Essays on What's at Stake in a Post-Vampire World* (Jefferson, NC: McFarland and Co., 2011), pp. 209–23.

Truffaut, François, 'A certain tendency of the French cinema', *Cahiers du Cinéma* in English 1. Originally published in French in *Cahiers du Cinéma* 31 (1954).

Turk, Tisha, 'Metalepsis in fan vids and fan fiction', in Karin Kukkonen and Sonja Klimek (eds), *Metalepsis in Popular Culture* (New York: De Gruyter, 2011), pp. 83–103.

Turnbull, Sue, '"Not just another Buffy paper": Towards an aesthetics of television', *Slayage: The Journal of the Whedon Studies Association* 4/1–2 (2004). Available at http://slayageonline.com/PDF/turnbull.pdf (accessed 3 March 2014).

The Twilight Zone, created by Rod Serling (2001, UPN, prod. by Paramount Network Television), television.

Tyree, J.M., 'No fun: debunking the 1960s in *Mad Men* and *A Serious Man*', *Film Quarterly* 63/4 (Summer 2010), pp. 33–9.

Wald, Gayle, 'Just a girl? Rock music, feminism, and the cultural construction of female youth', *Signs: Journal of Women in Culture and Society* 23/3 (1998), pp. 585–610.

——, 'Clueless in the neocolonial world order', in Frances Gateward and Murray Pomerance (eds), *Sugar, Spice, and Everything Nice: Cinemas of Girlhood* (Detroit, MI: Wayne State University Press, 2002), pp. 103–23.

——, '"I want it that way": teenybopper music and the girling of boy bands', *Genders* 35 (2002). Available at http://www.genders.org/g35/g35_wald.html (accessed 3 June 2012).

Waggoner, Erin B. (ed.), *Sexual Rhetoric in the Works of Joss Whedon* (Jefferson, NC: McFarland, 2010).

Walker, Rebecca (ed.), *To Be Real: Telling the Truth and Changing the Face of Feminism* (New York: Anchor Books, 1995).

——, '"Becoming the third wave", from *Ms* magazine', in Leslie Heywood (ed.), *The Women's Movement Today: An Encyclopedia of Third-Wave Feminism*, vol. 2 (Westport, CT: Greenwood Publishing Co., 2006), pp. 3–5.

Walkerdine, Valerie, *Daddy's Girl: Young Girls and Popular Culture* (Cambridge, MA: Harvard University Press, 1997).

——, Helen Lucey and June Melody, *Growing Up Girl: Psychosocial Explorations of Gender and Class* (New York: New York University Press, 2001).

Watcher Junior: The Undergraduate Journal of Whedon Studies. Home page. Available at http://www.whedonstudies.tv/watcher-junior-the-undergraduate-journal-of-whedon-studies.html (accessed 3 June 2012).

West, Michelle Sagara, 'For the love of Riley', in Glenn Yeffeth (ed.), *Seven Seasons of* Buffy*: Science Fiction and Fantasy Authors Discuss Their Favorite Television Show* (Dallas, TX: BenBella Books, 2003), pp. 65–71.

Whelehan, Imelda, *Modern Feminist Thought from the Second Wave to 'Post-Feminism'* (Edinburgh: Edinburgh University Press, 1995).

——, *Overloaded: Popular Culture and the Future of Feminism* (London: The Women's Press, 2000).

White, Emily, *Fast Girls: Teenage Tribes and the Myth of the Slut* (New York: Simon and Schuster, 2002).

White, Jessica, 'Is Margaret Thatcher really worth redeeming?', *Al Jazeera*, 20 April 2013. Available at http://www.aljazeera.com/indepth/opinion/2013/04/201341882140384449.html (accessed 15 June 2013).

Wilcox, Rhonda V., '"Show me your world": Exiting the text and the globalization of *Buffy*', keynote address to the *Staking a Claim: Global Buffy, Local Identities Conference*, 22 July 2003, University of South Australia, Adelaide.

—— (ed.), *Why* Buffy *Matters: The Art of* Buffy the Vampire Slayer (London: I.B.Tauris, 2005).

——, 'In "the demon section of the card catalogue"', *Critical Studies in Television* 1.1 (April 2006), pp. 37–48.

——, '"Set on this earth like a bubble": Word as flesh in the dark seasons', in Lynne Y. Edwards, Elizabeth L. Rambo and James B. South (eds), *Buffy Goes Dark: Essays on the Final Two Seasons of* Buffy the Vampire Slayer *on Television* (Jefferson, NC: McFarland, 2009), pp. 95–113.

Wilcox, Rhonda V. and David Lavery, 'Welcome', Fifth Biennial *Slayage* Conference on the Whedonverses (2012). Available at http://www.slayageonline.com/SC5/SCW5_Program_Final.pdf (accessed 5 August 2013).

Wilcox, Rhonda V. and David Lavery (eds), *Fighting the Forces: What's at Stake in* Buffy the Vampire Slayer (Lanham, MD: Rowman & Littlefield, 2002).

Williams, Linda, 'Why I did not want to write this essay', *Signs* 30/1: *Beyond the Gaze: Recent Approaches to Film Feminisms* (Autumn 2004), pp. 1264–72.

Winchell, Meghan K., 'Whedon takes "the scary" out of feminism', in Jodie A. Kreider and Meghan K. Winchell (eds), Buffy *in the Classroom: Essays on Teaching with the Vampire Slayer* (Jefferson, NC: McFarland, 2010), pp. 73–82.

Winslade, Jason, '"Have you tried not being a Slayer?": Performing Buffy fandom in the classroom', in Jodie A. Kreider and Meghan K. Winchell (eds), Buffy *in the Classroom: Essays on Teaching with the Vampire Slayer* (Jefferson, NC: McFarland, 2010), pp. 22–34.

Wood, Robin, *Hitchcock's Films Revisited* (New York: Columbia University Press, 1989).

Wollen, Peter, *Signs and Meaning in the Cinema* (Bloomington, IN: Indiana University Press, 1973).

Woodhull, Winnie, 'Global feminisms, transnational political economies, third world cultural production', *Journal of International Women's Studies* 4/3 (2003), pp. 76–90.

Woofter, Kristopher Karl, 'Little Red Riding ... Buffy? "Buffy vs. Dracula" in explorations of intertextuality in Introduction to College English', in Jodie A. Kreider and Meghan K. Winchell (eds), Buffy *in the Classroom: Essays on Teaching with the Vampire Slayer* (Jefferson, NC: McFarland, 2010), pp. 169–85.

Young, Cathy, 'Margaret Thatcher and feminism', *Real Clear Politics*, 18 April 2013. Available at http://www.realclearpolitics.com/articles/2013/04/18/margaret_thatcher_and_feminism_118018.html (accessed 17 June 2013).

Zaslow, Emilie, *Feminism, Inc.: Coming of Age in Girl Power Media Culture* (New York: Palgrave Macmillan, 2009).

Zubernis, Lynn and Katherine Larsen, *Fandom at the Crossroads: Celebration, Shame and Fan/Producer Relationship* (Newcastle upon Tyne: Cambridge Scholars Publishing, 2012).

Zweerink, Amanda and Sarah N. Gatson, 'www.buffy.com: cliques, boundaries, and hierarchies in an internet community', in Rhonda V. Wilcox and David Lavery (eds), *Fighting the Forces: What's at Stake in Buffy the Vampire Slayer* (Lanham, MD: Rowman & Littlefield, 2002), pp. 239–49.

Index